Getting Institutions Right
for Women in Development

Getting Institutions Right for Women in Development

Edited by Anne Marie Goetz

ZED BOOKS
London & New York

Getting Institutions Right for Women in Development was first published in 1997 by
Zed Books Ltd, 7 Cynthia Street, London N1 9JF, UK, and
Room 400, 175 Fifth Avenue, New York, NY 10010, USA

Distributed exclusively in the USA by St Martin's Press, Inc.,
175 Fifth Avenue, New York, NY 10010, USA

Typeset in Monotype Garamond by Lucy Morton, London SE12
Cover designed by Andrew Corbett
Printed and bound in the United Kingdom
by Biddles Ltd, Guildford and King's Lynn

A catalogue record for this book is available from the British Library

Library of Congress Cataloging-in-Publication Data
Getting institutions right for women in development / edited by Anne
Marie Goetz.
  p. cm.
  Includes bibliographical references and index.
  ISBN–1–85649–525–6 (hb). — ISBN–1–85649–526–4 (pb)
  1. Women in development. 2. Women in politics. 3. Women—
Government policy. 4. Organizational change. 5. Organizational
behavior. 6. Communication in organization. I. Goetz, Anne Marie.
1961–
HQ1240.G47   1997
305.42—dc21

ISBN 1 85649 525 6 (Hb)
ISBN 1 85649 526 4 (Pb)

Contents

Acknowledgements

This volume of reflections on gender and institutional change was built up over several years of debate amongst feminist academics and activists. It began as a workshop held at the Institute of Development Studies, University of Sussex, in November 1994, titled, like this book: 'Getting Institutions Right for Women in Development'. One objective was to generate some cross-pollination between theorists and activists, through debate between academics, management specialists, civil servants, and members of development organizations, many of whom offered 'insider' accounts of strategies to get their own organizations 'right' for women. Many of the papers from that workshop were published in the July 1995 issue of the *IDS Bulletin* (vol. 26, no. 3), and updated versions of some of these are reprinted in this collection. I am grateful to Kirsty Milward and Felicity Harrison for their research assistance and administrative support during this workshop, and to all the participants for contributing to lively discussions.

The next step in the genesis of this volume was one of the many seminars held in China in September 1995 at the NGO Forum of the Fourth UN Conference on Women. A team of feminist academics from the IDS and the School of Development Studies of the University of East Anglia prepared a workshop: 'Breaking In; Speaking Out: Making Development Organizations Work for Women'. The team consisted of Cecile Jackson and Ruth Pearson from the UEA, and, from the IDS, Sally Baden, Sheelagh Stewart, Lyla Mehta, Bridget Byrne, Kirsty Milward, and myself. We were joined, for the workshop, by Tina Wallace of the University of Birmingham, Inez Smyth of Oxfam, and Tahera Yasmin of the Canadian International Development Agency in Bangladesh. Presenters and participants braved the hottest and most humid day of the NGO

Forum, in a makeshift tent-cum-seminar room on an increasingly muddy field, to engage in a stimulating debate for an afternoon. I am grateful to everyone on the IDS/UEA team, and the other presenters, for contributing to focusing that debate on what had emerged as a central theme of the entire Conference: the dilemma of how to institutionalize gender equity concerns in development without either having the gender interest co-opted to serve, instrumentally, other development goals, or retreating to a devalued enclave concern on the margins of development processes.

In compiling the present collection, papers have been taken from the original IDS workshop and the Beijing workshop, and a few chapters have been contributed by researchers who were unable to participate in either event. As with the original workshop, this book retains an interest in representing perspectives of theorists and practitioners; some of the contributors are academics, others are or have been civil servants, gender trainers or NGO activists.

I am grateful to Robert Jenkins, Elizabeth Harrison and Sally Baden for helping me with editing some of the chapters, and I thank Louise Murray, the Zed Books editor, for her patience and enthusiasm. Thanks are due to Terry Pearce for her untiring help with typing and formatting. And special thanks to Robert Jenkins and Jeanette Goetz for their constant encouragement and support.

1

Introduction:
Getting Institutions Right
for Women in Development

Anne Marie Goetz

'Getting institutions right' has today become as central to development discourse and practice as getting prices right was in the 1980s. The focus has shifted from changing supply signals to understanding the politics of how institutions regulate and coordinate societies, how people's needs are interpreted by policy-makers, how resources are allocated. The purpose of the focus on understanding institutions, at least in most contemporary 'good governance' debates, has been to promote institution-building, to encourage the efficient use of public resources, and to encourage private investment (Moore et al., 1994: 8); getting institutions 'right' for market efficiency. What might be involved in getting institutions right *for women* is a question not often asked. It should be. In developing countries, Gender and Development policy objectives have, at least in principle, been accepted by the development establishment for some time now, yet the fact that social institutions and development organizations continue to produce gendered outcomes which can be constraining or disadvantageous for women means that we must investigate these institutions and organizations from a feminist perspective.

It is important to stress that institutions have not necessarily been 'right' for men either, shaping choices for them in limiting ways according to gender, class, and race in a variety of contexts. The focus in this book on getting institutions right *for women*, however, is meant to signal that a concern with gender justice should be a core value when analysing institutions and organizations and making proposals for change.

This book examines the project of institutionalizing gender equity in the development context. This is sometimes known as 'mainstreaming' gender equity concerns in development institutions. The contributions to this book provide theoretical and empirical discussions of gendered features of a range of development organizations, from NGOs (non-governmental organizations) to state bureaucracies. They consider the relationship between gendered aspects of organization, and gender-discriminatory outcomes in the development process. In the end, the project for gender-sensitive institutional change is to routinize gender-equitable forms of social interaction and to challenge the legitimacy of forms of social organization which discriminate against women. The contributors to this book also offer strategies to make gender equity routine in development organizations. The objective is to promote accountability to women in development institutions by identifying the organizational and political conditions under which economic and political gains for women in developing states might be achieved and sustained.

From WID to GAD and 'Mainstreaming' Gender in Development

'Women in Development' (WID) and 'Gender and Development' (GAD) refer to critical approaches to development policy-making from a feminist perspective. These approaches have a near-thirty-year history in the context of policy-making for social and economic change in developing countries. WID policies have been promoted by feminist policy entrepreneurs within development agencies, and by critics from outside development institutions, since the early 1970s. These policies to improve women's educational and employment opportunities, political representation and participation, and physical and social welfare have been given a high profile by periodic global UN Conferences for Women since 1975. In the developing world, these efforts were prompted by the observation that women were being excluded from new social and economic opportunities afforded through development efforts (Boserup, 1970), or worse, that women were being involved in development processes in ways which deprived them of their independent rights, roles and access to resources, 'domesticating' them into a Western vision of womanhood (Rogers, 1980).

When assessing these decades of WID policy implementation, feminists have pointed out two broad problems – problems which reflect on the ways these policies have been institutionalized. The first is that although WID policies have been to various degrees successful in improving women's material condition, they have been much less effective in improving women's social and economic power relative to men in development contexts. The second is the persistent political marginalization of women's views on the development process, especially at the level of development planning in institutions such as state bureaucracies and development organizations from multilaterals to NGOs. The first problem – the slow progress in equalizing power in gender relations – led to the shift from WID to GAD. More than a change in terminology, this represented a reassessment of concepts, analysis, and approaches in gender equity policies. WID approaches had been based upon a politics of *access* – getting women into development agencies, including more women as recipients or clients of development programmes, ensuring that more development resources reached women directly. However, sluggish rates of change in women's material condition led to the conclusion that women's lesser power in social relations, which is institutionalized in gender relations (as well as class and race relations), was inhibiting their capacity to profit from improved access to social and economic resources. The GAD approach recognizes the importance of redistributing power in social relations.[1] Beyond improving women's access to the same development resources as are directed to men, the GAD approach stresses direct challenges to male cultural, social and economic privileges, so that women are enabled to make equal social and economic profit out of the same resources. It involves levelling the playing field, in other words, by changing institutional rules.

The second problem, the persistent marginalization of women's perspectives on development objectives and on means to achieve them, relates to the institutional politics of pursuing feminist policy ambitions, and is the subject of this book. The implementation history of WID and GAD policy has always depended upon the institutional location of these policy efforts and the political strength and legitimacy of the women's movement. Moser's well-known description of the five most common incarnations of WID policy – 'welfare', 'equity', 'anti-poverty', 'efficiency' and 'empowerment' (1989) – broadly traces what happens to policy according to the ways it is interpreted and processed in different institutional contexts. WID policies to solicit women's involvement in 'anti-poverty' and 'efficiency' policies, for example, have been described as an instrumental use of women's labour by development institutions preoccupied with rapid economic growth (Kandiyoti, 1988). Investment in women's education or income-generating capacity can be justified on the basis of its positive externalities in terms of improved family and community welfare – as a benefit for development, rather than as a contribution to women's capacities to control their life choices – but this may have negative consequences for its contribution to women's autonomy. This way of justifying WID policy can be a consequence of the absence of women's own perspectives in decision-making in the institutions in question. It is no accident that, in contrast, the 'empowerment' approach to women's development interests emerged from a critique by women of developing nations, concerned to respect women's interests and identities in an unequal global economic order.

Over the last decades, WID/GAD policy entrepreneurs have attempted various combinations of strategies to foster commitment to women's interests in development. In the organizations which 'dispense' development policy, such as state bureaucracies and non-governmental organizations, much GAD research and activism has involved mobilizing constituency support to press for change from the outside, or on internal strategies such as encouraging the hiring of more women development professionals, increasingly sophisticated policy development, and the collection and provision of data on women's situation to help promote change in the knowledge environment informing decision-making. Deep-seated resistance has hampered these efforts. Policy-makers remained unmoved by empirical demonstrations of the importance of the gender issue, and in spite of significant increases in numbers of women development professionals, they cannot all be assumed to sympathize with the gender equity cause, and in any case, there are still few women in the upper echelons of decision-making in development organizations. Since the mid-1980s there has been a focus on centrally mainstreaming the gender equity concern by promoting it in all of the organization's pursuits, rather than pursuing it through separate WID bureaux and WID projects. These efforts have also come up against significant resistance.

In response, GAD advocates have produced carefully tailored training packages, guidelines, analytical frameworks and methodological 'tool kits' for development decision-makers. The training approach implicitly identifies the problem as attitudinal; it assumes that once sexist attitudes are changed, resistance will vanish. The search for simple formulae and tools to integrate gender-sensitive data and practices to projects and policies implies faith that technique can override forms of prejudice embedded in organizational cognitive systems and work cultures. Both approaches underestimate the role of discriminatory gendered patterns in the incentive systems, accountability structures, and bureaucratic procedure in derailing GAD efforts.

There have been a few feminist heralds in the GAD field who have pointed to the importance of understanding the gendered nature of development organizations and of their broader institutional environments: researchers such as Kathleen Staudt, Jane Jaquette and Nüket Kardam. But it is only recently that their ideas have been taken up by GAD policy advocates concerned to institutionalize gender equity more effectively. As yet there is little theoretical and empirical work available to illuminate gendered features of organizations and their links to unsatisfactory outcomes. In this book, however, we hope to contribute conceptual reflection and case material to expand on our understanding of gendered institutional politics in the development context.

Institutional Contexts of Development Organizations

This book sets out to investigate gendered features of development organizations and their institutional environments, and yet these are not normally considered to be highly gendered arenas. With regard to gender, the family is most commonly identified as the primary institution in which women's entitlements and capabilities are so distorted as to undermine their capacity to manage transactions to their advantage in other institutions. Other institutions tend to be seen as relatively gender-neutral territory. Institutions such as the market mechanism are assumed to manage transactions efficiently on the basis of voluntary contracts. Public-sector institutions are assumed to have nothing to do with the structural and systemic nature of women's disadvantage, which is seen to be the outcome of transactions in other institutions like the market and household. Recently, however, a much stronger appreciation has developed of a gendered dynamic shaping institutions beyond the household, where gender relations are understood to *constitute* institutions such that these institutions reproduce gendered inequities to varying degrees. In other words, we can now talk of specifically gendered market failures and gendered public-sector institutional failures: markets fail to invest in and reward women's productive and reproductive work; public institutions fail to include women equitably amongst the 'public' that they serve. These gendered preference systems are more than discriminatory attitudes or irrational choices on the part of individuals, or unintended oversights in policy. Nor are they deliberate policy outcomes. They are embedded in the norms, structures and practices of institutions.

It is helpful at this stage to make a conceptual distinction between institutions and organizations. In English, unfortunately, 'institution' can mean anything from an organization to the vague sociological notion of recurrent patterns of human behaviour. While this range of meanings is too broad to be analytically useful, it is difficult to settle on a definition of institutions which is much more precise. Following the economist Douglas North, institutions are best understood as frameworks for socially constructed rules and norms which function to limit choice. They are 'humanly devised constraints' (1990: 3) which reduce uncertainty and provide structure to everyday life, making certain forms of behaviour predictable and routine, *institutionalizing* them. The project for gender-sensitive institutional change is therefore to routinize gender-equitable forms of social interaction and to challenge the legitimacy of forms of social organization which discriminate against women. Recognizing the *human* dimension in the construction of institutions alerts us to the fact that they are not immutable or 'natural' approaches to organizing human relationships, and also to the fact that all institutions embody a history of social choices by particular groups. A critical analysis of institutions can show how these choices are sometimes socially sub-optimal, not made with either equity or efficiency in mind, but rather made to preserve the power of particular groups.

Other definitions of institutions emphasize their role in generating experience. The sociologists Anthony Giddens and R.W. Connell suggest that by setting limits to, or boundaries around, social practice, including thought, institutions shape human experience and personal identity (Giddens, 1986; Connell, 1987). The experience of gender difference, therefore, can be seen to be a *product* of institutions, where it is the outcome of institutionalized patterns of distributing resources and social value, public and private power.

Understanding institutions as historically constructed frameworks for behavioural rules and as generators of experience contributes to under-standing why it is that when new agents (such as women) and orientations (such as concerns with gender equity) are introduced to institutions, outcomes can seem so little changed. Institutional rules, structures, prac-tices, and the identities of the agents which animate them may continue primarily to serve the political and social interests which institutions were designed to promote in the first place.

Gender redistributive policies have characteristics which tend to create resistance and opposition within the organizational and broader institu-tional environment. Policies to mainstream women in development activities previously reserved for men – such as those which enhance women's rate of market engagement – involve participants in activities designed to change people's most unquestioned behaviours and deeply cherished beliefs. The business of expanding women's access to and control over resources, and of revaluing their roles in the rural economy, disrupts traditional interpretations of gendered need and worth upon which patterns of female exclusion and denial are based. Unsurprisingly, given the importance of systems of gender inequality for individual, kin and community identity, such policies can attract significant hostility from target communities.

This hostility stemming from cultural norms exists, of course, within bureaucracies as well. Amongst bureaucrats, it may be expressed in the circumspection and equivocation which can fracture gender policy rhetoric; in the insistence, for example, on gender-role complementarity and the denial of conflicting gender interests, or in the use of gender policy to service other objectives, such as family planning or efficiency goals. Diffidence towards the gender-transformatory aspects of policy can also be reflected in the tendency to downplay the empowerment-related objectives of such programmes and to focus instead on the 'technical' matters of quantifiable input provision, in a process which turns a blind eye to issues of women's actual control over these inputs. Or it can be expressed structurally through resource allocation patterns which leave gender-related programmes stranded on the peripheries of regular government development budgets, as short-lived, foreign-funded pilot initiatives.

The familiar analogy between institutions and the 'rules of the game' in competitive sport (cf. Schiavo-Campo, 1994; Evans, 1993) is helpful in expanding on this problem. 'Rules of the game' are adapted to the capabilities of the players; they challenge players, and allow for fair and manageable competition between particular categories of players. However, there may be completely new contestants entering the game at a much later stage whose capabilities are not reflected in the parameters of the game. Like pygmies competing with the Harlem Globetrotters on a conventionally designed basketball court, they will be unable to win, because they cannot change some of the basic 'rules' – like the height of the net or the size of the court. Most often, new participants have to adapt their behaviour to the existing rules. They may learn to win, but often at the cost of bringing their 'different' needs and interests to play – as when over-achieving managerial women become 'sociological males' (Kanter, 1977). After all the trouble of 'breaking in' to institutions, new participants find it surprisingly hard to 'speak out' in their own voice.

An alternative, of course, is to opt out entirely – to create new forms of institutions and organizations. Women's organizations represent this kind of response. They are oriented to developing new structures and organizational cultures which reflect women's needs, interests and behavioural preferences. It is no accident that women's organizations the world over often concern themselves with gender-specific problems which find unsatisfactory response from public or private institutions – problems such as sexual violence and personal physical security in the home. The chapters by Tahera Yasmin, and Sheelagh Stewart and Jill Taylor, discuss women's organizations and ask whether women approach organization and power in a different way from men. One observation they make is that these women's organizations continue, inevitably, to operate within the broader institutional contexts of the state, community, and the international environment for financing development operations, an environment which imposes dominant interests in development on the internal incentive structures and organizational forms of local organizations.

Organizations are formed within the environmental constraint represented by institutions, they create the concrete mechanisms through which formal and informal rules are applied, societies are regulated and coordinated, resources are distributed, and cultural systems are validated and reproduced. Over time, however, they can have a transformative impact on the institutional arena, changing underlying rules, systems and incentive structures. Douglas North suggests there are three main institutional arenas which provide a general normative 'environmental constraint' for organizations. These, and the organizations they embrace, are:

- *The state* This is the larger institutional environment for the public service administration, the legal system, and organizations which manage coercion such as the military and the police. Public service bureaucracies of particular importance in impinging on people's capacities to realize their endowments include: the educational and health system, marketing boards, agricultural research and extension systems, infrastructure, energy, irrigation and water supply. Also important is the nature of political institutions which shape patterns of representation and accountability (single versus multi-party systems, the organization of local government, etc.).
- *The market* The framework for organizations such as firms, producers' cooperatives, and financial intermediaries.
- *The community* The context for the organization of families or households, kin and lineage systems, local patron–client relationships, village tribunals or other organizations presiding over customary law. Organizations or associations of 'civil society' exist in this arena: NGOs, women's organizations, civic organizations.

Most of the contributions to this book focus on development organizations, looking at the gendered constitution and outcomes of organizations operating in the public arena. The market and institutions in the 'domestic' arena such as the household are not discussed directly.

Different institutional arenas each structure social transactions and maintain social order through different dominant dynamics or norms. According to Moore, the state and its bureaucracies respect the principles of hierarchy, the market is structured around notions of competition, and community-level transactions often respond to notions of solidarity (Moore, 1992: 66). The public sector will have a normative environment shaped by bureaucratic values and methods stressing impartiality and accountability; market organizations will be based on principles of exchange on the basis of voluntary contracts; and the community may be shaped by ideologies of intra-familial altruism, shared identities on the basis of religion, gender, region, ethnicity, lineage or generational groups, or shared problems and concerns over matters such as community welfare, environmental protection, labour rights, and so on.

For policy purposes, the organizations in each institutional arena pose different challenges for gender-sensitive change. The public sector is usually seen as the easiest to penetrate given the much more obviously humanly constructed (as opposed to seemingly ascribed, 'natural', or 'God-given') nature of its rules and norms. The formal impartiality of bureaucratic norms based on merit, and inclusiveness of democratic principles (if and when they are positively espoused by states) seem to offer women a chance to participate as part of the 'public' served by the public sector. The market, on the other hand, is perceived as a notoriously hostile arena in which to achieve gender-equitable outcomes, given the disadvantages women entrants face with their lower human and capital resource endowments. Some organizations based on principles of solidarity – such as NGOs – are regarded as particularly promising sites for gender-sensitive change strategies, out of faith in the responsiveness of egalitarian value-driven cultures to women's needs and interests.

Frustration with the pathologies associated with state bureaucracies, including their susceptibility to capture by elite interests, asymmetrical principal–agent relationships allowing for little participation by clients, and a notorious indifference to equity issues in status-conscious civil service cultures, has led aid donors to prefer working through NGOs, whose decentralized command and communication structures, and investment in participatory decision-making processes, are promoted as models for the public administration (Korten, 1987; Fowler, 1990; Buvinic, 1989). There is a largely unexamined assumption that these organizations are also more receptive than state bureaucracies to the problems of the poor in general, and to poor women. This seems to be based upon the assumption that collective as opposed to corporate management approaches should admit of greater involvement of subaltern groups, as should other structural features which reverse information flows from the top down to the bottom up, which expand on fieldworkers' decision-making power, which enhance the participation of local groups in decision-making. Some recent studies, including chapters by Brooke Ackerly, and Aruna Rao and David Kelleher in this volume, challenge this presumed comparative advantage of NGOs with regard to their gender sensitivity. NGOs can be as deeply structured by male privilege and preference as other organizations, and indeed, can be as bureaucratic and hierarchical as public-sector institutions. NGOs which appeal to notions of a 'moral economy' and community solidarity often reproduce deeply gendered aspects of community institutions.

Gendered Outcomes

The persistence of gendered outcomes of everyday decision-making in both state and non-governmental organizations, often in spite of policy rhetoric promoting gender-sensitive changes, has led to the conclusion that institutions themselves are gendered; that relations of administration in the public sector, or exchange in the private sector, are gendered. In deconstructing institutions by gender, it is easiest to begin by identifying their gendered effects, or their 'gendering' outcomes, and move from there to understanding how they are actually *constituted* by gender difference. It helps to work through an example, so here we take the case of rural development. In most countries, striking gender differentials persist in efforts to integrate women to development programmes in the productive sectors, particularly agricultural production. Analysis of implementation patterns show that women's identity for policy is often limited to those features of their lives which centre on their contribution to family welfare, and on their needs as dependants of men, rather than their needs as agricultural producers. Table 1.1 schematizes gender-dichotomous patterns in rural development programmes. It is an adaptation of a method used by Nancy Fraser (1989) to deconstruct public policy from a gender perspective, and it has the institutional environment of government rural development programmes in South Asia in mind.

The table, obviously, is a very abstract representation of dichotomous patterns in policy interpretation and implementation, and it makes generalizations which obscure great complexities in policy interpretation. Nevertheless, the general point can be made that there are often gendered sub-texts and dichotomies in institutional practices and outcomes. There can be an implicitly 'masculine' mainstream system of development programmes addressing the needs of primary producers, while an implicitly 'feminine' sub-system is tied to household and community management, and is geared to mothers and their dysfunctional (that is, malnourished, poorly educated, sometimes female-headed, or simply too large) families, and sometimes their degraded environments. 'Producers' such as 'farmers' are implicitly men. Agricultural development policies rarely involve training and recruiting women extension agents, research in crops which women grow, and ensuring that market information and new production inputs reach women farmers. Instead, there are projects to enhance women's kitchen gardening or homestead-based income-generating efforts. Policies for women differ markedly in the justifications appealed to for policy legitimacy (community development problems instead of national production targets), in monitoring and implementing agencies, and in their funding base. They differ, too, in the degree of autonomy and rights they

Table 1.1 Policy benefits and delivery practices compared for men and women's rural development programmes

Differences in:	'Mainstream' economic development system	Subsidiary community welfare sub-system
Central orientation	To address the production needs of 'farmers', of 'primary' workers, or 'household heads', and 'breadwinners'.	To improve household and community management, addressed to 'subsistence', voluntary, or 'secondary' labour; geared to 'mothers' and their dysfunctional families.
Justifications appealed to for policy legitimacy	Macro-economic planning considerations in national priority policies.	'Basic needs' considerations in projects.
Monitoring and implementing agencies	Ministries of Agriculture, of Local Government, or of Rural Infrastructure	Separate women's bureaux within line Ministries, NGOs, and women's organizations.
Significance of benefits	Individual access to modern agricultural technology, to the modern banking system, etc.	Group-based access to appropriate small-scale technology and micro-enterprise training.
Degree of autonomy accorded beneficiaries	Active subjects participating in policy-making.	Passive objects on whom change is visited.
Funding base	Permanent government budgets for national development priorities.	Foreign-funded pilot projects.

accord beneficiaries, with male producers' associations more likely than women's associations to be consulted in public decision-making.[2]

These differences send unambiguous messages to policy clients about their social identity, their relative importance, and social worth. Such programmes can enhance women's survival chances within the traditional family. But in doing so, they can help reinforce the traditional assumptions about women's roles which contribute to their lower entitlements and capacities for self-development, although this will depend on the ways women themselves receive and react to policy messages. Such policies hardly provide women with an institutional alternative to dependence on the family, which employment rights or equitable participation in the market might do. They institutionalize a profound gender division in public policy clientship which reinforces notions that women's and children's needs are rightly matters for private, male, provision.

It is important to note that gender differences in policy delivery approaches should not be seen as necessarily discriminatory. For example, group-based approaches to delivering credit, training or appropriate technology to women may be much more appropriate than a more individualized approach. A group approach may allow women to build a sense of solidarity for mutual support, something which men may not need as badly because of their greater social power individually, or which they may have already developed through class-based mobilizing. *Sameness* is not required in policy delivery approaches but, rather, sensitivity to difference, respect for equal rights, and a commitment to outcomes which are empowering for women. Thus, a group-based framework for delivering resources to women is not a problem if one objective is its contribution to women's collective empowerment. It is, however, a problem if it is merely an instrument for more efficient development practice; a means of managing controlled and uniform resource delivery.[3] It is also a problem if organizations assume women's identity for public policy as being conditioned by their social relationships as dependants of men, and construct their interpretation of women's needs and interests accordingly. Two contributions to this volume (Ackerly and Goetz) trace the ways implicit assumptions of this kind are expressed through the implementation practices of fieldworkers in rural credit programmes, and how they affect women's capacity to assert autonomous control over development resources.

The Gendered Constitution of Institutions

The general example of gender-differential outcomes in the organization of rural development suggests that institutions do not just passively mirror gender differences in social organization; they also *produce* gender differences through their structures and in their everyday practices. With the exception of the organization of families and kinship systems, it is not always obvious how institutional norms and the organizational structures and relationships which enact them are constituted by gender, particularly since norms embedded in bureaucratic impartiality or voluntary exchange appear, on the surface, to be gender-neutral. In the family, by contrast, the foundational institutional contract – marriage – is clearly gender-ascriptive. The conjugal contract is made between a woman and a man, and the language of kinship (sister, brother, uncle, aunt, etc.) is explicitly gendered. But there is an ideological and conceptual split between 'public' and 'domestic' or 'private' institutions, where a foundational principle is that public relations of production, exchange, and administration are indifferent to gender difference. A classic tenet of the Weberian view of bureaucratic organization, for example, is that public bureaucracies are insulated from the social and political relations in which they are embedded, and in particular, abstracted from patrimonial, and by implication, patriarchal relations. The absence of explicitly gendered organizing principles disguises the salience of gender divisions of labour, power and desire as organizing principles in these contexts (Connell, 1987). As Kabeer notes:

> Despite the separation of domestic institutions from the public domains of production and exchange, familial norms and values are constantly drawn on to construct the terms on which women and men enter, and participate, in public life and in the market place.... Both within and across institutions, gender operates as a pervasive allocational principle, linking production with reproduction, domestic with public domains, and the macroeconomy with the [local]-level institutions within which development processes are played out. (1994: 62)

Each major institutional arena is gendered in its male bias – its failure to value, recognize or accommodate reproductive work, defining it as 'unproductive', or basing effective participation on a capacity to attain freedom from the reproductive sphere. Institutions are gendered in their active male preference; they exclude women as members or clients/ recipients; or, alternatively, they actively 'feminize' women's participation to entrench their secondary, nurturing, supportive roles, or dependence on men, in institutions outside the household.

All institutions beyond the household or domestic sphere are gendered to the degree that they are located in a 'public' and 'productive' economy, while neglecting the human resource subsidy which the 'domestic' and 'reproductive' economy provides to the 'productive' economy (Elson, 1994: 39). Because the sexual division of labour relegates reproductive functions primarily to women, men are better able to pursue their interests in the 'productive' economy, while women's participation is always conditioned by the way their roles in the reproductive economy have shaped their endowments. This socially constructed and gendered split between 'public' and 'private' is then deeply reinforced – institutionalized – through the formation of social networks or shared understandings and conventions of exclusion and inclusion, justified ideologically, which privilege the participation of the particular social group that has freed itself from reproductive work (ibid.: 37). In the market, for example, while conventional economics explains social norms in producer relationships as mechanisms to monopolize sources of labour or capital for efficiency purposes, critical social scientists have demonstrated that contractual arrangements for social exclusion and inclusion actually function as techniques of social control, maintaining the social and political standing of one gender, or a particular class (Evans, 1993; Bardhan, 1983; Hart, 1991). These social norms are often not explicit, but rather, are embedded in the structures and hierarchies of institutions, in the conditions and requirements for access and participation, in their incentive and accountability structures.

A good example of embedded gendered exclusion in institutional structures and practices is the way financial intermediaries have excluded women (and the poor in general). The successes of special credit institutions in challenging this demonstrates directions for positive institutional change to include women. High barriers to equitable participation by the poor, and especially women, in financial markets are maintained through basic rules of participation which favour propertied male producers. The collateral requirement in borrowing excludes women who often do not own land; the transaction costs involved in loan processing and management procedures means that small loans, especially consumption loans, which women may prefer, are not favoured by banks. The physical location of banks requires travel away from home, which may be difficult for women, and basic application procedures may require a degree of literacy not attained by many women producers.

Innovations in financial intermediation pioneered by organizations like the Grameen Bank in Bangladesh have demonstrated the enormously positive gender-sensitive impact which changes to these structures and practices can have. Replacing collateral requirements with peer monitoring of loan use and repayment, and on-the-spot loan approval, has cut loan access transaction costs to the woman borrower and loan management costs to the lender, while also making it possible to lend smaller amounts. Bringing banking to the village eliminates the social and economic costs of mobility to women. The elimination of complex application procedures requiring literate borrowers, and the waiving of requirements for male guarantors for women's loans, allows women access to the financial system in their own right.

Structures and Agents

From this point on in this chapter, the discussion focuses mainly on organizations, rather than institutions more generally. The key to devising strategies to change organizations to enhance their receptivity and accountability to women whether as citizens of the state, participants in development programmes, or staff members in organizations, is to understand the gendered dynamics of decision-making and organizational functioning. Norms, legitimating ideologies and disciplinary foundations are imprinted on organizational structures such as management hierarchies. These produce everyday procedures and practices which inform incentive systems, formal performance standards and informal organizational cultures, which direct the behaviour of individual agents. Human agents, participants in organizations, do not simply passively respond to incentive systems or policy directives, however. They bring their individual ideologies and behavioural patterns to their work in ways which can eventually change practices and structures.

As Cecile Jackson points out in this volume, the role of individual agents in affecting institutional functioning is often neglected, partly because of structuralist assumptions which over-determine the impact of power relations and resource endowments on individuals. Whether within the family or in a state bureaucracy, individuals have agency affecting their response to institutional incentives. In development service institutions individual agents have important roles in affecting the impact of policy, nowhere more so than at the implementation level. This partly explains how progressive gender policy goals can be subverted in implementation processes, as the critical arena for the realization of the spirit of policy commitments is at the interface between development workers and the organization's membership.

Individual agents in organizations may or may not share in a general institutional ambivalence to gender-redistributive policy, but given the precariousness of their career positions within their organizations, their options are limited to compliance with dominant attitudes, or a very risky commitment to more 'counter-cultural' policy goals such as gender equity. At the lower levels of development bureaucracies, organizational agents constantly interact with beneficiaries and because of this are in a position to retain an awareness of the real needs and capabilities of their beneficiaries. Organizational agents receive authoritative interpretations of the needs of women beneficiaries from their superiors (who have themselves 'translated' the interpretations of policy elites), interpretations embedded in the programme inputs which they are expected to dispense, and in the delivery practices which they are expected to pursue. But their own perspectives on legitimate needs and programme practices may vary according to their own interactions with beneficiaries, their notions of their own identities, and their individual positions within class, organizational, and gender hierarchies.

Several chapters in this volume examine the importance of individual discretion in promoting gender equity within resistant institutions. Jackson demonstrates the ways fieldworker responsiveness to women's needs in a farming project in eastern India resulted in the legitimation of activities designed to assert women's rights. Anne Marie Goetz explores differences in the receptivity to women's needs shown by women and men fieldworkers in rural credit programmes in Bangladesh. And the chapters by Georgina Waylen, Shirin Rai and Virginia del Rosario examine the ambivalent role of women within the state; some acting according to their class and party interests; some taking risks as 'femocrats' to challenge state-institutionalized sexism.

A Gendered Archaeology of Organizations[4]

The process of understanding the gendered nature of organizations engages researchers in an 'archaeological' investigation; it involves disinterring and reinterpreting histories, and scrutinizing artifacts such as favoured concepts, terms of inclusion or exclusion, symbols of success or failure. It involves investigating the traces which gendered patterns of privilege leave in the organization and architecture of space and time, and in behavioural patterns which are tolerated or punished. Here, eight elements of a 'gendered archaeology' are outlined.

1. *Institutional and organizational history*

A starting-point in analysing organizations by gender is to identify the gender interests which have, over time, shaped their broader institutional frameworks. This is not a particularly easy task. Take the case of the state, which is the broader institutional framework for individual development bureaucracies in the public administration. In the West, studies of the history of the definition of the modern 'public' sphere, by Carole Pateman and others, have shown that women were excluded from public citizenship in the sense that its definitional criterion was some form of 'independence' defined in terms of the male experience, including property ownership, bearing arms and 'employment' (Pateman, 1988; Okin, 1991; Gordon, 1990: 20). The resulting gendered split between public and private came to institutionalize women's exclusion from the concerns and practices of public institutions.

Understanding the history of how a particular group has established an institution can illuminate how patterns of exclusion became institutionalized, and this helps in identifying critical points for change. But feminist analysts run into the same difficulties as Marxist functionalists if they substitute gender for class and assume a conspiracy of male interests monopolizing certain institutions. For example, Mies's argument that the state is a 'general patriarch' (Mies, 1986), an executive of men as a group, suggests a homogeneous and passive tool for a monolithic larger interest. It underestimates the complexity of the state, with its many different organizations with sometimes conflicting interests, offering differing prospects for feminist incursions. It obscures histories of women's struggles, and makes it hard to explain genuine victories achieved in women's interests.

Also, 'men's interests' are presumably just as difficult to identify 'objectively' as women's,[5] nor is the category of 'men' any more valid as a universal than is the category of 'women'. The historical record, however, does show that men tend to act, across divisions like class or race, more cohesively than women do in defence of certain gender interests, and they do so in ways which mean that public institutions help to forge connections between men's public and private power. In part, this is due to their longer occupation of public office and to their literal dominance of decision-making and decision-enforcing. It is also due to the historical embedding of their needs and interests in the structures and practices of public institutions. Attention to the historical processes through which certain institutions come to promote male dominance and female dependence should help illuminate the mutability of dominant interests through politics and contestation.[6]

Attention to gendered institutional histories also illuminates the gendered sub-texts of apparently neutral organizing structures, practices, and ideologies, to help explain why these prove so resistant to women and their interests. The past cannot be changed, but new interpretations of established histories can be empowering for change processes when the historical construction of contemporary 'givens' or 'facts' is understood. Taking the history of the Western state again, we know that women's voice was initially explicitly excluded from institutional procedures for ensuring participation, such as the vote, and processes underlining political legitimacy, such as securing popular consent. This gives grand concepts like democracy a gendered sub-text, defining women out of equal and effective public participation (Phillips, 1991). In the labour market, investigations into the history of agricultural labour processes, or trade-union formation, illuminate points at which the active exclusion of women was part of the negotiation of men's economic security *vis-à-vis* employers (Hart, 1991; Cockburn, 1983). These examples point to the need to redefine the meaning of concepts such as citizenship and 'production' in order to give women's civil rights an equal foundation.

In this book, Katherine Fierlbeck's insightful analysis of the relationship between accountability, consent and interest articulation investigates the gendered history of the concept of 'consent' underlining political arrangements. She reminds us of the ambiguities of 'consent' for women, where their presumed free consent to arrangements (such as marriage) which diminish their individual rights, obscures the role of institutional 'contexts of choice' in circumscribing their autonomy as freely choosing individuals. This comes as a timely warning in the context of governance debates. Democracy, participation and accountability may not automatically allow for the expression of women's interests, divorced from changes in the institutions of private property or the labour market which might make women's participation more meaningful.

2. The gendered cognitive context

The ideologies and disciplines that animate organizations can institutionalize strong gender biases. Conventional economics, for example, which guides thinking in many development organizations, has been identified as 'fundamentally disabled' in its capacity to understand women's inequality as a function of gendered power relations because of its choice-theoretic analytical framework (Elson, 1994: 39). Elizabeth Harrison's discussion of the FAO (Food and Agriculture Organization) in this book shows how disciplines related to agricultural production have fundamentally masculinized the notion of the agricultural producer. Organizations oriented to social and human development have been more open to the inclusion of gender perspectives, but until recently women have tended to be included in 'feminized' ways, as objects of family welfare policy. Feminist critiques of disciplinary frameworks from economics to anthropology have contributed conceptual and theoretical revisions to allow for the inclusion of gendered perspectives. These critiques have been important in efforts to valorize and legitimate women's perspectives on the ways institutions conceptualize their environments and roles. Nüket Kardam's chapter illustrates the importance of institutional cognitive frameworks in affecting the prospects for receptivity to gender equity concerns.

3. Gendered organizational culture

Some feminist analysts of bureaucracies, such as Kathy Ferguson, argue that literal male dominance is embedded in distinctive features of bureaucratic culture such as the valorization of instrumental rationality, top-down command and communication systems, specialization, as well as aggressive, goal-oriented styles of management. The suggestion that these represent innate sexual characteristics is highly contentious, as indeed is its corollary: the suggestion that these features of administration necessarily exclude positive outcomes for women. Stewart and Taylor's chapter gives an example of this in its description of working with the police in Zimbabwe – a strongly masculinized and hierarchical institution – to promote better responses to problems of domestic violence. In spite of serious problems with the male culture of the police, the centralized structure and discipline of the police force, along with its strong logistical capability and extensive network of outposts – all aspects of rigid hierarchy and strict command relationships – were a positive advantage in expanding the coverage of the project and ensuring a uniformity in the application of new gender-sensitive procedures.

4. Gendered participants

All institutions have privileged participants, included and excluded groups, superiors and subordinates. Identification of the gender of 'winners' and 'losers' in the market, or of decision-makers versus decision-takers in organizations, is important in determining which group's interests are served by a particular institution. Men tend to dominate most formal public-sector institutions, and most private-sector market institutions, as well as most socially significant civil society associations. Whether more women in decision-making positions would re-orient institutions towards responsiveness to women's gender interests remains a hypothetical question, as there are few empirical cases of women dominating public institutions. Conversely, the mere fact of male dominance does not necessarily preclude men from representing women and acting in their interests. In actuality, however, men as a group do appear to act to defend their interests as a gender, even across class divisions, particularly in terms of defending male employment security and privileged market access. The tantalizing possibility that a greater physical presence and more tangible participation of women in public institutions might change the character of these institutions, however, is behind the focus on women bureaucrats, fieldstaff, and politicians in some of the chapters of this book. Most of these chapters (by Waylen, del Rosario, Rai and Goetz) cannot reach a conclusion about the capacity of women 'insiders' to promote women's interests, because they are investigating contexts in which women are in a dramatic minority and lack structured external support such as might come from women's organizations. However, Ackerly's study of credit programmes in Bangladesh, and the chapters on women's organizations by Stewart and Taylor, and Yasmin, strongly imply that investing in the confidence and security of women staff has been a key to successful efforts to promote women's empowerment in development programmes.

5. Gendered space and time

The physical and social capabilities of those who dominate institutions will be reflected in performance or success criteria, and in the physical and social – or spatial and temporal – structure of an organization's work. Men's social capacity to achieve relative liberation from child care and domestic responsibilities allows them more time for work or institutional interactions beyond the home, while their social independence gives them cultural rights to mobility and autonomy outside the home. Institutional time management of working hours, and life-cycle/career trajectories, will reflect these capabilities, as will the physical location of the institution. Thus institutions from markets to schools can be particularly inaccessible to women if they are distant from home, open only during hours when women are doing work for which there are few labour substitutes, and if they fail to provide space for children. An example of gender-friendly changes to institutional space and time is China's post-1986 approach to community-managed primary education, in which measures such as flexible schooling hours, sibling care facilities at school, and special schools for girls, accommodated girls' space and time constraints (World Bank, 1995: 60).

In this book, Yasmin's chapter goes into the most detail about organizational approaches to structuring space and time. Comparing a women's development NGO to mixed NGOs in Bangladesh, she demonstrates how it is possible to overcome seemingly intractable constraints on women staff's capacity to travel and live away from home through gender-sensitive provisions for women's accommodation and mobility. These efforts have transformed the public space of the office into a comfortable quasi-domestic space, with provision for child care, for eating and sleeping; bringing the private into the public, the home into the office. Other NGOs in Bangladesh, such as BRAC, also have offices-cum-living quarters in rural areas. There is a marked difference in their character, however, with many aspects of the 'domestic' – particularly children – excluded or concealed; the public space remains relatively 'unpolluted' by the domestic. Although the women's organization's approach makes the public arena much more accommodating of women, it tends to be derided by outside observers such as donors, who regard its offices as 'dowdy', with the implication that there are efficiency costs to this domestic informality.

For changes to space management to contribute to women's empowerment, rather than being experienced as paternalistic forms of control or protection, considerable time must be invested in raising women's self-confidence and capacities to defend their rights. Yasmin shows that this time investment is usually considered wasteful and inefficient by 'mainstream' organizations. Just as a substantial time investment is critical for embracing new staff, so too is it an important element of working for women's empowerment on the level of programme implementation, where work to unseat internalized feelings of inferiority, and to build up solidarities and resource bases as alternatives to dependence on men, takes tremendous amounts of time. These, too, are activities mainstream organizations prefer to sacrifice in favour of easily measurable, quantifiable achievements such as quantities of credit disbursed and recovered, numbers of new members registered, numbers of people trained in particular skills.

6. The sexuality of organizations

One aspect of the gendering of public space is the way the sexed body is perceived in that space. Though ostensibly absent from non-'domestic' spaces, sexuality is inevitably an element of human interaction in any location, and the way various 'permitted' forms of sexuality are managed, as in the military, or ignored, as often the case in school settings, will have implications for women's physical security or ability to gain respect as equal participants, rather than as sex objects (Hearn et al., 1989). The chapter by Rao and Kelleher addresses this issue most explicitly, in raising problems of the harassment or 'teasing' of women staff by men in BRAC, and in discussing management efforts to accommodate certain expressions of female sexuality such as maternity and menstruation, as well as efforts to control (hetero)sexuality by discouraging liaisons between staff.

The contribution of women both individually and as a group can be devalued by invoking the symbolic significance of the public–private divide to associate their presence and affectivity in the organization with their private identities. Sex-typed tasks signal this, but its most insidious expression is the problem of sexual harassment, which deeply undercuts the identity and effectiveness of women as autonomous and equal public agents.

7. Gendered authority structures

On the one hand, gendered ideologies and disciplinary structures can leave little space for women to validate their perspectives, and on the other, gendered ways of organizing space, time and sexuality can make it difficult for women to compete effectively with men, or to thrive and succeed in certain institutional environments. Gendered authority structures can further undermine efforts to establish direction and vision in

women's gender interests because of the lack of cultural association between women and 'public' power, and because of the ways male authority
is entrenched in hierarchies and command and control systems. The
greater significance assigned to male achievements and forms of expression, as a consequence of their near-monopoly of control in organizations, is reflected in organizational value systems, the gendering of
particular skills, and in particular, in the gendering of authority symbols.
This makes it difficult for women to command authority for their
approaches and views in organizations, and results in the familiar
phenomenon of women having to take on sociologically male attributes
('male' authoritative behaviour, power dressing, minimizing the demands
of home and family, etc.) in order to gain recognition in male-dominated
power systems. Goetz's chapter discusses how gendered authority systems
affect the nature of relationships between male fieldstaff and beneficiaries,
not just producing greater deference on the part of women beneficiaries,
but also institutionalizing a pattern in which male staff first seek women's
husbands' permission before working with women, making men the
mediators between the project and village women.

8. Gendered incentive and accountability systems

Together, the above gendered dimensions of organizational practice within
institutions add up to the creation of gendered incentive and accountability systems. Incentives may be tied more to quantitatively measurable
performance targets than to qualitative matters such as promoting empowerment processes. Accountability may be oriented towards more
vociferously demanding constituencies (such as funders, or well-organized
clients such as producers' associations) rather than downwards or
horizontally towards women's groups. The near-global mood of neo-
liberalism in the management of public institutions, with the imposition
of commercial contracts for services which may be hard to measure in
monetary terms (such as counselling victims of domestic violence,
consciousness-raising work, community care, or academic reflection) has
meant the introduction of new principles, relationships, and incentives
which can marginalize many concerns and projects associated with
women's empowerment.

Kardam's chapter deals centrally with incentive systems, demonstrating
the accountability failures which result from conflicting or incompatible
incentive systems at the interfaces between different institutions, such as
large international NGOs and small local organizations. Stewart and
Taylor's chapter details the bureaucratic and hierarchical relationships
introduced to a Zimbabwean women's organization when it began

receiving foreign funding. The new preoccupation with financial account-ability meant a shift in accountability towards funders, away from the organization's primary stakeholders, its female membership. Ackerly's chapter details how this operates for the financial incentive and account-ability systems in credit organizations. Performance incentives in small-scale credit delivery services are increasingly tied to the speed with which money is moved, rather than to its impact within the household. Pressure to disburse and recover money rapidly will relax concerns to ensure that credit contributes to women's financial autonomy.

Interest Representation

This book sets out to develop a feminist critique of organizations and institutions. Such a critique has to be based upon a notion of women's gender interests in assessing the gender-sensitivity of organizational responses to women. But defining women's gender interests is a particu-larly vexed problem in feminist theory. Maxine Molyneux has provided a practical guide to this question by distinguishing between women's (and men's) practical gender interests, which arise from their lived realities as socially gendered individuals, and strategic gender interests, which are deduced from an analysis of women's subordination and are oriented to transformation of the relations between the sexes (1985). Anna Jonasdottir situates the discussion of women's interests in the context of feminist institutional change efforts, by distinguishing between women's interests in gaining 'simple access' to institutions and establishing a 'controlling presence' within them, as women acting in a corporate, not merely numerical, sense (1988). This does not necessarily point the way to en-suring that institutional change is occurring in ways which promote women's strategic interests in changing gender relations, as it is not im-possible to imagine a non-feminist corporate expression of women's interests – the successes of the anti-feminist women's lobby in the US in challenging abortion rights or undermining the Equal Rights Amendment are indicators of this possibility.

This problem is discussed in Fierlbeck's chapter, which focuses on the *contexts of choice* in which women determine their political interests. She highlights the importance of determining whether the choices institutions create for women are gender-constrained, in the sense that they create environments which embed women's perceptions of their own interests in a narrow range of gendered subjectivities. The importance of ensuring meaningful conditions for choice – which include material and political equality – puts paid to sunny assumptions that more democratic govern-ance will automatically enhance accountability to women, without attention to the contexts in which women consent to particular distributions of social and political power. Feminist theorizing has acknowledged and embraced the importance of social difference as a source of variation in women's life experiences and hence in their political perspectives. The problem with cultural identity politics for feminist capacities to make judgements about the justice of institutional arenas is partly that it raises the spectre of relativism. Also, in the context of celebrating cultural difference, there can be a tendency to conflate social or cultural identity with political opportunity and choice, a point made by Fierlbeck. This is a form of conceptual slippage which has very conservative implications. It comes back to a problem of associating a rather limited and sex-typed range of political and social interests with women. Ackerly illustrates this problem in her chapter when she shows that some observers would argue that a woman who ignores her own needs in order to repay a loan is acting in an empowered way. However, her 'choice' to deprive herself lacks the institutional context for empowerment. She has no alternative, especially in a culture that validates maternal self-sacrifice.

Since one objective of investigating gendered features of organizations is to identify ways organizations can consciously change institutions of gender disadvantage, it seems inescapable to hold, if only as a temporary analytical device, a feminist notion of women's interests in mind, one which privileges women's rights to make choices in conditions of personal autonomy. This feminist notion of women's interests could then be used as a measure against which to assess institutional change. This is a contentious suggestion, given the obvious cultural bias inherent even in the notion of privileging 'personal autonomy'. The implications of cultural differences for the meaning of feminism (not that there is one meaning of feminism) have been chastening in terms of the differences between feminists in different parts of the world. Jackson's contribution to this volume suggests that it is better to leave the content of interests open, to leave that to women themselves in particular historical and cultural contexts, and to avoid pre-judging the potential for realizing feminist goals in particular cultures. No culture is monolithic in its repressive capacity, and women often create considerable room for manoeuvre for themselves within these cultures. She says this is 'an admittedly messier' view, but it is better able to accommodate the diverse and sometimes contradictory interests that women express and pursue.

In the end, as Nelson and Chowdhury (1994) suggest, probably a good guide to assessing the interests expressed in institutions is an analysis of the gender ideologies implicit in institutional outcomes. Gender ideologies include personal theories about power and agency, and express views on the extent of desired individual and social change. The key would be to interrogate these ideologies for the potential they display for transforming the unequal distribution of resources, social value, and agency between women and men. This does not erase the dilemma of establishing a feminist 'bottom line' for judging institutional outcomes, something which few chapters in this volume avoid.

Organization of the Book

Accountability to women: theoretical perspectives

The first two chapters, by Fierlbeck and Kardam, provide frameworks for considering problems of accountability to women. Fierlbeck's chapter cautions against accepting institutional arrangements justified on the basis of women's 'consent', given the deeply constraining institutional contexts in which most women exercise choice. Nüket Kardam's article provides a framework for situating inter- and intra-organizational issues in a broader, cross-institutional context. She stresses the importance of under-standing divergent gender politics and institutional incentives which operate in three important contexts: the political, the organizational, and the cognitive. These will affect incentive structures of interacting agents in development: NGOs, the state, multilaterals and target populations. Where performance incentives respond to different political, organizational and cognitive imperatives, accountability failures result. Harrison's chapter illustrates this problem by examining the fate of gender equity policy at the interfaces between a multilateral, a national government and a local community. She shows how confusion about, resistance, or indifference to the relevance of gender issues within the fish-farming sector of the FAO was reinforced in Zambia at the level of national institutions such as the agricultural extension system by the lack of awareness of gender issues and the lack of women extension agents. This was met at the community level by a reluctance to undermine the 'moral economy' with the suggestion that there are significant gender differences or conflicts.

Institutionalizing gender equity in state bureaucracies

Three chapters discuss efforts to institutionalize gender equity concerns at the state level. Waylen and del Rosario's contributions analyse formal bureaucracies for promoting women's interests in Chile and the Philippines respectively, and Rai's contribution considers issues of women's representation in the context of moves to set minimum quotas for women's representation in local, and perhaps soon federal, government in India.

In Chile and the Philippines a recent regime change from an authoritarian dictatorship to popular democracy has provided opportunities to institutionalize a place for women in the state. The broad legitimacy base of both new regimes, as well as the role of women in the struggles for democracy, has opened up new, though still uneasy, opportunity spaces for the expression and legitimation of women's concerns in state institutions. These chapters, particularly Rai's, address the tensions between formal systems of interest incorporation and representation (including the party system), and the generally weak political impact of women in the absence of institutionalized forms of representation in the state. The former often leads to co-optation. The latter, women's grassroots activism, can be effective at the local level, as in Chile, but tends to be oriented to organizational forms which do not translate well into effective participation in broader political processes. The Philippine case illustrates one of the most effective examples of national women's machinery in terms of institutionalizing a place for women to express interests at policy-making levels. Even here, however, accountability and representation remain key problems, as expressed in difficulties in cultivating a sustained dialogue with the women's movement. The chapter on the Philippines also traces a range of characteristic patterns in the management of public institutions which undercut the potential for mainstreaming gender concerns. These include the high boundaries maintained between different sectors in public administration, conflicting and competing sectoral concerns, and problems of isolation and marginalization of gender policy representatives.

Institutionalizing gender equity in NGOs

The chapters by Ackerly, and Rao and Kelleher, scrutinize NGO structure and management from a gender perspective. Both contributions discuss NGOs in Bangladesh, a country with an enormous amount of NGO activity. Rao and Kelleher describe an organizational change project which involved moving beyond gender training to challenging, sometimes painfully, deep-seated gendered features of everyday practices and incentive structures. Ackerly's contribution examines the impact of programme design and organizational structure on outcomes, scrutinizing in particular their consequences for women's empowerment. She demonstrates that goals such as women's empowerment are not always consistent with other goals such as rapid loan recovery. Both chapters challenge assumptions that NGOs are necessarily more receptive to gender equity concerns by virtue of their presumed egalitarian values. In other words, management democracy and egalitarian ideologies alone do not add up to an institutional comparative advantage for NGOs in prioritizing gender equity.

The role of individual agents

The two chapters by Jackson and Goetz take a closer look at the inter-face between organizations and their clients, with a view to investigating the degree of divergence between top-level policy directives and actual project outcomes. They investigate the space for manoeuvre at the micro-level, where fieldworker discretion can either promote gender equity or undermine it. Jackson also looks carefully at the role of women project clients in responding to the project, in ways often very distant from the intentions of planners. Her chapter discusses a project which, on the outside, appeared to offer few prospects for gender-equity concerns, being focused on agricultural technology, with few women staff and lacking a strong gender policy. That fieldstaff and women clients were able to appropriate project resources for activities barely related to formal project objectives – such as agitating against men's alcohol abuse – suggests that the importance of formal organizational structures and intentions should not be overestimated in the light of women's agency to appropriate project resources for their own devices.

Women organizing for themselves

The last two chapters look at how women organize differently. Yasmin's contribution illustrates a range of alternative approaches to personnel management and programme organization employed by a women's or-ganization in Bangladesh. She also shows, however, that this organization was unable to resolve problems of power conflicts, particularly those stemming from age-based status differences and centred around manag-ing succession in the leadership of the organization. This demonstrates problems in the often-noted almost anarchic distaste for institutionalizing power differences in women's organizations. Power differences are in-evitable, and some degree of hierarchy and bureaucracy can help in controlling their effects (Phillips, 1991). Stewart and Taylor's discussion of a women's NGO in Zimbabwe illustrates some of the problems of trying to develop a participatory and consensus-based management style in a culture structured on strong gender differences in approaches to expressing authority and demonstrating competence. Their chapter also illustrates a powerful strategy for small women's organizations tackling massive social problems – in this case domestic violence. The organiza-tion was able to leverage its influence on the Zimbabwean police force by playing on the police's legitimation anxieties in order to encourage a positive change in their responses to policing and prosecuting domestic violence.

Clearly, 'getting institutions right' for women in development entails feminist political activism across all social institutions and within individual organizations. As Bernard Schaffer (1984) has shown, drawing on postmodern social theory, administration is not a technical instrument but a political situation – composed of knowledges and social relationships which encode a history of contestation. What the above unravelling of organizations shows is that there are many different points for positive interventions, but the social relations embedded in social institutions and development organizations cannot be changed just by getting a structural blueprint right – in the end, it is a matter of political struggle.

Notes

1. For an excellent account of the conceptual shift from WID to GAD and the institutional politics of this shift, see Razavi and Miller, 1995a.

2. A similarly dichotomous map could be developed to trace the institutionalization of poverty-alleviation measures, with many poverty programmes funded on a pilot basis by outside donors, differing dramatically in the resources and rights accorded to participants.

3. Increasing concern is being expressed about the problem of instrumentalism in efforts to promote gender and development policy – where, for example, resource provision to women or girls is justified on the grounds of positive externalities such as women's apparently greater propensity to invest in household well-being, or fertility control (Jackson, 1996; Baden and Goetz, 1997). It is important not to be too doctrinaire about this problem, however, as to do so denies women's agency and capacity to take advantage of new resources for their own needs, whatever the objectives of policy-makers.

4. I am grateful to Maxine Molyneux for suggesting that this is an 'archaeological' approach to exploring organizations.

5. For discussions of women's gender interests, and in particular, whether 'objective' or 'strategic' interests can be identified for women as a gender, see Molyneux (1985), Jonasdottir (1988), and Fierlbeck, in this volume.

6. This suggests a model of the state such as that proposed in 'state-centred' approaches, cf. Skocpol and Amenta (1986), Evans et al. (1979), or Block's conflict model of the state (1987).

Part 1

Accountability to Women: Theoretical Perspectives

2

Getting Representation Right for Women in Development: Accountability, Consent and the Articulation of Women's Interests[1]

Katherine Fierlbeck

The frustrated cry that the institutions which so deeply affect women's lives in so many countries simply aren't accountable to them belies the simple but ubiquitous belief that human beings ought to be able, individually and collectively, to determine the nature of the structures which govern how they live their lives. The modern demand for accountability is both a recognition of the existence of qualities which distinguish humans from other sentient creatures and, more importantly, a potently useful instrument for protecting and (sometimes) nurturing those qualities (dignity, hope, love, respect) that define our humanness.

Do the institutions most influential in determining development strategies deny accountability to women? As with the questions addressing the democratic nature of any regime, institution, or process, the answer will invariably depend upon how the term is understood. This is not merely a semantic quibble, as a great deal of political power can lie in the ability of political actors to define the terms of discourse in their own terms; and it is useful to remember that institutions such as the World Bank are manifestly not managed by women.[2]

The question of the extent to which a governance-oriented approach facilitates accountability to women *qua* women is irreducibly caught up in the question of the extent to which it ought to do so. My first task is to describe how the criteria of governance (as accountability) are firmly grounded upon the concept of consent as the principal prerequisite of legitimate political authority; my second, to note how consent has played an uncomfortably ambivalent role in the ability of women as a social grouping to achieve (or even articulate) distinct political goals. My argument is that while we can use the idea of a 'context of choice' (which underlies the expression of women's *subjective* interests) in order to make the (politically essential) concept of women's *objective* interests both useful and palatable, situating this context of choice too firmly within a discussion of identity as a primary good has very unenticing disadvantages for those concerned with changing the current conditions of women rather than merely legitimizing them.

The recent emphasis upon governance by institutions such as the World Bank as a framework for policy-making (World Bank, 1992 and 1994; OECD, 1993; Bratton and Hyden, 1992; Williams and Young, 1994) has slightly but perceptibly shifted the terms of evaluation for programmes from efficiency and economic growth to whether the individuals affected by such programmes find them credible and worthy of support. Part of this trend has been purely pragmatic, in so far as it is difficult to implement and administer effective programmes over a long period of time without broad-based support.[3] But the demise of Cold War ideological polarization, coupled with the limited achievements of more orthodox development approaches to date, have obliged (and permitted) such powerful institutions to think hard about the reasons why certain policies manifestly lacked wide-scale support.

The World Bank's 1992 document *Governance and Development* duly noted that the Bank 'has learned from its experience that participation is important for the success of prospects economically, environmentally, and socially' (27). Bound by its Articles of Agreement not to take political positions, the Bank has been able to phrase its support for participation not as an inherent component of liberal democracy, but as a vital requirement for 'efficiency'. Two years after *Governance and Development*, *Governance: The World Bank's Experience* added that 'accountability is at the heart of good governance' (1994: 12) and that 'the effective voice of local people' could best be increased by permitting greater freedom of association in various non-governmental groups (1994: 43). The OECD, not constrained by the same restrictions as the World Bank, asserted quite forwardly that

> certain principles seem inherently desirable. These revolve around the concepts of consent, legitimacy, and accountability to the people: whether participatory processes exist, whether the government is governing with the consent of the governed, whether the latter are allowed an effective voice in the government's conduct and have the possibility of withdrawing their consent and participating in a peaceful replacement of one government with another. If sections of the population like women and minorities cannot participate fully in these processes, the governed do not have an effective voice. (1995: 11)

But the current emphasis on governance has given rise to at least two discernible sets of objections. The first is that too precipitous a rush to achieve popular participation could destabilize already tenuous political

administrations. As Jeffries argues, the call for stronger grassroots participation is frequently based upon the assumption that the power of the
state is excessive. Yet, in many African states, the problem is that 'the
state *qua* state is so hopelessly weak. Government is frequently authoritarian because it is so markedly non-authoritative' (1993: 32). By weaken-
ing the ability of the state to stabilize the political and economic infra-
structure necessary for development, '"democratic" politics is likely to
exacerbate rather than reduce problems of corruption, wastefulness and
short-sighted economic policy formation' (1993: 20).

The second objection asserts that the identification of governance 'as
the primary source of the problem (explaining the lack of success of past
benevolence), and as the basis for solutions (justifying new conditions
and limitations on this benevolence)' is a none-too-discreet promotion of
liberal-capitalist ideology. As donors still anchor 'political conditionalities
within the good-governance regime to orthodox economic conditionality
and the fundamentals of "market-friendly" development' (Schmidtz, 1995:
68, 71), client states are quite restricted in how they wish to accomplish
(or even define) development. Despite the rhetoric, according to this
account, such an approach is hardly democratic in so far as it fails to
respect 'peoples' rights freely to choose their own modes of development
and to decide their own public policies' (ibid., 73).

Regardless of the broader debates over donor agencies' governance
policies, however, the focus upon participation, pluralism, and accountability seems to indicate that greater efforts will be made both to listen
to women's voices, and to facilitate the participation of women in policy-
making at institutional and local levels. Yet the stress upon widespread
acceptability as the pre-eminent standard of political legitimacy nonetheless
poses potentially serious threats to WID programmes. This is because
the fundamental idea underlying the authority of concepts such as participation, accountability, pluralism, and so on (that is, traditional liberal
ideals) is consent: certain practices are acceptable – and thus carry political
authority – because all involved have agreed to them. But the emphasis
upon consent in place of the achievement of more objective and concrete
standards can itself be utilized to validate and to entrench the status quo.

Despite the obvious appeal of policy-making based upon a principle
of individual and collective self-determination, one ought to pay close
heed to the ambivalent role of consent-based accounts of governance
upon which liberal-democratic polities are grounded. From the seven-
teenth century on, for example, the doctrine of consent as the *sine qua
non* of political legitimacy (and thus political obligation) was frequently
used as a means to justify growing material inequalities between classes
(and to reinforce the unequal power relationship between adult women

and men). As feminists within liberal polities have become increasingly wary about offering unqualified support for consent-based accounts of legitimacy in policy-making, it is perhaps useful to discuss the double-edged nature of this concept within the context of the WID strategies and objectives which risk becoming undermined by selective (but common) interpretations of consensual legitimacy. Women cannot afford to dismiss the value of consent or consent-based theories, as they provide a strong basis for individual autonomy and political strength. But consent is, nonetheless, an ambiguous term that must be understood clearly, and used judiciously.

Provision and Agency as Competing Bases of Political Authority

The evocative appeal of democracy has frequently rested upon its role as stalwart champion of the disadvantaged: 'majority rule was originally attractive because it was an ideology of opposition, an ideology that was not about government but rather about displacing entrenched elites, undermining the powerful, and empowering the powerless' (Wertheimer, 1990; Shapiro, 1990). But the assertion that the powerless ought to be empowered stems as much from the visceral evidence of the consequences of their powerlessness as from an abstract belief in the value of human autonomy. That basic needs are simply not being met is much more direct and compelling evidence of egregious bad government than the circumscribed scope of political participation in an educated, well-fed and healthy population.

The gradual acceptance of democratic political norms globally would seem to augur well for those concerned with the well-being of women. But democracy as a specific account of justifiable authority is not, in its more formal manifestation, about meeting the physical needs of those who are the most disadvantaged: it is about securing the consent of the majority in order to act on behalf of the polity. The two accounts do not always coincide. And, as democratic (or consent-based) principles increasingly define political legitimacy, those accounts of representation not explicitly based on consent are more and more frequently spurned or devalued. But consent is far more difficult to measure satisfactorily than material standards of living; and specific interpretations of what constitutes consent (as well as cultural variations concerning the value of consent) make the concept formidable to apply in practice. The brutal paradox is that while the least controversial evidence of women's marginalization is the striking physical and economic disparity they experience,[4] such disparity is increasingly dismissed as relevant proof of marginalization as long as women are perceived to have 'consented' to such conditions. Thus the recent emphasis upon democracy and consensual policy-making as the undisputed standard of organizational legitimacy could, ironically, undermine the authority of WID groups who expect that greater democratization will bolster their attempts to further the interests of women who are physically, economically and culturally marginalized. If democratic governance becomes the principle by which programmes are evaluated, the political battle for WID will increasingly be to articulate women's consent in a way that does not reinforce their social and economic marginalization.

One of the few undisputed characteristics of democracy is the claim that the legitimacy of representation in the modern world rests unequivocally upon the assertion that the body claiming representative authority is democratic. Rather than narrowing down the field of what can be considered legitimate representation, however, this has merely expanded the claims of what constitutes democracy. In many instances this willingness to probe and to question the nature of democracy and liberalism has facilitated the goals of WID: the assumption that the problems addressed by development theory are neutral, for example, has been shown in a very detailed and concrete way to be an instance of epistemological myopia. Women have been cut out of, or disadvantaged by, development programmes because of the lack of crucial information regarding women's roles, values, and preferences; this information was not collected because women's roles, values and preferences were considered either unimportant or identical to accounts articulated by men. This assumption of sameness has been increasingly challenged; but the political results do not seem to be commensurate with the formal acknowledgement of the relevance of these epistemological challenges.

That women, as an identifiable group, are manifestly disadvantaged materially *vis-à-vis* men within their own societies can be understood to be unacceptable for different reasons. One common claim, for example, is simply that it is wrong that their material and physical needs are not being met; another is that this marginalization is evidence that women do not have an equal voice in determining the way in which their society ought to be governed, and that this political exclusion is wrong. The argument that political legitimacy depends upon meeting the physical needs of a group is one of the oldest justifications of any particular political authority. John Locke made this point quite clearly when addressing the assertion by Sir Robert Filmer that the power of sovereigns was paternal in nature, and thus absolute. Locke's argument against absolute sovereignty based upon divine right was that religious tenets made it quite clear that the sovereign was responsible to God to look after the welfare of the subjects: just as shepherds were employed by farmers to look after the well-being of the flock, and did not have the authority to harm them at will, so too was the sovereign in a fiduciary trust with God to ensure that the needs of all God's subjects were met as effectively as possible (Locke, 1960). Thus the authority of a monarch was not simply God-given, but depended more substantially upon the ability of the sovereign to meet the terms of the fiduciary trust placed upon him by God.

While modern liberal democracies assume electoral accountability to underlie the legitimacy of their regimes, the criterion that voters frequently use to judge the relative merit of competing representatives is the extent to which they deem that a candidate or party will facilitate (or has already facilitated) the material prosperity of the polity (or the subgroup in which the voter classes herself). It is arguable, too, that the perceived illegitimacy of formerly communist states was grounded as much upon the failure of such states to provide material goods as effectively as market states, as it was upon the inability of most citizens to participate in establishing the rules governing their polity. A few contemporary states do partially justify their authority upon their ability to provide for the basic needs of their populations. That a regime has increased the health and educational levels of its population, the agricultural productivity of the land, the strength of the economy, and the stability of the social order cannot summarily be dismissed as a claim to good governance, especially when the argument is presented that the provision of basic goods and services would not have been possible within a state where political power is not strongly centralized (see, for example, Jeffries, 1993). Macpherson (1965) has argued that this is itself a justifiable form of democracy in which the emphasis is 'on ends, not means': '[i]t is to make the criterion of democracy the achievement of ends which the mass of the people share and which they put ahead of separate individual ends. And this of course is the classic, pre-liberal, notion of democracy...'

Problems arise, however, when basic needs are seen to have been met, and further demands are placed on political actors. Once the population is literate, healthy, educated and well-fed, which (or whose) needs ought to be addressed?

The increasing wealth and political fragmentation of seventeenth-century England led many political theorists to argue that the optimal form of political association was one based upon the consent of all individuals. But the normative force of consent as the basis of political authority, according to Macpherson (1962), must be understood within the context of a nascent capitalist economy. The authority of the market required the assumption that those engaged in commercial exchanges did so of their own volition, were aware of the obligations imposed by contract, and agreed to be bound thereby. If human beings were presumed to be hierarchically ordered, with some individuals being naturally more gifted or deserving than others, the argument could be made that any exchanges entered into were not equally binding on all parties (just as a contract negotiated between an adult and a young child is never strictly enforced because of the inequality in competence between the two). For capitalism to be seen as fair, the contracting parties had to be understood to be equal, the contract had to be seen to be freely entered into, and – most importantly – being responsible for contracts freely entered into *regardless of the outcome* was to be taken as the ultimate principle of justice. Capitalism could only function if inequalities were seen as just; and therefore justice had to mean accepting responsibility for the consequences of one's actions.

It was justice in the economic realm, then, that influenced the interpretation of legitimate political representation as representation to which individuals consented directly. As the ideal of consent increasingly became accepted as the standard of political legitimacy, liberal regimes could less convincingly argue that women's voices were irrelevant because their interests were self-evidently met by fathers and husbands; or that colonial territories' interests were addressed by imperial regimes. If each individual entity were equal in what was fundamentally important, then each individual was entitled to consent or dissent regardless of any other criterion. Disallowing the vote to women or denying a colony self-determination had been justified ideologically on the basis that they were better provided for under the guidance and authority of their masters: but the normative force of individual autonomy was effectively engaged to contest the justifiability of constraining individual agency.

The moot point, of course, was determining what, precisely, constituted consent (see, for example, Pitkin, 1965). As the political manifestation of consent – voting – became increasingly delineated and institutionalized, the conditions under which consent was assumed to exist within the sphere of commercial contract were usually unarticulated and so the dynamics of power within consensual market relations were not formally addressed. The past decades' experience of political rule in command economies may have illustrated the possibility that consent, which requires some formulation of meaningful choice of alternatives, may be difficult, if not impossible, without some underlying market system that permits a strong diffusion of political power. Simply to assume that exit is an acceptable form of voice is, of course, unappealing for a number of reasons. But economic sovereignty, both of producers and consumers, is one of several very useful choices or strategies in articulating the absence of consent; and especially so when one finds oneself in a political minority. However, if the usefulness of a market should not be underestimated in determining the context of consent, so too should it not be overestimated. The more credence a society places upon 'consent' as the requirement for legitimate governance, the more the society must investigate conditions in which consent is presumed to have been given.

Interests and Identities: Constructing the 'Context of Choice'

How ought consent to be understood? Carole Pateman (1988, 1992) has explored the way in which women have been presumed to consent to a status to which rational, autonomous male citizens would never submit:

> The presumed consent of a woman, in a free marriage contract, to her subordinate status gives a voluntarist gloss to an essentially ascribed status of 'wife.' If the assumption of natural subjection did not still hold, liberal democratic theorists would long ago have begun to ask why it is that an ostensibly free and equal individual should *always* agree to enter a contract which subordinates her to another such individual. (1988: 9)

But what women putatively consented to were not the terms of a negotiable contract, but 'to a status which in its essence was hierarchical and unalterable'. To what extent was the decision not to get married within the confines of such a contract an authentic choice? If the essence of womanhood were defined by her status as a wife and mother, then an unmarried and childless woman would be a freakish monstrosity without any social identity; and any decision to accept this unpalatable alternative could itself well constitute proof of an irrational disposition.

It is in this way not the definition of women's interests but of *meaningful choice* which has become the most difficult theoretical obstacle for feminists. 'The most heavily charged conflict within the discourse about the concept of interests in modern times,' writes Anna Jonasdottir (1988), 'concerns the question of *objective and subjective interests.*' The reasons for this conflict are by now quite well known: to say that women as a class do have objective interests which must be addressed despite individual preferences devalues their own subjective articulation of what is important to them; while to admit only that women have subjective interests makes it all but impossible to address the disparities and attitudes that disadvantage women *qua* women. The accounts offered by theorists such as Jonasdottir (1988) and Molyneux (1985) to resolve this conflict have of themselves been quite persuasive: the solution to the dilemma of interests, of course, has been to distinguish between agency (or subjective interests) and the context within which agency can properly be said to be exercised:

> The main advantage of such a distinction is that it permits the resolution of the conflict surrounding objective and subjective interests. The concept's *formal*

aspect becomes primary so that the content of needs and desires is, from the point of view of interest, an *open question*. In a certain way this means that only 'subjective' interests exist ... [and yet] [u]nderstood historically, and seen as emerging from people's lived experiences, interests about basic processes of social life are divided systematically between groups of people in so far as their living conditions are systematically different. Thus, historically and socially defined, interests can be characterized as 'objective'. (Jonasdottir, 1988: 41)

In other words, it is possible to speak of objective interests in so far as the formal or subjective aspect of interest-articulation is limited because certain individuals, by virtue of their membership within an identifiable group, are denied a range of reasonable choices. The ability to exercise choice without paying a high price for doing so can be said to be in women's objective interests without delimiting the content of their choices for them. But this resolution raises further queries about precisely *which* conditions must exist for subjective interests to be reflectively chosen rather than unconsciously preferred. For, while the provision of certain material goods and formal political institutions would seem to constitute a basic requirement for the exercise of agency, many feminists and thoughtful liberals are changing the contours of the discourse surrounding the context of choice to argue that, in addition to material equality of condition and formal political equality, the assumption of choice is empty without a strong conception of identity within which choice is constructed.

'Consider,' asks Charles Taylor, 'what we mean by *identity*':

It is who we are, 'where we're coming from.' As such it is the background against which our tastes and desires and opinions and aspirations make sense ... my discovering my own identity doesn't mean that I work it out in isolation, but that I negotiate it through dialogue, partly overt, partly internal, with others. (1991: 34)

Why is identity important? It is a fundamental aspect of any political system that holds choice and choosing to be crucial in determining the best life to live, in constructing a coherent account of political obligation, and in solidifying political legitimacy and authority. Liberal theory holds that 'the freedom to form and revise our beliefs about value is a crucial precondition for pursuing our essential interest in leading a good life' (Kymlicka, 1989: 163). But where do these beliefs about value come from?

The decision about how to lead our lives must ultimately be ours alone, but this decision is always a matter of selecting what we believe to be most valuable from the various options available, selecting from a context of choice which provides us with different ways of life. (Kymlicka, 1989: 164)

Thus we cannot expect that people can make definite choices unless they have a conception of what is valuable to them; and they cannot construct a framework of value unless 'they fit into some pattern of activities which is culturally recognized as a way of leading one's life' (Kymlicka, 1989: 165). The political force of consent, based as it is upon choosing one particular alternative rather than any other within a range of choices, thus requires a 'situated' account of value.

But what is the implication of this for women? To the extent that female identity is wrapped tightly in reproductive functions or the emotional nurturance of others, and male identity is not, the political legitimacy of consent (based on the availability of choice, which is itself firmly grounded in traditions that entrench the hegemony of maternal identity), will only structure women's choices in a way that reinforces the current division of power between genders. Moreover, such a division will increasingly be considered legitimate because women have consented to such roles within an ostensibly open context of choice. There is no basis for challenging gender-based inequality if it is a result of free choice. If women understand that they *can* choose unattached lives free from the physical, psychological, and material demands of spousehood or motherhood, but then still choose more traditional roles, then we simply cannot explain this away through references to women's own lack of consciousness of oppression. That women 'internalize' certain sentiments or values (Staudt, 1990: 305) is no longer a claim of false consciousness that negates the claim of consent; it is a perfectly acceptable formation of a decision made within a specific context of choice which emphasizes the validity of the consensual choice made by women. But if a young woman has the formal choice to become an unattached professional, or to become a wife and mother first and foremost, to what extent is this a free and conscious choice if the woman's mother (or family, or society) professes disappointment (or disdain, or hostility) at the prospect of a single and barren daughter? To what extent does the free choice to engage in traditional roles diminish the 'free' choice of a minority not to do so? And to what extent should this framework of choice be legitimized simply because this is the social context within which a woman's identity has developed?

The resolution to the problem of objective/subjective interests offered by Jonasdottir works only as long as the context of choice is considered to be purely formal or material. But if Taylor (1991, 1992), Young (1989, 1990), and Kymlicka (1989) are correct in arguing that a stable social and cultural environment is yet another crucial variable in determining personal choices (because 'it's only through having a rich and secure cultural structure that people can become aware, in a vivid way, of the options available to them, and intelligently examine their value'

(Kymlicka, 1989: 165)), then women's value specifically as mates or mothers becomes emphatically pronounced. The problem is not that women lack consciousness of themselves as women but that they are all too conscious of themselves as women, when being a woman means fulfilling a specific socially defined role. If we then accept, as Jonasdottir urges us, the primacy of subjective interests, once we have determined that a viable 'context of choice' exists, then we are obliged to accept that women's own declaration of their interests as wives and mothers is what is truly important to them. And if they themselves articulate this account of interests, it becomes even more difficult for other women to argue that these choices, based as they are upon the same social context, are not valuable to *them*.

Accepting cultural membership as a primary good in the formation of a context of choice means that women will face increased difficulty in justifying why they wish to take advantage of opportunities that do not recognize their cultural value as women. Thus, rather than alleviating the feminist dilemma of choosing between the objective and subjective interests of women, Jonasdottir's account together with current arguments for the normative force of identity (determined within social contexts) only reinforces the claim that women are in unequal positions because they have chosen to put themselves there. And because they have so chosen (understanding what the alternatives are), they are obliged politically to support the resulting social and political relations.

Conclusion: Choice, Autonomy and Respect within a Framework of Accountability

If the most tangible and emphatic proof of the necessity for WID programmes is the material conditions of women *vis-à-vis* men, this evidence becomes ineffective as a means of contesting the legitimacy of policy processes as long as inequalities are deemed to have been the product of consent. Accountability, if it is to be accepted by women's groups as the new standard of political legitimacy, must involve a great deal of discussion regarding the particular nature of consent involved. The assumption of liberal democracy as a neutral context of choice has rightly been challenged (Young, 1990). But as long as a legitimate context of choice is perceived to be situated within existing social contexts, where the identity of women is structured upon reproductive roles, the value of consent for women will not be fully realized.

In liberal theory, the normative force of consent carries with it a grim and disagreeable price: the obligation not to challenge decisions made by autonomous agents which we may find tremendously unpalatable. If the moral foundation of consent as the basis of political authority derives from the claim that individual adults are responsible agents who can – and must – take responsibility for their actions, then we cannot deny them the self-determining (but unappealing) choices they make. The current debates within liberal theory that offer the most rich and provocative contributions to intellectual thought are those which ask under what conditions consent (or the selection of meaningful choices) can be said to obtain. And it is here that liberalism reaches its most thoughtful potential by reaching into the other two most alluring and influential schools of twentieth-century thought – socialism and postmodernism – and confronting *their* discomforting challenges to the complacent assumptions of consent.

Although Marxism seems to have been politically discredited by its economic inadequacies and its severe circumscription of political liberty, its most discerning insights will be powerfully relevant as long as political authority and market systems coexist. As long as significant material inequalities remain, the potential for distortions of acceptable relations of power will exist between formally equal individuals. This does not negate the possibility of constructing a political system based upon consent; but it does oblige us to monitor and debate the situations under which material conditions unduly influence the calculation of consent.

More inchoately, but perhaps more devastatingly, the ragged but vociferous postmodern movement has presented an even more serious challenge to the doctrine of consent as the basis of legitimate authority. While the coherence of an argument grounding political legitimacy upon consent rests upon the premise of individual autonomy in decision-making, an increasing number of theorists have challenged the intelligibility of this assumption. Rather than existing as self-contained agents wafting through a universe of endless choices, we are situated creatures who are continually and insidiously affected by the more fundamental emotional and psychological ties which we require in order to perceive choices in the first place. Loneliness or social censure or insecurity are formidable obstacles to an individual's ability to make specific choices even when formal political and substantive economic equality exists.

Thus I wish to deny neither the philosophical force of the accounts offered by theorists such as Jonasdottir or Kymlicka, nor the normative resonance of political authority based upon the idea of consent. On the contrary, I desire only to caution that we must be fully cognizant of what types of variables constitute limitations upon our ability freely to choose the types of political constraints within which we agree to live our lives.

Women as a group may, paradoxically, expand their context of choice if they are more willing to view themselves as individuals within arbitrary and contingent environments rather than as members of the class of women simply because women, as a group, have been socially and culturally defined for too long. The value of such a radical individualist approach is not in its atomistic premises but in its ability to make us aware of the extent to which we unquestioningly accept our society's choices as our own. Only when we consciously acknowledge the extent to which our social bonds themselves construct our context of choice can we realize that changing this context is itself a possibility; and it is only when we can effectively influence this web of contingencies within which our lives are shaped that consent can become a forceful basis of political authority for women.

Consent, as a basis of political authority, remains a forcefully compelling principle because it recognizes so many of the human qualities – autonomy, dignity, responsibility – which we collectively value. But to revere the concept of consent means that we must respect the unpalatable decisions made by others and respect, in turn, means than we cannot ultimately challenge the autonomy of the decision-makers. Thus the more we respect consent, the less capable we are of investigating the context of choice; and the less satisfied we are with the context of choice, the less respect we have for the principle of consent in practice. To break this circle we must be willing to probe and to query the choices and decisions of 'autonomous' agents; for consent itself is not only a moral construct but, more tangibly, a potently political device for ensuring obedience. Instruments of such palpable power must always be carefully and consistently scrutinized, and we must be brave enough to say whether consent has been won at too high a price.

Notes

1. A version of this chapter first appeared in 'Getting Institutions Right for Women in Development', *IDS Bulletin*, vol. 26, no. 3, July 1995. This article was written with the intrepid research assistance of Eva Thurlow.
2. 'Since completing an internal study in 1992, the World Bank has increased the number of women in management to 11 per cent from 9 per cent. It hopes to reach its short-term goal of 15 per cent by 1997. But a glass ceiling remains: women account for 98 per cent of secretarial staff, 26 per cent of professional staff, 11 per cent of management and one of 22 executive positions.' *The Globe and Mail* (8 October 1994), A10.
3. Williams and Young (1994) give five specific reasons for the emergence of the governance issue within the Bank: experience with adjustment lending, internal bank factors, academic influences, current fashion, and relations with NGOs.
4. That women are disadvantaged *vis-à-vis* men by specific development strategies is discussed by, e.g., Myra Buvinic (1983) and Barbara Lewis (1991).

3

Making Development Organizations Accountable: The Organizational, Political and Cognitive Contexts[1]

Nüket Kardam

Development projects usually include several actors: bilateral and multi-lateral development agencies, non-governmental organizations (NGOs) and governments (including government agencies at national and local levels), and recipients. The effectiveness of a project depends on the cooperation of all these actors. If we assume that (a) motivation based on incentives determines performance in organizations, that (b) different kinds of organizations use different incentive structures, and that (c) ineffectiveness is the result of the failure to relate incentive to performance on a fair yet compulsory basis, then we need to clearly understand the differences in the incentives of bilaterals and multilaterals, NGOs and recipient governments. In addition, in each sector, incentives are linked to different sanctions. For example, in the public sector the state expects public officials to be motivated by vocation and thus carry out orders. In exchange, it guarantees incomes, recognizes professional autonomy and creates internal accounting systems, while forcing the minister to account to citizens at elections.

The enforcement of sanctions requires *accountability*: service providers have to be motivated to deliver the desired type and level of performance. This can be done by ensuring that the influence of the concerned stake-holders is reflected in the monitoring and incentive systems of service providers. If we accept that accountability is essential and that its 'effectiveness' will depend on whether effective sanctions exist through which that accountability can be enforced, then we need to know what conditions limit as well as promote accountability, in this case gender account-ability in different agencies. I define gender accountability as responsiveness to women's interests and the incorporation of gender-sensitive policies, programmes and projects in state institutions and donor agencies. What are the options open to stakeholders – in our case, beneficiaries, donors, members, governments? As an example, Hirschman's (1970) concepts of 'exit' and 'voice' can provide useful tools in evaluating options.[2]

NGOs (international or domestic) and government agencies obtain resources (development assistance) from the state and from multilateral or bilateral donor agencies and provide services in exchange, and as such they are involved in explicit or implicit contracts in which their output must measure up in some way to what they have received.

> Accountability then becomes the mechanism through which this relationship is regulated, one between principals and agents in which the former must create a system in which they can obtain the information required to monitor performance and create the incentives and sanctions required to ensure that the agents meet the obligations created through the receipt of funds or support. (Brett, 1993: 278–9)

Most of the development literature considers accountability either as a political or an organizational issue and few consider it as a cognitive issue. All three must be examined in order to acquire a broader understanding of accountability. Accountability has to do with the organizational characteristics (goals, procedures, staffing, incentive systems) of all agencies involved, as well as with the political context, that is, the political commitment of the stakeholders to a project, whether the options of 'exit' and 'voice' are available and whether democratic accountability exists. Finally, accountability cannot be discussed without understanding the 'discourse' underlying a particular policy area, in our case gender policy. How do different stakeholders define 'gender issues'? On what basis should resources be allocated to women? The perceived cause of gender constraints will also determine what solutions are proposed. To what extent is there agreement between different stakeholders on the nature of the issue and the proposed solutions? These are some of the questions we might ask as we explore gendered institutions. Therefore, I will begin by analysing the conditions that limit and promote accountability[3] within these three major categories: the organizational context, the political context and the cognitive context.

What Conditions Limit Responsiveness to Gender Policy?

The organizational context

Conflicting objectives of stakeholders

The world of development assistance is populated by a large number of actors: NGOs (both as donors and beneficiaries), beneficiary populations, bilaterals and multilaterals, and host country governments. Since each of these parties has differing and sometimes conflicting interests and leverage, difficult problems of monitoring and enforcement arise. Each actor would like to ensure effective performance, though their needs and criteria as well as their sources of information will differ. While the donors attempt to ensure appropriate performance, the recipients will wish to maximize their autonomy and resources.

Even when there is a seeming fit between project objectives and broader recipient and donor goals, effective performance cannot be guaranteed because such a fit doesn't reveal whether the project is a priority for the recipient or not. If it is not considered a priority (this means that either the project objective specifically fits into policy priorities of recipient institutions and/or is supported by top officials in relevant recipient institutions), the project may serve implicit or unofficial priorities instead of official ones. In the case of developing country bureaucracies, securing autonomy – the power of independent action – is a priority and this can only be accomplished through the acquisition of resources. A high proportion of these resources are expended in maintaining the organization itself rather than in achieving specified goals. A very common way to 'maintain oneself' in developing countries is through patronage politics; resources are secured to acquire and maintain allies.

In order to capture resources, bureaucracies may accept unwanted projects. Once resources are secured, there is a tendency to abandon implementation and turn to the competition for the next round of resources on the part of high-level government staff. This means incentives for effective performance are vastly reduced. In the case of projects for women, governments may accept funds for such projects but may not necessarily have the interest or the will to implement them. We know that many projects that incorporate women are externally funded and it is not clear how sustainable they will be in the long run. Harrison's chapter on an FAO (United Nations Food and Agricultural Organization) fish-farming project in sub-Saharan Africa illustrates the different and at times conflicting perspectives of the donors, the local-level bureaucracies and the recipients themselves. While donors promoted gender analysis in a fish-farming project, the local-level bureaucracies found this policy 'incomprehensible', and the inclusion of women was mostly accepted to attract funding and promote good relationships with the donors. Unofficial priorities are not just characteristics of recipient institutions; donor agencies may also have implicit goals such as the timely delivery of projects through the pipeline. One example is the World Bank: as a Bank, it is a profit-making institution and therefore maximizing the number of loans made in the shortest amount of time possible may take priority. This emphasis on feeding the project pipeline encourages front-end planning, that is, focusing on project design, preparation and appraisal rather than implementation and evaluation. This situation further weakens incentives for performance and its monitoring. As formal and informal goals diverge, commitment may be lost, communication problems may increase, and central direction may weaken.

A World Bank vocational training project in Turkey that ran into difficulties satisfying its objectives illustrates some of these organizational issues (Kardam, 1992). The project objective, 'improving the supply of well-trained labor for manufacturing industries through vocational training' was in line with the export-oriented development strategy of the government, as well as the World Bank strategy to incorporate developing countries into the world market economy through increased exports. Yet most of the instructors who went abroad to be retrained (in areas of export business) returned to their previous jobs. This situation is partly derived from the lack of interest in the project by the Turkish authorities. There is no comprehensive human resource development policy in Turkey that establishes the links between education–employment–certification. If vocational education were a priority area for the Ministry of National Education, perhaps broader policy reform that links education and employment could be established. Even though it is a declared goal, using education to increase socio-economic development is still secondary to its service to promote citizenship and national ideology. Vocational education in Turkey has a definite secondary status, since universities have been the avenue to respected, white-collar jobs. This lack of interest was reflected in the low involvement by high-level bureaucrats in this project. It also affects the lower echelons of Turkish bureaucracy, who are unlikely to devote attention to a project unless they get the appropriate signals from their superiors.

Decentralization

The world of development assistance is very decentralized. For example, the United Nations consists of a myriad of agencies that may be involved in the same project. Projects are implemented by international or national NGOs. The governments are further involved either as recipients of assistance, or, in the case of the UN, as contributors of funds to their own projects. In my research on the UNDP's response to gender issues (Kardam, 1992), I found that the decentralized nature of the tripartite system (consisting of UNDP, UN specialized agencies and member governments) contributed to the slow response. Within this tripartite system, the UNDP is required to give first consideration to project execution by UN executing agencies with the appropriate specialization. Donor governments have a voice in UNDP affairs as contributors of funds, and recipient governments have come to regard the Indicative

Planning Figures (IPFs) as firm commitments to their countries. Further-more, recipient governments contribute funds to UN projects, which gives them a voice in the process. This system may lead to a lack of definition of responsibilities (with commensurate authority) in project management. In the case of gender issues, I found that this has led to 'passing the buck', a disavowal of responsibility syndrome. The decentral-ized system has not been entirely unfavourable to the consideration of gender issues, however. It has at times allowed gender-sensitive UNDP staff to play the role of 'instigator' by bringing donors and recipient governments together to sponsor particular activities.

Procedures of stakeholders and finding indicators for success

Procedures, broadly defined, include skills, knowledge, training of employees (including the approaches and strategies used) and decision-making techniques (such as economic analysis, technical analysis, or analysis based on social science techniques). Particular procedures also provide staff members with particular perspectives or world views on issues. Both donor and recipient procedures influence the project process and shape the project team's operations. Since gender policy formulation takes place within institutions, it is of the utmost importance to pay attention to specific organizations' goals and procedures in order to promote gender-positive institutional change. Whether gender policy is introduced in a way consistent with the goals and procedures of an organization influences its response.

In my analysis of three development agencies, the World Bank, the UNDP and the Ford Foundation, I found that policy advocates took care to define gender issues in accordance with each agency's goals. For example, the World Bank's goals are to increase its profitability as a financial institution and to promote economic growth for developing countries (with reliance on the market mechanism). To the extent that women in development (WID) issues were presented and justified in a way instrumental to these goals, they have been acceptable. Ultimately, the consideration of WID issues depends on the ability of its advocates to demonstrate greater benefit to cost ratios in order to elicit more resources. On the other hand, the Ford Foundation's more extensive response to WID can be explained by the greater consistency of WID with the Foundation's goals and procedures. The Foundation's goal of finding innovative solutions to social problems rests on a value system that emphasizes equity and anti-discrimination. The root of social prob-lems is seen as stemming from the unequal treatment and discrimination of some groups in society. Given that the objective of WID advocates is to enhance women's ability to contribute to and benefit from develop-

ment on an equal basis with men, the relevance of gender issues is justified on the basis of the Foundation's goals and values (Kardam, 1991).
The Ford Foundation's procedures emphasize the search for and solution
to social problems. In fact, staff members are primarily social scientists
with backgrounds in academia and research organizations. Finding solutions to social problems has meant support for the production of new
knowledge. When the Foundation enters a new area, it makes grants for
basic research, applied research and action programmes, in that order.
This has proved to be an advantage in women's programming because
research by and on women clearly helped identify areas where action
regarding women's programming was needed.

Procedures that are control-oriented tend to hinder flexibility and
response to unforeseen circumstances, qualities that are especially needed
in new areas like gender policy. Control-oriented procedures discourage
frequent consultations between the donor, recipient and the project team,
and may lead to misunderstandings and resentments. Procedural differences affect the project process even more if the organizations involved
operate in different cultural and economic contexts, as they do in development projects. Project teams are accountable to several masters, that is,
they have to work with at least two different organizations with quite
different procedures. Even seemingly small procedural differences, such
as differences in payment of foreign consultants and their local counterparts, may create enough resentment to reduce motivation and incentives
for effective performance considerably.

Monitoring mechanisms also present problems. Monitoring is especially
costly where donors are funding services in remote foreign areas about
which they have virtually no independent information. Official aid agencies
subject to public scrutiny and accountability need to ensure that services
are properly performed. Formal evaluations carried out by large donors
are sometimes the most rigorous processes to which NGO projects are
subjected. Yet these exercises are difficult in themselves since evaluators
have limited time, local situations are very complex, and both fieldworkers
and beneficiaries will have a vested interest in ensuring that the service
continues. They may therefore collude to conceal failures from evaluators.

Perhaps the major problem in the public sector is the difficulty of
devising and enforcing rational success indicators. In the case of gender
policy this is especially relevant, as there is disagreement on how it should
be defined and implemented.[4] As Brett points out:

> As long as non-market agencies are used for many purposes, we will have to
> make allocation decisions on the basis of imperfect success indicators which
> involve calculations based on subjective ideological judgments as much as on

objectively measurable quantities.... Where objectives are in conflict – for example where participatory processes reduce the output derived from a given investment – the final assessment must be based upon a sum of the gains and the losses. This involves difficult philosophical and practical problems evaded in traditional economic analysis, but in real life social choices are commonly made on the basis of competing and incompatible objectives where non-material values often take precedence over material gains. (1993: 280–81)

Many of the chapters in this volume (Harrison, Ackerly, Rao and Kelleher) illustrate the difficulty of defining and finding appropriate indicators for gender analysis.

Internal policy advocacy

For a new issue to gain acceptance, a consistency or 'fit' with the organization's goals and procedures is necessary, though not sufficient for acceptance. A new issue which may be consistent with goals and procedures but without advocates willing to bargain on its behalf will not automatically be incorporated. Without the conscious effort of some people, sometimes called policy advocates or policy entrepreneurs who strive to introduce a new issue in a consistent manner with general goals, policies may never be formulated or implemented (Kardam, 1992). For example, Waylen argues that SERNAM, the Chilean women's bureau established in 1990, succeeded because it consciously sought to achieve outcomes fitting in with the agenda of the government, that is, measures associated with poverty alleviation, rather than ones which threatened to alter gender relations directly.

Polsby (1984) suggests that policy innovations are initiated by interest groups and persons who actively identify new issues and who specialize in acquiring and deploying knowledge about them. He calls these people 'policy entrepreneurs' who, by the skilful mobilization of facts that serve to justify action, and through the accurate identification and thoughtful cultivation of allies (political clout), bring a policy into being. A good example of successful policy entrepreneurship is presented in the chapter by Stewart and Taylor. The Musasa project, a Zimbabwean NGO which focused on the problems of rape and domestic violence, established a successful working relationship with the Zimbabwe Republic Police in combating rape and violence. In my research on the response to environmental issues at the World Bank, I found that an alliance between environmental NGOs and Bank staff members promoted greater attention to such issues (Kardam, 1993).

By virtue of being inside an agency, policy advocates also build in accountability mechanisms by reviewing and revising policy documents, providing input to policy documents, attending high-level management meetings, suggesting new policies to the management and interviewing job candidates. Strategies to present facts as a basis for action range from holding seminars, writing background papers, inviting outside speakers, holding staff meetings, and providing input into programme development, to showing how a new issue fits the goals and procedures of the organization. If agencies don't have gender policy advocates working from within, then instigating gender-positive institutional change will be relatively more difficult.

The political context

Political commitment of stakeholders

If politics means, according to one well-known definition, 'who gets what, when and how' or the distribution of power in terms of both resources and influence, then the politics of international agencies, as well as the politics at both national and local levels will affect gender policy outcomes. Given the time constraints and the competing issues demanding attention from international and national bureaucrats, the question becomes 'why should one pay attention to gender issues at all?'

Lack of political commitment to a project hampers effectiveness because sanctions are ineffective or are not imposed, performance is not monitored and incentives for performance are weakened. In the development literature, lack of political commitment to a project by the recipient country is usually emphasized (Grindle, 1980). Obviously, developing country elites' (this includes both the responsible implementing agency and top government officials) commitment to the project increases the chances of success. If the project is not considered important, implementation will suffer; bureaucrats who are responsible will not give it priority. A discussion of political commitment should not just focus on the recipient side, however. Donor agencies are part of the political context of projects as well. As Heaver puts it:

> It cannot be stressed too strongly that it is a non-issue to raise a question whether agencies should be involved in the sort of recipient bureaucratic activity.... It is a non-issue because agencies have no choice: they *are in* the political game.... If funding agencies choose to adopt a do-nothing strategy, this is effectively a political decision to accept the present position. If agencies are serious about their official goals, the question is ... not whether they play politics, but how to be better at it than others. (1982: 39)

Donor agencies may need to mobilize support among the government agencies and various groups in society in order to achieve project objectives. Parker and Friedman point out:

In spite of the differing interests, all these organizations are linked not only through their shared goal of enabling development but also because each entity needs the support of others for its change process to have a positive impact. For example, if an international U.S.-based development organization makes a strategic change in its primary goals in favor of directly addressing unequal gender power relations, it cannot carry out this goal unless its donor organizations value and support such an approach. (1993)

Sensitivity to external pressure

At the international level, the rise of the WID movement pressured development agencies and governments to put gender issues on the agenda. The United Nations recommendations resulting from several conferences on gender issues, the establishment of WID offices at many development agencies, and the WID bureaux and units within many governmental bureaucracies are the outcome of these pressures. More recently, at the International Conference on Population and Development in Cairo, gender issues were put on the agenda clearly and centrally. The Programme of Action adopted by delegations from 179 states includes a chapter on 'Gender Equality, Equity and Empowerment of Women':

> This chapter calls on countries to empower women and eliminate inequality between men and women, eliminate all forms of discrimination against the girl child and the root causes of son preference; increase public awareness of the value of girl children, beyond their potential for child bearing, and promote equal participation of women and men in all areas of family and household responsibilities. (Populi, October 1994)

At the same time, movements are at a disadvantage when it comes to institutionalization, including the establishment of accountability mechanisms, because the issues need to be broadly formulated to gain acceptance and because they generally are instituted from the outside rather than from within. Furthermore, development agencies' sensitivity to external pressure depends on their independence from their environment. Those actors that are relatively more independent would be less likely to be influenced by external pressure than those that are more dependent. The degree of independence has to do with an international organization's range of accountability to other actors. The narrower the circle of accountability, the more independent an international organization would be. For example, international non-governmental organizations in the field of international development, such as the Ford Foundation, seem to be relatively more independent because their circle of accountability is very narrow: they are directly accountable only to a board of directors. The World Bank, on the other hand, is probably not as independent as the Ford Foundation in its policies, but is nevertheless more so than most

United Nations agencies. The World Bank has a weighted voting system and is therefore accountable to those member states who provide the highest capital subscription. Many UN agencies, on the other hand, are much less independent, because their circle of accountability is quite wide: they are accountable to all member countries since the decision-making process is based on a one member, one vote system. They are thus much more permeable and open to influence by all member governments, as well as by NGOs. Naturally, external influence, such as that exercised by the international women's movement, would have a different impact on different international organizations, depending on their relative independence within the international development assistance regime. It is not necessarily the case, however, that more accountability is accompanied by increased effectiveness. Too much public voice can bring service delivery to a halt; excessive accountability may diminish effectiveness considerably. In fact, both the US Agency for International Development and the US State Department have been named as organizations where accountability to diverse interests has reduced their effectiveness.

Even when international development agencies have become responsive to gender issues, there is no guarantee that they can, in general, elicit compliance from recipient governments. We know that promoting compliance for international norms and rules is a problem for all international regimes. According to Oran Young (1989), the lack of well-entrenched and properly financed supranational institutions in international society ensures that international regimes must rely heavily on the ability and willingness of individual members to elicit compliance with key provisions within their own jurisdictions. I have argued elsewhere that international norms and rules may be very influential in prompting policy changes in a particular country, but whether these policy changes are more than words on paper depends on relationships between state and society (Kardam, 1994). It is important to note that proposing that states make changes regarding women's roles and status creates deeper problems than just those of verification and policing. Proposing changes in the relationship between the state and its subjects is especially sensitive, for as Krasner points out, prevailing international norms and practices place few inhibitions on a state's discretionary control over its own subjects (1985: 118). Yet, support for women's movements from outside the state is crucial for the survival of many national machineries for women that were established in response to the UN Conference in Nairobi in 1985. Alvarez (1990) points out that, in the past, international feminist solidarity successfully brought pressure to bear on the international development establishment, indirectly pushing developing states to open up some political space, however minimal, for the articulation of progressive gender discourses and policies.

State–society relationships

States possess political institutions. These traditionally include constitutions, institutions of power such as legislatures, executives and judiciaries, and a means of promoting political views, often seen in the form of elections. Even though most of these elements are present in Western democracies, as well as authoritarian regimes, in non-democratic settings, questions may arise regarding the extent to which these institutions are held accountable for gender policy, as well as other policies. Southern states struggle to achieve certain goals: 'The central political and social drama of recent history has been the battle pitting the state and organizations allied with it (often from a particular social class) against other social organizations dotting society's landscape' (Migdal, 1988: 27). Within this context whose who make the rules acquire social control. In relatively new states, rules of the game are not necessarily agreed upon. State elites try to penetrate society, regulate social relationships and extract resources with varying degrees of success. For example, the seemingly inconsequential conflict in Mustafa Kemal's Turkey over what kind of hat men should wear was, in fact, about who had the right and ability (religious elites or bureaucratic elites) to make rules.

The question of accountability becomes very important when introducing the term 'civil society' to the discussion of the state. If we define civil society as those institutions and groups below the state level that can challenge the state itself on certain issues, then the type of state must be considered. Presumably, a state that permits such groups to exist and advocate opinions in an unfettered manner can be classified as a democracy, or at least possessing democratic values. Authoritarian regimes, in contrast, would probably not allow such groups to exist at all, or only under strict control. The relationship between the state and civil society becomes particularly important when speaking of a system in transition, or a transition to democracy. One must consider not only the institutional developments, but the existence of, or potential for, a civil society. For the latter to exist, the state must be receptive to possible sources of opposition, and allow its population to participate actively. There must be a political culture conducive to political action.

The accountability of state institutions for gender policy will increase to the extent that regimes are democratic and to the extent that there are women's organizations within civil society who demand it. For example, Alvarez argues that in transitional regimes gender-specific demands may stand a greater chance of being met if women's mobilization is seen as necessary to consolidate the regime, solidify its legitimacy and achieve larger developmental goals (Alvarez, 1990: 270). Waylen's chapter also supports this argument by showing how the Chilean women's movement succeeded within the wider context of the Chilean transition to democracy.

The uneven power balance between beneficiaries and agencies

The beneficiaries of many development projects, especially where women are involved, are typically poor, ill-educated and vulnerable, with limited access to information. But accountability in development projects is generally directed not towards the beneficiaries but towards the donors. As Brett points out:

> in deprived environments, for example in Africa, neither exit nor voice are realistic options for the poor. Some NGOs try to 'empower' beneficiaries through participatory structures which encourage local communities to identify priorities, develop programs.... These are commendable efforts, but they are time-consuming and depend on the goodwill of the agency. They do not give consumers any independent authority over the agency; only donors enforcing a budget can exercise such authority, so that in terms of evaluation, donors have to be seen as surrogates for consumers. (1993: 292–3)

Brett goes on to suggest that local NGOs, once they have access to external sources, acquire a privileged position in the local community while potential beneficiaries may not know what their entitlements should be. Furthermore, once NGOs become successful and expand their operations by scaling-up, this may lead to a preoccupation with growth rather than with beneficiaries.

Professional technicians and government bureaucrats are not rewarded for being responsive to local conditions or contributing toward the development of local institutional capacities. They are accountable to actors different from the clients and this substantially reduces the incentive to be responsive to client interests. As Korten puts it:

> The fact is that USAID is accountable to the US Congress and to agencies such as the Office of Management and Budget. Not surprisingly, the USAID programmer is more likely to be preoccupied with the needs and involvement of the groups that arbitrate his program than with those of the poor beneficiaries. (1980: 484)

Governments may be more easily adaptable to local problem-solving but may lack the political will. To what extent would governments be interested in involving women beneficiaries in programmes and projects? It is clear that new participation changes the nature of the influence structure. Participation is inescapably political. Broader participation by women is likely to change the use and allocation of resources in society. Indeed that is why it is often advocated. Ackerly's chapter in this volume emphasizes how empowerment is mistaken for, for example, the number of loans made to women. She suggests that promotion of women's empowerment requires that planners design incentives for workers, borrowers and husbands that prompt them to choose empowerment as their goal.

Cognitive context – the discourse of gender

The 'definition' of gender issues by stakeholders

In order to promote any new policy, a gap between reality and the desired state has to be seen. Furthermore, reasons for the existence of such a gap need to be elaborated so that one can devise ways to overcome it. There is a wide diversity of views regarding why there is a gap between what exists and what the ideal state of gender issues in development should be, as well as how this gap should be overcome (see Goetz, 1991; Jaquette, 1990 and Kardam, 1987).

The theme of gender and development combines two broad theoretical issues: women's social, economic and political roles in society, and the nature of development itself. As is well known, international development agencies, governments and NGOs differ on the definitions of both these issues. The international WID movement itself has not been able to reach an agreement on any norms, mostly because the definitions had to be left broad and ambiguous in order to elicit cooperation from different actors. Looking briefly at gender relations, most would agree that the power relations between men and women are unequal and what women do is generally undervalued, but the reasons why this is the case and the policy recommendations that stem from these differ vastly.

If the reasons are seen as the infiltration of Western norms that undermine traditional roles and the accompanying respect for women, then the policy recommendations that follow would certainly not include exposing more women to the public sphere and to competition with men. Instead they would include ways to maintain the 'equal but separate' status of women. This, for example, is how religious conservatives in Turkey generally view gender relations. If the reasons for unequal gender relations are seen as being caused by exploitative economic relations, as socialist feminists view them, then policy recommendations would include different treatment of women from different socio-economic backgrounds. Thus different policies for, for example, urban middle-class women, urban factory workers, domestic servants and peasant women in rural areas would be devised. On the other hand, if the crux of the issue is seen as the lack of opportunity for women within male-defined institutions, then policies are targeted to establishing space for women, and rewriting laws to promote women's interests.

The discourse on development, like the discourse on gender relations, also presents a vast and colourful array of definitions and policies that flow from these definitions. Since the issue is not gender issues *per se* but gender and development, gender policy and practice have been interpreted, analysed and justified differently, depending on the discourse on development. When efficiency and economic growth are emphasized, the economic contributions of women to development are brought on the agenda. Policy recommendations then include ways to improve their contribution to national development through programmes and projects in training, education and employment for women. It is suggested that patriarchal norms, principles and institutions be dismantled to the extent that they interfere with women's contributions to economic growth. When equity, basic human needs and welfare issues dominate the discourse, the discussion turns to women in poverty and lacking in basic human needs. Recommended programmes and projects for women within this discourse include increasing literacy, providing loans for small-scale enterprises for women, providing upgraded technology to reduce hours of work and the like. More recently, with the introduction or the term 'empowerment' into development, *women's* empowerment has become a topic of discussion. Policy recommendations that flow from this discourse are broader than the first two. Women's empowerment now includes achieving control over one's life through expanded choices. The policy recommendations that would flow from this view deal with ways of resolving conflicts between women's productive and reproductive roles, for example, child care, and men's share in the maintenance of the family, as well as women's participation overall in the redefinition of gender relations and the meaning of development itself.

All policy is focused on the allocation of resources. How is allocation of resources to women viewed? The institutions one targets for change depend on whether the basis of such allocation is equality, merit or need (Jaquette, 1990). Those who argue for equality would focus on legal institutions, while those who argue for a market allocation for resources would focus on how women could elicit more responsiveness from market institutions. If allocation to women is argued for on the basis of need, then welfare bureaucracies constitute the target. Therefore, it is very important to analyse the gender discourse in specific contexts so that it is clear from which institutions one demands responsiveness. Many of the chapters in this volume show how institutions are gendered. Rosario points out how progress towards gender accountability is slow because it requires challenging the assumptions of policy-makers and political institutions as a whole. Rao and Kelleher discuss how BRAC (the Bangladesh

Rural Advancement Committee) is gendered because of the deeper sense of devaluation of women in both men's and women's socialization.

Strategies for Gender-positive Institutional Change

The exercise of leadership and the formation of alliances

Effective leadership is necessary to move any issue forward. In the case of gender issues, Northern European donors have taken the lead and encouraged other donors to consider gender issues. Initiatives have also come from NGOs both North and South. WID entrepreneurs can request the assistance of gender-sensitive allies both within their agencies and outside. Leadership is a matter of entrepreneurship; it involves a combination of imagination in inventing institutional options and skill in brokering the interests of numerous actors who support such options. Expanding accountability will require a new coalition of gender-sensitive donor agencies, development practitioners in donor and recipient countries, as well as governments and NGOs. Women's NGOs need to become more sophisticated in understanding how institutions work and how to promote change within them. As Korten points out:

> Those VOs [voluntary organizations] with women in development programs are coming to appreciate the full potential of women as a development force and the extent to which their liberation may be a key to unlocking cultural constraints to needed economic and political change. This creates the natural basis for alliances with organizations engaged in the women's movement. (1990: 200)

In addition, international commissions can be set up to monitor compliance; a base for this exists in the series of international covenants on women's issues, managed by the UN Commission on Human Rights.

Improved communication between women's groups and state institutions

Further democratization of societies will play a large role in eliciting responsiveness from governments. In this process, women's groups can play a very important role in promoting the strength of civil society and improving communications between themselves and the government. Unfortunately, in many authoritarian systems, states have been reluctant to allow voice to groups within society, and such groups have shunned government initiatives due to fears of co-optation.

The strengthening of civil society should lead to an improved voice for women. Improved voice comes with empowerment. Uphoff and Esman point out that locally responsive organizations are facilitated by, and may indeed depend on, relative equity in the ownership and control of land, since this reduces the risk that they will be captured by established elites. Likewise, there is danger in including in the same organization groups with inherently conflicting social and economic interests, such as incompatible ethnic groups or landowners and landless workers. In other words, the interest of certain groups in society may impede rural development efforts that involve the poor, including women. This is more the case in a stratified society.

Higher level of education for women

A higher level of education for women will clearly increase women's empowerment and their 'voice' both within society and within institutions. Women who are educated not only have fewer children but also are more aware of the options available to them. This would lead to increased representation of women in state institutions. Clearly decisions emerging from state institutions would more nearly approximate the wishes of women if the staff of these institutions reflect the demographic characteristics of the general population.

Commitment to a transformational development

In order to achieve accountability for gender policy, ultimately, the definition of development needs to change. Thus, besides practical strategies, a redefinition of the development discourse and its acceptance into mainstream development policy is required for long-term change. Such a discourse would start with 'people-centred development'. As Korten has defined it: development is a process by which the members of a society increase their personal and institutional capacities to mobilize and manage resources to produce sustainable and justly distributed improvements in their quality of life consistent with their own aspirations (1990: 67).

Increased accountability will come partly from the political consciousness of women and the practical strategies they use to demand it, but that is only half the story. Increased accountability is also a function of the values of the power holder. Is there such a thing as the responsible use of power; and, if so, how can it be attained? If egoism and greed are deeply embedded in human nature, the human spirit needs to be strengthened so that power is redefined in positive-sum rather than zero-sum terms. Korten suggests that 'this new consciousness must view power not as a club to be used in the service of personal aggrandizement, but rather as a gift to be held in stewardship to the service of the community and the human and spiritual fulfillment of all people' (1990: 168).

In conclusion, it is clear that a discussion of accountability is crucial to making development organizations work for women. Furthermore, it is also crucial to understand the nature of gender relations and their incorporation into bureaucratic and political ideologies. This chapter argues that accountability to gender issues is very complex and is central to making development organizations work for women. Considering accountability from three different perspectives, the political, organizational and discursive illuminates and clarifies some of these complexities.

Notes

1. A version of this chapter first appeared in 'Getting Institutions Right for Women in Development', *IDS Bulletin*, vol. 26, no. 3, July 1995. I would like to thank the participants of the Institute of Development Studies, Sussex Workshop on 'Getting Institutions Right for Women in Development', 3–5 November 1994 for their valuable comments and suggestions; I would also like to thank Jeffrey Yake for his research assistance.

2. The preceding two paragraphs draw upon E.A. Brett's article 'Voluntary Agencies as Development Organizations...', *Development and Change*, Vol. 24: 269–303, which I found very useful.

3. I will use 'responsiveness' and 'accountability' interchangeably in this article.

4. I will discuss these issues in more detail in the section on the 'cognitive context'.

4

Fish, Feminists and the FAO: Translating 'Gender' through Different Institutions in the Development Process[1]

Elizabeth Harrison

Over the last fifteen years or so, feminist analyses have apparently influenced both thinking and practice in international development agencies. The language of gender and development has been widely adopted. For example, awareness of the differences between practical and strategic gender needs[2] is evident in the policy documentation of many multilateral and bilateral donors. However, the tendency of projects for women to 'misbehave' noted by Buvinic in 1985[3] is now replicated by the tendency of 'gender planning' to slip subtly and imperceptibly into the much older 'projects for women'. A relational approach to gender is replaced by a focus on women, while male gender identities lie unexamined in the background. The problem of institutionalizing gender analysis, making it more than a nagging concern on the margins, is as acute as ever: 'despite the energy and resources allocated to this work for more than a decade, Women in Development (WID) still most frequently remains an "add-on" to mainstream policy and practice' (Moser, 1993: 4). The commitment to gender analysis only rarely becomes gender-sensitive practice. More frequently it is translated into 'targeting women' and gradually exchanged for the practical exigencies of project reality.

This chapter traces the process, through a case study of one donor – the United Nations Food and Agricultural Organization (FAO) – and one of its projects in sub-Saharan Africa. The project is not specifically for women, nor does it focus mainly on gender issues. It aims to promote small-scale fish farming as a diversification and supplement to rural livelihoods. However, gender issues gained a high profile in the stated aims of the project. I examine how these are articulated and mean different things to different people in the policy process, from headquarters in Rome to local-level bureaucracies and the farmers in contact with the project.

The example shows how divergent interests contrive to reinforce the continued marginalization of gender issues. I am not suggesting that there is anything especially heinous or different about the FAO or its associated project. Indeed, the efforts that have been made to incorporate gender are often extremely well intentioned. However, processes observed in this case arguably reflect tendencies which are taking place in many similar organizations. Kardam (1991) argues in a study of the World Bank, the UNDP and the Ford Foundation that the integration of gender issues is constrained by both structural and individual choice factors. The different organizations show different capacities and respond in different ways. Without advocates willing to bargain on their behalf, issues such as gender analysis are not automatically incorporated.

Explanations

Two related influences are important in the apparent marginalization of gender issues. First, it can be explained by the different perspectives of different stakeholders in the process. Policy regarding gender is interpreted in diverse ways by different people. This is influenced not only by their position within an organization, but by a wide range of other characteristics. Age, gender, ethnicity, personal history, all influence how people act on and interpret the policies they are required to implement (Long and van der Ploeg, 1989).

Gender is often portrayed as a technical concept which, if only better understood, could be integrated into the planning process. However, an understanding of gender issues from a feminist perspective introduces questions of power, control of resources, and conflict, which are potentially challenging and certainly difficult to deal with. Staudt (1985) comments on male resistance to analyses of gender which threaten male privilege. There is, however, more than a crude dichotomy of interests at issue. For both men and women at all levels in any organizational structure there is also a need for simplification which conspires against any full comprehension of the construction and operation of gender relations. On the one hand, there is a body of knowledge and argument pointing out the variety, complexity and flexibility gender analysis should encompass. By their very nature, because gender relations are socially constructed, they are subject to change and influenced by other aspects of differentiation. On the other hand, development practitioners are unable and unwilling to deal with such complexities. They need a kind of conceptual shorthand – 'simple principles' and 'methodological tools'. In the course of such simplification, recognition of the potentially contentious and inherently political (as opposed to technical) aspects of gender relations is usually the first to go.

The second and related influence in the process is a proliferation of information which is not used and is of highly varying quality. According to many donors, the biggest barrier to addressing gender issues is a shortage of information, not what is done with it. One of the significant achievements of feminist scholars in the 1970s and 1980s was to illuminate the blindness of most development interventions to the different needs and interests of men and women. However, questions need to be asked about the context and the use of such information. There is clearly a difference between 'feminist knowledge', which is challenging, and 'data for development' (Goetz, 1994), which is not. Merely collecting more information will not address the inequities it may reveal. This seriously misconstrues how projects work and assumes a commonality of interests of different actors which is unlikely to exist. As Bierschenk (1988) notes, it is more accurate to see development projects as arenas of negotiation by strategic groups.

Gender and the Crisis of Rural Fish Farming

Fish farming has been promoted in Africa since at least the 1940s. Most frequently, farmers are encouraged to construct earthen ponds, and to manage them as part of their farming system in combination with other crops. From the point of view of donors, fish farming has the potential to meet gaps in protein availability, provide an extra source of income and assist in diversifying rural livelihoods. In these respects it is analogous to many other strategies for rural development.

Currently the promotion of fish farming in Africa is facing a crisis. The donor optimism of twenty years ago is being replaced by a wish to explain the 'failure' of African aquaculture. From the perspective of donors, this failure is manifested in a variety of ways. Farmed fish production from Africa is tiny compared to world totals (less than one per cent). Projects both fail to meet their immediate objectives and are unsustainable. In the light of this waning optimism, two things have happened: there has been a reduction in international assistance to African fish farming, especially in the 1990s, and there has been a mounting interest in gaining a better understanding of the rural communities into which the technology is introduced. One aspect of this is the wish to better understand gender issues.

The Case Study: From Rome to the Fish Ponds

Fish and feminists in Rome

Fish-farming projects are promoted from within the fisheries department at the headquarters of the FAO in Rome. The manner in which the department has addressed issues of gender is a response to a combination of influences: the personal motivation of individuals, the pressure from donors to include sensitivity to gender in project activities, and the constraining realities of both time and money.

Most of the expert staff in the fisheries department have a background in biology or fisheries management. Their main professional interest is fish – how to make sure they grow, how to manage stocks of them, and how to negotiate competing claims for them. They may have strong motivations regarding the well-being of fish consumers, but success criteria in their jobs generally relate to technical concerns.

Furthermore, there is a serious gender imbalance within the fisheries department. This is more pronounced than in the organization as a whole where, of 1,087 professional staff in Rome in December 1993, 219 (21 per cent) were women. On the other hand, women make up 1,311 of the 1,904 general service staff. Women in the professional grades tend to be clustered at the lower end of the salary scale. In the fisheries department there are 13 women in professional grades as compared to 77 men (14.4 per cent). Of these, none are in the senior grades of directors of division or chief of service (13 posts). In the Inland Water Resources and Aquaculture Service, which has primary responsibility for aquaculture development, none of the ten professional staff are women.

The gender imbalance in the department does not of itself imply inability or unwillingness to take gender issues seriously. However, the people occupying senior positions are not neutral, value-free implementers of policy. They bring to their post personal priorities, perspectives and experiences. Influencing these, though not necessarily either visibly or consciously, is a dominant and male-oriented view of the world.

Within the department, however, specific measures have been taken to integrate gender issues in its work. These have included the establishment of a Core Group on Women and Fisheries, the organization of conferences concerned with women and fisheries and women and aquaculture, and the publication of guidelines for planners to ensure that women are included in project preparation. The Core Group on Women and Fisheries includes representatives from all parts of the department. Its tasks are to review projects to check for the inclusion of women, to organize and promote workshops and to 'sensitize counterpart experts and decision makers in recipient countries on gender issues' (Sen et al., 1991: 59). The implication is arguably that sensitization on gender issues in headquarters has already been achieved. The group's activities have, however, been limited because it had no funds allocated and has had to raise money through the different divisions.

In 1987 the Core Group, with financial assistance from NORAD, helped to organize the FAO's first conference on Women in Aquaculture (FAO, 1987). All of the presentations to the conference were made by women. The opening address to the conference was made by the then head of the Aquaculture Development and Coordination Programme (a man). One paragraph warrants quoting in full:

> I have been criticized for the organization of this workshop on two counts. First, I have been criticized (and only by women, no less) for not inviting men as principal participants. But I have no good reason to do so. Frankly, even in this small workshop of thirty carefully selected participants, there is probably not one question I can ask about aquaculture which cannot be answered by one of you. Thus, if during the next three days you need to know the typical labour force of a shrimp hatchery, or the organization for a credit programme in Africa, or the requirements of a project development document for UNDP, someone here among you will have the answer. (FAO, 1987: 6)

This statement reflects a view which is often only implicit: that 'women' can be dealt with separately and the process of technical planning can go on as before. Male gender identities are not questioned. Participants at the conference were predominantly academics and representatives of women's departments in international organizations. Some of them approach issues of gender from a feminist perspective in that they see the relations between men and women as hierarchical and potentially conflictual. The conference document thus illustrates how very different interpretations and perspectives on gender can co-exist within the overall policy-making process. The process of incorporation accompanying persistent marginalization is key in the continuing slip from gender analysis to projects for women.

In his discussion of a development project in Lesotho, Ferguson (1990) argues that the kind of guide to action produced by academic analyses is of no use to development agencies (in his case the World Bank), because they do not provide a charter for the sort of intervention that the agency is set up to do. In the case of Lesotho, analyses suggesting that the causes of poverty are political and structural are 'unhelpful' because development agencies are not in the business of promoting political realignments or supporting revolutionary struggles. The picture becomes more complicated when, as in the example above, the 'unhelpful analyses' are included within the mainstream. Rather than being rejected as useless, they are adopted and ignored.

Gender in the Field Programme

Despite the efforts of individuals, gender policy in the fisheries department in Rome remains little more than the collection of information. There is no institutionalized training for either Rome or field-based staff.

This situation occurs in the face of mounting evidence of the need for such training. The calls for more and more information which character- ize most of the Rome-produced documents about women serve to by- pass more difficult questions of gender and power. The result is 'unsystematic and ad hoc measures being implemented and in some cases, the marginalization of gender issues in project activities' (Sen et al., 1991: 60). The marginalization of gender issues at the level of projects cannot, however, simply be blamed on failures in gender training or failure to commit funds at central level. A more complicated process is taking place as the meaning of gender is shifted and translated.

In 1986, the FAO initiated a programme for aquaculture development in Southern Africa. Aquaculture For Local Community Development (ALCOM) was designed to move away from earlier unsuccessful develop- ment models and to be more 'participatory'. ALCOM was developed partially in response to a conclusion in the FAO's Thematic Evaluation of Aquaculture (FAO, 1987) which suggested that the limited sustained impact of fish culture projects was due to a lack of understanding of the socio-cultural and socio-economic motivations behind small-scale farm- ers' decisions to adopt aquaculture. Accordingly, much of the programme's work has involved the execution of studies and 'methodology develop- ment'. Pilot projects have been set up in most of the countries of the Southern Africa Development Community (SADC) region. These are coordinated from a headquarters in Harare, Zimbabwe.

The programme has received funding from several donors: the Swedes, Norwegians, Belgians, and Japanese. The greatest contribution has come from the Swedish International Development Authority (SIDA). Within SIDA, a number of significant measures have been undertaken to institu- tionalize gender issues. The organization has had a WID office (now called the Gender Office) since 1979. The office undertakes training in gender awareness, attempts to strengthen the position of people responsible for gender at the country level, and develops methodological tools to be used in SIDA's planning cycle. Although not provided with a substantial budget, gender issues have a fairly high profile within the organization.

From ALCOM's inception, the role of women in aquaculture has had a high profile. In the programme's initial preparatory phase, 'women and youth' was identified as a separate target area. No specific budget was allocated 'as ALCOM has always stressed the need for a multidisciplinary approach' (Sen et al., 1991: 77). The aim was, through literature and studies, to identify options and activities to be included in project activities.

Programme management in Harare was increasingly under pressure to respond to two, not necessarily compatible, demands: to produce fish and to exhibit gender sensitivity. On the one hand it was important to address an apparent failure of the programme to produce tangible results, and to find ways of using the results of studies. On the other hand, the need to be seen to be doing something about women remained strong. The result was two-fold. First, a series of studies and meetings were undertaken, and publicity material continued to focus on the important role of women. Second, gender issues remained largely absent from the rest of the programme's activities.

In November 1990, ALCOM hosted an international meeting at Victoria Falls to discuss gender issues in fisheries and aquaculture development. Following this workshop, and in response to its recommendation for more disaggregated information, the Japanese International Co-operation Agency (JICA), agreed to fund a sub-project within the ALCOM programme, 'Enhancement of the Role of Women In Fisheries and Aquaculture Development'. The aim of the sub-project was the incorporation of gender issues in projects for inland fisheries and aquaculture development in southern Africa. Intended outputs were the production of gender-specific data, guidelines and checklists for collecting gender-specific socio-economic information, and the formulation of pilot projects.

In the synthesis paper to the Victoria Falls meeting various policy approaches to gender issues over the last twenty years are discussed. Approaches advocating equity and speaking in terms of subordination are contrasted with efficiency and poverty focused approaches. Equity approaches are dismissed. '[T]his approach (the "equity" approach) proved unpopular mainly because it sought to change the social relationship between men and women through a redistribution of power. Politically, therefore, the approach was not acceptable, nor was it easy to implement' (Sen et al., 1991: 63).

A focus on data collection avoids such contentious issues. Hence this is the main outcome of the gender project – and its main finding. According to the project final report, the principal conclusion of studies carried out in Tanzania, Zimbabwe and Zambia but unrelated to project activities was that: 'there is a severe gap in some gender related information, particularly on the division of labour between sexes, access and control over productive resources and responsibility for decision making' (FAO, 1993: 3).

Guidelines for filling the information gap were therefore needed. These were drafted by FAO personnel and consultants and begin from the premise that there has been little change in sectoral planning regarding gender issues because there is insufficient information on such issues. Furthermore, planners are not certain how or where to obtain such information. Given this premise the guidelines are surprisingly full of sweeping generalizations about both men and women. While lamenting the lack of information, the guidelines do not address other reasons causing planners and host governments to ignore gender issues, particularly those arising from their own motivation. They do not consider why and under what conditions issues of gender may be relevant. As with the studies, and with the recommendations produced by the Victoria Falls workshop, the vast amount of documentation, methodologies and guidelines fails to articulate the problem of women's position in a way that would be challenging or contentious. Despite the obvious fact that a fair amount of information about women in aquaculture has been produced, the issue of why it is not translated into practice is bypassed.

While the guidelines and the meetings failed to confront the essentially political nature of gender relations, ALCOM's publicity machine continued to produce plenty of evidence for the programme's gender-sensitivity. Several editions of *ALCOM News* have contained articles on women and fish farming. In January 1992, the front-cover story was devoted to a photo essay about women and fish farming in Luapula Province, Zambia. It starts: 'Fish farming hasn't ushered in a blue revolution. It has in fact meant a dawn-to-midnight grind for some rural women. But it has given them another income alternative. It has stimulated an upbeat spirit in them. A new hope for tomorrow' (ALCOM, 1992: 9).

The article provides a response to those who question the tangible benefits of fish farming, and express concern that it is so manifestly a technology taken up primarily by men. The emphasis is on family harmony in fish farming, to the extent of caricature. The complexity of the sexual division of labour is simplified to '"my wife helps me with everything" says Stanislaus proudly' (ALCOM, 1992: 8). Gender is thus highly visible and apparently important to ALCOM. However, in the same way that fish farming is a technology largely promoted by men for men, gender issues are construed, by both men and women, as something articulated by women for women. Hence, ALCOM publications which are not specifically about women still tend to assume that the farmer is a man, decisions are made by him, and benefits reach all members of the household equally. At a staff meeting in Harare, gender issues had a place on the agenda as 'the women project'. It was relegated to 'any other business' in the list of priorities, but in the end not discussed because a socio-economist had not been appointed.

Discussion of 'gender' and 'women' does not disappear the closer to the fish ponds and rural communities one gets. At the same time as people from Rome and from Harare bring these debates to the villages, they are re-articulated by both men and women in these villages. It is at the level of the pilot project, the interface between the interveners and the supposed beneficiaries, that questions of strategies and personal priorities become most pertinent.

Local-level Bureaucracies

In 1991–92, I carried out field work in Luapula Province, Zambia. The research was funded by the Overseas Development Administration (ODA), but hosted by ALCOM. They had been implementing a pilot project in the area since 1989 and my role was to provide socio-economic inputs to the project as part of a wider research project. My research was to build on existing studies carried out by ALCOM staff and consultants. Among these were two which had specifically considered gender issues in fish farming (Mbozi, 1991; van der Schoot, 1989).

The pilot project had initially involved the posting of two expatriate workers, an aquaculturist and a socio-economist, to the province. They were to work with Department of Fisheries extensionists, conducting trials and studies and developing extension materials. The province was initially thought to be a success story for fish farming as there had been a rapid expansion in pond construction. However, management practices were not technically optimal and the extension service was so under-resourced as to be ineffective. Both of the first two project workers had left by early 1991 and were replaced by a new aquaculturist in mid-1991. He arrived at about the same time as I did.

The new project worker was in a complex position and had to respond to a number of imperatives. In the first place, he was in his first job in Africa and needed to make a success of it for his own career reasons. He quickly understood that efficient management of ponds and the production of fish were increasingly important success criteria for his employers. Second, he had to address a legacy of ill feeling which had developed between the ALCOM project and the local fisheries department. People in the department expressed resentment that the project did little more than conduct studies and certainly did not come up with important tangible goods: vehicles, allowances and equipment. Third, he had to respond to the pressure to include women in his work. For one thing there was me, reminding him that it would be wrong to assume joint household utility. For another, he had to host the occasional forays of the ALCOM publicity machine. The issue of *ALCOM News* devoted to women and fish farming in Luapula involved a four-day visit by the ALCOM information officer.

For the aquaculturist, spending time with fish farmers every day, certain facts became clear. Most fishpond owners in Luapula, as elsewhere in Africa, are men. Men have better access to land, much more free time, and are more likely to be adept at gaining access to extension services.

Historically, as with many other innovations, fish farming was promoted as a technology for men. Women do contribute labour to male-owned ponds, but such labour contributions are determined largely by women's perceived benefit. They cannot necessarily be taken for granted and depend on the complicated and negotiated nature of intra-household relations. To complicate matters further, household form in Luapula is not fixed and unchanging. Although the most common household form is that of two adults and their dependent children, unstable marriages and frequent temporary migration mean that today's nuclear household may not always be identical to tomorrow's.

However, awareness of these complexities in the face of a need to get farmers to produce fish is not very useful. As Villareal points out, the front-line worker who has the mission of presenting a package and making it work has to work out appropriate strategies, possibilities, and constraints. It is therefore not surprising that those who are targeted and therefore subject to the benefits of the project are those who are 'willing, able, and at hand' (Villareal, 1992: 251). For the aquaculturist the most sensible way of dealing with limited resources and producing the goods was to work directly with the most visible farmers, those prepared to put themselves forward. These were almost all men.

The pressure to include women in the work was not completely ignored though. Rather it was adopted as just that – the inclusion of women, rather than as a concern for gender relations. On a 'fish-farmer exchange', in which farmers were taken to visit the ponds of other farmers, the itinerary included a female fish farmer. The woman visited was many miles' drive from all of the others. She had two huge dry ponds which had been professionally excavated, although on poor soil. She was a former provincial governor. The relevance of her experience to the semi-subsistence farmers who came to visit her was unclear. She was, however, a woman.

For the extensionists, this apparent insistence on the inclusion of women was largely incomprehensible. All but one of the extensionists in Luapula were men. The one woman was not from the area, and was transferred away after only a year. For these men, the prevailing view is that women are weak, powerless, and unable to participate in decision-making: 'Traditionally, women are known to be weak to men. This therefore puts them off most of the activities, for instance fish farming. In short, inferiority complex is a hindrance for women.'[4]

Although this view does not tie in with evidence that women in Luapula do the majority of physical labour (Allen et al., n.d.), or visible evidence of their activity in fish farm maintenance, it is strongly held by extensionists. The pressure to include women in everything is therefore seen as at best an oddity, but more commonly as an inconvenience. In the first place, extensionists and more senior personnel in the department have limited means with which to do their jobs. Only one extensionist in the province has a motorbike, and the rest make do with broken bicycles or rely on transport from the project. There is one departmental vehicle, which is also used for capture fisheries work. In the face of mounting inflation, government workers' salaries are also increasingly worthless. Therefore, the arrival of a donor-funded project brings the prospect of both a greater ability to carry out one's job and possibly perks through the provision of allowances. In the case of ALCOM, however, there was a perception that the donor arrived with an imposed target group which was both irrelevant and used up scarce resources. At the same time, the expected benefits were not forthcoming. To extensionists, there are only doubtful benefits in seeking out women all the time, and this is what they perceived ALCOM's interest to be. In practice the analysis of gender becomes translated to the inclusion of women, a dictate which, when imposed on men who cannot see the point, is resented.

Community and Household

From the FAO in Rome, to ALCOM and the Luapula pilot project, notions of gender relations and the role of women in fish farming are developed, changed and reinterpreted according to the perspectives of different actors. But this process does not stop with passive recipients at the end of the chain in the villages of Luapula. The language used within the project suggests passivity. Women are a target group. So are poor farmers, and model farmers. But the target groups themselves use and manipulate the inputs of the project. As Olivier de Sardan (1988) has argued, the symbolic as well as material and economic benefits of projects are the subject of tension, manoeuvring, and competition.

In Luapula certain farmers wish to be associated with development and progressiveness. This has deep historical roots. Moore and Vaughan (1994) note for neighbouring Northern Province that letters from aspiring 'progressive farmers' in the 1940s show the way a discourse of development had become a shared discourse between colonial officials and certain groups of African men. They argue that 'it should not surprise us then, that when people respond to new development schemes and policies, they bring their history with them' (Moore and Vaughan, 1994: 234).

For the farmers in Luapula, the material gains to be made from association with the ALCOM project are by no means obvious. There is, however, a long history of donor and government intervention in the area. The legacy of this is a tendency to associate projects with material support. One effect is the consistent – and indignant – requests for loans, assistance, and inputs. Some farmers also respond strategically to the ALCOM project as they have done to predecessors. In particular they adopt the kind of language and concepts promulgated by the project and others before it. At a meeting for the distribution of loan forms for fish farming, I overheard the following conversation:

> A: We must learn to show that we are a good community to get these loans.
>
> B: No, that is not what is important now. They are interested in individual farmers now. We must each show that we have a good plan. Then we will get the loans.[5]

Another farmer still believed that community participation was the important catchword. He was the owner of a large vegetable garden, supported with private sponsorship. He took Ministry visitors to see it and proudly told them, 'this is our community vegetable garden'. Crehan and van Oppen note a similar phenomenon elsewhere in Zambia, where 'we are your sons and daughters, you are developing us' means 'we have legitimate claims on you' (Crehan and van Oppen, 1988).

Not all farmers enter the discourse of development in this way. Those that do tend to be better educated, slightly better off, and more likely to be men. In general, women are less likely to attend meetings, or to make claims on extension services. However, there are signs that women, like men, are beginning to learn the possible strategic importance of adopting the gender agenda. In certain villages in Luapula, there has been a succession of visitors (not only from ALCOM) whose primary concern seems to be 'women'. Often this concern has been manifested in the formation of women's clubs. Clubs are recognized by many as a means of access to development assistance because they have often been the principal means through which loans and grants have been distributed. It is not surprising, therefore, that in the village of Chibote, which had received at least four researchers asking questions about women (including myself), the ALCOM information officer taking photographs of women, a German nutrition project for women, a Swedish health clinic with a focus on women and children, a Danish sewing project, and an ALCOM 'mutual feeding centre', women will come together as clubs at the least encouragement. Unlike in other parts of the province, a number of women have dug and managed fish ponds. On my arrival in the village, I was immediately greeted by a group of women, asking me to 'register' them as a club. They explained: 'We are women. We have dug ponds. We must be a club now. We need to be registered.' They said that they had received many visitors interested in fish farming who had promised them a club but still nothing had happened.

It may be wrong to suggest a neat causal relationship here; that women dig fish ponds more because of the prospect of development assistance than because of any benefit from the pond itself. As Jackson (this volume) points out, intentions cannot necessarily be read from action because the factors shaping choice are themselves obscure. Rather than 'manipulation', it may be more appropriate to see these actions as the result of the partial internalization or hybridization of externally induced values. It is nevertheless clear that several women and men in the village are aware of, and ready to respond to, the interest in gender which is articulated by the various projects, including ALCOM. Conflicts over resources within the household and disputes in access to community resources are not part of that agenda by the time it has filtered through the project process. Nor are they part of the shared discourse between interveners and intervened.

While developers speak in an undifferentiated way about households, assuming a sharing and harmonious unit, that picture is reflected in the responses of both men and women in the villages. They are happy to confirm the picture. There is every chance that Stanislaus did say 'we share everything' proudly. True or not, there is nothing strange in it being unacceptable to speak publicly of dissension or disharmony within the household. As Wilson notes for a community in North London: '[i]t was clear that in virtually all marriages, there was a conspiracy of silence where inspection would have challenged the dominant ideology of marriage – the shares were not fair' (Wilson, 1991, cited in Kabeer, 1994: 227).

Behind the image of unity is a much more complex state of affairs. The transitory nature of many marriages in Luapula means that many men and women adopt separate economic strategies, or at least try to ensure possibilities for independence in the event of changes in marital status. There is an identifiable division of labour according to certain tasks, but a flexible and varied control over the products of the labour according to the nature and apparent stability of the marriage tie. Often a shift towards greater separation in farming activities, and to women taking exclusive control of particular fields, is a precursor to marital breakdown. Women and men farmers in Luapula may not talk in terms of gender analysis, but the negotiated and shifting nature of gender relations, the incorporation of both conflict and harmony, are still critical to them.

Conclusion

From the fish ponds in Luapula to Rome, 'women' becomes shorthand for 'gender analysis'. In the process, the political implications of a gendered analysis fade away. The influences at work in the process cannot be neatly read off as male resistance or organizational inadequacies. Among the stakeholder perspectives are those of men who believe that women should deal with things about women and that this is really not their concern. Such a view is reinforced by the fact that the widespread subordination of women is unsurprisingly reiterated as an important aspect of feminist gender analysis. As Sarah White has argued, regardless of discussions about the rightness of WID or WAD, GID or GAD, 'even if we use the term "gender", we almost always talk about it only in relation to women not men' (White, 1994: 98). Although there are very good reasons for this, there is a tendency to further the idea that it is women who need to do the changing. While there is still a need, therefore, for men to be aware of women's interests, claims and rights, it is equally crucial to make male gender identities themselves an issue.

From the point of view of the organization, the demands for simplification and categorization are strong. This is manifested in a thirst for information which there is no capacity to digest or act upon. On the one hand the variety of men's and women's interests eludes systematization. On the other, the goals, objectives and methods of the organization are not neutral and reflect these varying interests. Away from the headquarters, the priorities and incentives of individuals are different, whether they are project workers, bureaucrats or farmers. People use, manipulate, ignore and translate concepts of gender according to these priorities and incentives.

Notes

1. This chapter first appeared in 'Getting Institutions Right for Women in Development', *IDS Bulletin*, vol. 26, no. 3, July 1995.

2. The concepts of practical and strategic needs are developed in the work of Maxine Molyneux (1985) and Caroline Moser (1986, 1993).

3. By 'misbehave', Buvinic meant that projects' economic objectives evolved into welfare action during implementation.

4. From a presentation to the Seminar for Fish Scouts, Mansa, March 1991, by Mr H. Mwape.

5 Source: field notes 17 September 1992.

Part II

Institutionalizing Gender Equity
in State Bureaucracies

5

Mainstreaming Gender Concerns: Aspects of Compliance, Resistance and Negotiation[1]

Virginia O. del Rosario

Prompted by the declaration of the International Women's Year and subsequently the International Decade for Women, a number of governments have ratified international conventions regarding women, revised parts of their legal codes, passed new legislation or established departments or 'women's desks', as ways of signalling their acknowledgement of the importance of women's issues. In some instances such public, official acknowledgement may have been a strategic move, designed to access international funds which have been increasingly made available for women-specific activities and projects.[2] The establishment of 'national machineries' features prominently as one major achievement of governments during the Decade (Nijeholt 1991a). Set up in about 140 countries, these 'machineries' are purported to provide a structure for policy formulation, programme implementation, monitoring of women's status, and research and training, often with the explicit task of integrating women in development (UN, 1987: 20). However, while structures for mainstreaming gender concerns have been put in place, achievements towards the real integration of women in the process of development have been limited (Gordon, 1985). Despite the fact that integration of women in development is officially sanctioned by many governments, such machineries constantly face the problems of insufficient funds, understaffing, and marginality to the mainstream work of the institutions concerned (Newland, 1991: 124; Moser, 1991: 84). To uncover the reasons behind these problems, we need to look at the internal functioning of state development bureaucracies.

This chapter examines the institutional structure and contexts within which WID policy-making takes place in the Philippines, the agents involved and their practices. Drawing on the experience in the labour and employment sector, it is argued that while a government may appear to be successful in mainstreaming gender concerns in development and may well be seen as a model for gender-responsive planning and policy-making, the situation may be illusory. As we shall see, there are internal inconsistencies regarding the issue of gender within a particular state and its development bureaucracy. While these inconsistencies are a barrier to the goal of promoting women's interests in development, they also represent spaces for manoeuvring and strategizing within a bureaucratic system to push as much as possible for attention to gender issues.

The first part of the chapter provides an overview of Philippine policy on women and development, including its institutional framework. The second part, concentrating on the labour and employment sector, scrutinizes the major policies on women and development in the light of practice to unravel patterns of acceptance or resistance of particular policy-makers to the officially sanctioned 'mainstreaming of gender concerns'. Strategies of intervention by a group of women bureaucrats and the results are also discussed.

The discussion draws heavily on my working knowledge and experience as a former senior civil servant in the Philippine Department of Labor and Employment (henceforth referred to either as 'DOLE' or 'the Department'). Ten of my thirteen years in the Department were spent as Division Chief of the Standards Division in the Bureau of Women and Young Workers, the nucleus organization for policy and programme development for working women and youth. Part of my responsibility was as Chair of the Technical Working Group for institutionalizing or mainstreaming gender concerns in the labour and employment sector. This period of access to high-level discussions and meetings, allowed by my rank in the Department, equipped me with sufficient working knowledge to be able to reconstruct 'facts' concerning the subject of this chapter which are not found on official records. Official records necessarily and not unexpectedly reflect official views and interpretation. As they rarely report all that transpired in discussions or the real reasons behind decision-making they do not necessarily constitute the full facts.

Women In Development in the Philippines: National Policy and Institutional Framework

In the Philippines, the broad principles regarding women are embodied in the Constitution. Regardless of sex, age, race or creed, equality in employment, education and other social arenas is a basic provision of the Philippine Constitution. However, equality between men and women, together with women's maternal and economic roles and their special health needs, feature in the amended Constitution (1987) as explicit stipulations.

To give effect to the constitutional mandate regarding women, five major national instruments are particularly important:

* 1985 Labor Code of the Philippines as Amended;[3]
* 1987 Executive Order 227 (the New Family Code of the Philippines);
* 1989 Executive Order 348 (Approving and Adopting the Philippine Development Plan for Women 1986–1992);
* 1992 Republic Act 7192 (Promoting the Integration of Women as Full and Equal Partners of Men in Development and Nation Building and for Other Purposes);
* the Philippine Plan for Gender-Responsive Development 1995–2020.

Two major government institutions, the National Commission on the Role of Filipino Women and the Bureau of Women and Young Workers of the Philippine Department of Labor and Employment, are particularly relevant in so far as official policies for women in the labour and employment sector are concerned.

In direct response to the declaration of International Women's Year, the Philippine government created the National Commission on the Role of Filipino Women (NCRFW) in 1975. The NCRFW is the national coordinating body for policies and programmes on women initiated by both governmental and non-governmental organizations in the Philippines. However, it has no direct responsibility in policy-making or service delivery for women; that is the responsibility of other government departments.

Since its creation in 1975, the NCRFW has had the mandate of working 'towards the full integration of women for social, economic, political, and cultural development at national, regional and international levels on a basis of equality with men'.[4] Regardless of the government in power, it has remained under the office of the president, a factor of strategic importance both in promoting the commission's high visibility and enabling it to influence the government at the highest level. Similarly, its coordinating function between the governmental and non-governmental sectors has been maintained.

However, changes in its leadership have been quite extensive, with the leadership's composition during the Marcos administration contrasting with that since 1986 when Aquino became president. Prior to 1986, NCRFW Commissioners were mostly drawn from the government, with a minority from selected women's organizations. As those drawn from the government often occupied ministerial posts, this method of appointing of leaders was seen as an effective way of obtaining institutional commitment to women's issues. From 1986, the NCRFW's leadership gradually changed, moving towards greater representation of the non-governmental sector in its Board of Commissioners.[5] The change has had the advantage of providing the NGO sector with a more solid platform to affect government policies and programmes on women, though to my knowledge its effect on the commitment of government ministries has not been publicly discussed.

Mainly functioning as a central database for women and less effectively as a coordinating body during the Marcos era,[6] the NCRFW's work since 1986 has placed a greater emphasis on influencing policy and establishing an institutional mechanism (that is, 'national machinery') for women and development.[7] At the departmental level, WID institutionalization is attempted through establishing Focal Points and Technical Working Groups. The Focal Point and the Technical Working Group act as a nucleus and a pressure body in each government department for integrating women's concerns in its planning, policy-making and programme implementation.

The Department of Labor and Employment (DOLE) has responsibility for all workers. Irrespective of the government in power, labour policies and programmes have three major objectives: (1) promoting gainful employment opportunities and optimizing the development and utilization of the country's human resources; (2) advancing workers' welfare and protection through providing just and humane working conditions and terms of employment; and (3) maintaining industrial peace by promoting harmonious, equitable and stable employment relations that assure equal protection for the rights of all concerned parties. With DOLE's programmes and services being grouped according to these areas,[8] its concern for women workers can best be described as a department-wide responsibility with the Bureau of Women and Young Workers (BWYW) taking the lead role in addressing the group's particular requirements.

Unlike the NCRFW, the BWYW originated long before International Women's Year. It was set up in 1960[9] and since then has been one of the staff agencies[10] of DOLE. Historically, the BWYW has always had a woman director,[11] and its staff have been predominantly women. Playing an advisory role to the Department Secretary, it has prime responsibility for women and young workers which it carries out according to the policies of the Department. Its main activities include standards setting and review, policy and programme development and research, thus requiring it to relate closely with other governmental and non-governmental organizations concerned with women and young workers. With the establishment of the WID Focal Point and Technical Working Group in the Department in 1990, the BWYW additionally provides both a link and support to these structures in promoting the mainstreaming of gender concerns in the labour and employment sector. In short, the BWYW is the institution within the Department which ensures as much as possible that the specific needs of women workers are articulated both within and outside the Department.

WID in the Labour and Employment Sector: Policy vis-à-vis Practices

Programmes and targets for women specific to each of the various sectors of society and economy are laid out in a comprehensive document, the Philippine Development Plan for Women 1989–1992 (henceforth referred to as 'the Plan'). The Plan was intended to 'serve as ... a companion ... [to] the Medium Term Philippine Development Plan to ensure the main-streaming of women in development'.[12] Featuring additional chapters on migration, prostitution, violence against women, media, and arts and culture, the Plan can be said to be more comprehensive than the main, national plan and is in fact intended to be 'the government's major reference or "Bible" on gender and development'.[13] With respect to women in the labour sector, the Plan is purported to act as an encom-passing guide for policy-making, in the same way that it should be used as a guide by other government departments.

As in many other countries, policy-making for women in the labour and employment sector has historically reflected the conflicting values of equality (with male workers) and special protection. This largely stems from unresolved arguments and indecision within and between pressure groups and government agencies over certain aspects of women's employment. Prioritized themes of international development agencies at particular junctures contribute further to such indecision.

The Department of Labor and Employment (DOLE) responds to the provisions of the Plan through two packages of programmes: (a) DOLE's regular programmes, and (b) those planned and implemented by its various agencies alongside the four priority gender issues identified in the labour and employment sector. The former type of programme adopts an 'in-tegrated approach towards its clientele', an official phraseology which is a euphemism for women's issues being subsumed to men's issues. Whether designed before or after the Plan, such programmes follow the three major policy objectives of the Department and are the primary focus of efforts aimed at mainstreaming gender concerns. The latter type of pro-grammes address migration, homework, equal employment opportunity and sexual harassment, termed the 'four priority gender issues'; they represent, in reality, 'for women only' programmes or those with sharper focus on women workers.

Since 1990, efforts to mainstream gender concerns in the labour and employment sector have all been done within the functionally related structures of the Focal Point and the Technical Working Group, with the Bureau of Women and Young Workers acting as a linking and support organization. Under the instigation of the NCRFW, both the Focal Point and the Technical Working Group were created in 1990 to facilitate the implementation of the provisions of the Plan concerned with the labour and employment sector. Their membership is overwhelmingly female. Since their creation, both structures have been reconstituted and reorganized in order to be 'more responsive to the changing needs of the sector'.[14] The most recent reorganization took place in February 1994, shortly after the submission of DOLE's First Report of Compliance to the 1992 Act promoting women's equal participation. During the reorganization, a short-term 'Institutionalization Plan for Mainstreaming Gender Concerns'[15] was adopted and changes introduced to membership, both in terms of composition and number, although its predominantly female profile was maintained. It is notable that as a result of the latest reorganization, the Philippine Secretary of Labor and Employment no longer chairs the Focal Point. This change can be seen as a shift of this structure from being the ultimate policy-making body for gender concerns within the Department to that of merely assuming an advisory role in such matters.

By comparison with other government departments, DOLE has had one of the 'most active and successful' Focal Points and Technical Working Groups in the country.[16] It was also the first government department to embark on the pilot implementation of the Plan. Nevertheless, in its 1993 report to the Philippine Congress, DOLE states 'clearly the ultimate goal of mainstreaming gender concerns in the sector still has a long way to go' and identifies the major obstacles to the full achievement of this goal. The obstacles stated in the report are: (a) budgetary constraints, (b) inadequate sensitivity towards gender issues, on the part of both DOLE's clients and its internal staff, and (c) an insufficiently disaggregated database which makes it extremely difficult, if not impossible, to assess the differential impact on women and men of policies, programmes and projects pursued by various bureaux, offices and agencies of DOLE. Many of these problems are not restricted to DOLE or to the Philippines but apply widely in many contexts, including those within international agencies purporting to promote women and development (Harrison in this volume; Rathgeber, 1990; Newland, 1991). However, it is the unstated aspects of these problems which are equally crucial.

First, budget constraints are more complex than simply a lack of financial resources. Similar to many other areas of corporate planning in government bureaucracies, major decisions (especially on resource allocation) are largely influenced by attitudes of policy-makers towards particular programmes. In addition, as found in other situations, the question of personalities inevitably becomes a factor intruding on decision-making, with a particular bureau judged to be only as effective as the credibility of its director. It is notable that the openly and widely acknowledged concern for gender issues within DOLE does not match the budget allocation for the BWYW, which remains one of the lowest within the Department. The imbalance of resource allocation for the various bureaux reflects the low priority of programmes intended for women in comparison with other programmes, such as industrial relations (del Rosario, 1987).[17] In fact, since the beginning, the WID institutionalization programme of DOLE has been mainly financed by external, notably foreign, sources. In early 1993 when the need for allocating funds for women-specific projects was communicated to the heads of the different bureaux and branches of the Department, the announcement generally met with strong resistance, although during individual discussions with heads of bureaux the majority emphasized that they were 'supportive of mainstreaming gender concerns'.

The resistance of agency heads to allocating resources is not limited to financial issues. A similar, though unspoken and much more discreet, opposition displayed to mobilizing human resources. Heads of agencies showed a good record of compliance with the required agency participation in gender-related activities and, without exception, appointed a regular representative to the Technical Working Group, especially as the instruction memorandum emanated from the Secretary of Labor and Employment, who also chaired the Focal Point.[18] However, when participation required more than attending meetings (for example, report preparation, involvement in research, etc.) problems would arise. The agency representative would become overworked, having to cope with her responsibilities in the Technical Working Group, as well as her 'regular' responsibilities in her own agency. In short, gender concerns are not seen as being integral to an agency's regular work, and this could well be the reason why agency heads resist the idea of allocating funds for women-specific or women-related activities from their regular budget. Thus, as observed in similar situations, the BWYW and the WID institutionalization programme in general are under-resourced, which can be taken as a serious indication of a lack of real commitment on the part of many bureaucrats towards gender issues.

Second, there are differing reactions, especially of male officials, to the problem of inadequate gender-sensitivity. There seems to be an easy acceptance that the problem exists as it relates to the Department's clientele, but there is a very reluctant admission, if at all, of the existence of the problem in so far as DOLE officials are concerned. This difference in mind-set has engendered different responses to current and proposed measures to promote gender-sensitivity.

To promote gender-responsive planning in the Department, various types of gender-sensitivity training are given to its personnel.[19] It is notable that when a gender-sensitivity session was targeted particularly at DOLE officials, silent resistance was quite overwhelming, as evidenced in the extremely poor attendance of senior male officials.[20] The few who were in attendance often displayed a low level of interest in the session. Some even made snide remarks about the topic of the session.

However, when the target of measures was the clientele, the agency heads tended to be more supportive of implementing such measures. In fact, activities aimed at promoting gender-sensitivity of DOLE clients were implemented with the approval of agency heads, in lieu of conducting gender-sensitivity sessions for their own personnel.

The problem arguably runs deeper and has much to do with the basic assumptions informing both the organization within which policy-making takes place and the policy-makers themselves. Here, gender blindness and gender bias are key issues. Through their gender blindness, policy-makers (incorrectly) assume that the category 'workers' constitutes a homogeneous group of individuals and, as such, always represents a unity of interests. The corollary assumption of the 'male worker' is equally pervasive. The categories upon which policy-making is premised are, of course, difficult to sustain in the real world. Nonetheless, from their blinkered position many policy-makers are led to adopt the simplistic view that the goal of policy-making is rightly to address these unified 'workers' interests'. In the process, policy-makers not only negate the existence of equally salient needs and interests deriving from and imposed by other forms of social cleavage (such as by gender), but are able to justify a myopic organizational approach towards development – one that even reinforces gender and other social inequalities. As Newland points out, 'Development policies are set within male-dominated institutions which still see WID as an instrument rather than a goal in itself: a means for lower population growth, higher economic growth or more successful political mobilization' (1991: 130). The persistent sexist attitudes and beliefs especially of some top-level policy-makers, such as those noted earlier in this chapter, further exacerbate the problem. The end results are policies which subsume women workers' needs under those of male workers or, if 'women's interests' are ever considered, policies that again homogenize women and their interests, with the effect that they are often singly identified with their servicing role as mothers and homemakers. Instead of liberating women from their traditional role in society, policies actually reinforce this and invalidate any needs and interests which specifically derive from women's identity as workers, let alone their multiple needs and interests as workers and family members.

For example, income-generating activities are promoted by the Department as part of its employment policy. The projects, mostly targeting women, are aimed towards augmenting family income and are advertised as such. While it is true that material benefits can accrue to women and their families as a result of engaging in these projects, their design and manner of implementation buttress women's subordinate role and status as supplementary income earners. An even more basic deficiency of policies in the labour and employment sector derives from a narrow conceptualization of 'work' and 'women's work'.[21] 'Work' tends to be equated only with waged work. Worse, that work is often assumed to take place under the same conditions enjoyed by a male wage worker, that is, virtually free from the interference of domestic responsibilities. But this notion of work does not speak to the reality experienced by female wage workers who, in addition to engaging in paid work outside the home context, often have responsibilities for child care and other domestic chores and/or may also carry out some forms of home-based economic activities. Rather than seeing women's work in its totality, policy designers and implementers tend to view the economically productive activities that women do in isolation from their family life and the wider socio-cultural circumstances. The effect is not only to devalue and under-estimate the extent of work that women do, but to ignore women's multiple identities and interests as mothers, daughters, wives, factory workers and home-based workers. Furthermore, a redefinition of sex roles to alleviate the resulting double if not triple burden of paid work and family responsibilities on women is hardly given the priority and emphasis it deserves, especially given the Department's stated concern with the welfare of workers. The latter policy is thus contradicted, unless the issue of reorientation of traditional sex roles is taken seriously during the design and implementation of employment policies and projects.[22]

Some of the above issues have been addressed by the BWYW during the review of Labor Code provisions concerning women. The rigidity or resilience of state masculinism[23] embodied in these issues is put to the test as the BWYW awaits the action of the Labor Code Review and Drafting Committee on such proposals.

Third, and finally, the absence of a gender-specific database stems from the durable assumption that men's and women's experiences of development do not differ qualitatively and quantitatively. This erroneous assumption is reflected in the continuing resistance of many heads of line agencies of DOLE to collecting women-specific information.[24] As a result, however commendable policies are, the biggest obstacle towards achieving their desired objectives remains implementation (Smith, 1985), arguably compounded by lack of effective monitoring. The lack of an adequate and accurate information base means that 'rational' policy-making becomes a formidable task.

Overall, the practices of DOLE policy-makers in so far as WID is concerned are in a conflicting state of compliance and resistance. Faced with this contradiction, a number of female middle-rank managers committed to gender issues have formed an informal alliance, exploring spaces for action while at the same time having to toe the official line. Most of these women are also the regular agency representatives on the Technical Working Group and/or Focal Point. Clearly, their actions, whether individually or as a group, have been highly dependent on the 'availability and interaction of time, space and place' (Chhachhi and Pittin, 1991). Additionally, their experience has shown that specialized knowledge, and knowing how and when to use such knowledge, are important elements of women's strategizing.[25] In general, some forms of manoeuvring, formal as well as informal negotiations requiring varying degrees of persuasion or confrontation with colleagues and superiors, have proved possible. Achievements have been made in the following areas:

(1) Advocacy in the corporate planning process to ensure inclusion of gender issues in the mainstream policy-making machinery of the Department. This has involved parallel activities at the bureau/agency level and at the Departmental level. At the agency level, the Technical Working Group representative pushed for gender concerns in policy and/or programme planning within her own agency. Examples of results include the 'Gender Sensitivity in Voluntary Arbitration and other Voluntary Modes of Dispute Prevention and Settlement' for labour and management representatives and 'Gender-Responsive Trade Unionism'. As a result of these experimental inputs in July 1993, the module on gender has now become an integral part of DOLE-initiated seminars for management and trade unionists. At the Departmental level, the monitoring forms issued by the Planning Service to the different bureaux/agencies now include a section on women-centred programmes.

(2) Advocacy during the review of the 1985 Philippine Labor Code. The original intention of the Technical Working Group was to become part of the Labor Code Review and Drafting Committee. However, as this was not possible, it had to resort to submitting a written recommendation. Its major recommendation was to use non-sexist language in the drafting of the new code. It also endorsed the recommendations made by

the BWYW, especially the intent behind such recommendations (that is, to remove the sexist implications of existing Labor Code provisions).

Concluding Remarks: Confronting State Masculinism

Using the experience in the labour and employment sector regarding mainstreaming gender concerns, it has been shown that state structures are clearly not monolithic; they are composed of individuals with different perspectives on, and interests in, development. They therefore respond to WID differently. State masculinism assumes both a systemic and a localized nature in the realm of policy-making, with the two often inter-acting to produce effects which are detrimental to women's interests. It is not uncommon to find contradictions in government policies which in turn pose conflicting demands on women. Furthermore, the interactive relationship between systemic and localized masculinism has made state development bureaucracies shrink from any radical redefinition of wom-en's position that would legitimate women's claims *vis-à-vis* men's interests (Nijeholt, 1991b).

Despite this, it is clear that progress, though slow, has been achieved. This progress has come about neither spontaneously nor as a result of government benevolence. Instead, much has been achieved through sus-tained feminist engagement from both outside and within government bureaucracies. The government's official support for mainstreaming gen-der concerns, together with structures in place, have been utilized by female bureaucrats to advance gender issues. Spaces created by internal inconsistencies on the issue of gender within bureaucracies such as the Department of Labor and Employment have given women bureaucrats the necessary power base to effect change, however limited. Virtually every interaction has involved coming face to face with a different kind or hierarchy of masculinist power, engendering different kinds of re-sponses (negotiation, persuasion, confrontation) on the part of these women bureaucrats. Experience has shown that the prerogative power of agents of the masculinist state can sometimes be swayed to favour women. The barrier of state masculinism is not impenetrable.

Notes

1. This chapter first appeared in 'Getting Institutions Right for Women in Development', *IDS Bulletin*, vol. 26, no. 3, July 1995.

2. This possibility is not far-fetched, especially in the context of developing countries where domestic resources are scarce and, hence, access to external resources is at a premium. Nevertheless, suggesting that such actions may be calculated is not to undervalue their benefits to women in these countries.

3. The 1985 Labor Code underwent extensive review in 1993.

4. The Philippine Development Plan for Women 1989–1992: 6.

5. I am using the term 'non-governmental sector' to encompass all groups (including academia and trade unions) other than the government.

6. For a discussion of factors contributing to the ineffectiveness of the NCRFW as a national coordinating body during the Marcos era, see del Rosario (1987).

7. National Commission on the Role of Filipino Women – Office of the President, Term Report 1986–1992.

8. The various bureaux and agencies of DOLE are 'clustered' by programme area, function and nature of operations. There are six clusters in total: three according to programmes of the Department (i.e., employment, workers' protection and welfare, and industrial relations) and the remaining three according to nature of operations and function within the Department's organizational structure (i.e., regional operations, policy and international affairs, and management services). Each of the three programme clusters is headed by an Under-secretary. All the other clusters are headed by an Assistant Secretary. Within this organizational structure, the BWYW is under the direct responsibility of the Under-secretary for the Workers' Protection and Welfare cluster.

9. BWYW started as the Women and Child Labor Section in March 1925 under the then Philippine Bureau of Labor. After three decades, the section was expanded and elevated to become the Women and Minors Division of the Bureau of Labor Standards. In 1960, it was further elevated to the status of a bureau.

10. A 'staff agency', such as the BWYW, provides staff support to the regional offices in terms of technical supervision and policy direction. 'Line agencies' typified by the regional offices, are responsible for implementing labour policies and programmes and delivering direct labour services to clientele.

11. On one hand, the fact that the BWYW has always been headed by a woman is a matter to celebrate. On the other, this fact shows the persistent belief that women's issues are rightly women's affairs only. This attitude is reflected in other ways. For example, male officials expect only female officials to get involved in family planning programmes of the Department, whereas male officials expect to be involved in matters concerning industrial relations, as a high-ranking female official has complained to me.

12. S. Collas-Monsod (then Director-General, Philippine National Economic and Development Authority), 'Foreword', Philippine Development Plan For Women 1989–1992.

13. National Commission on the Role of Filipino Women – Office of the President, Term Report 1986–1992: 11.

14. Department of Labor and Employment, 1993, 'Highlights: First Report in Compliance to R.A. 7192', Manila: DOLE.

15. DOLE Administrative Order 86, Series of 1994 Amending Further Administrative Order No. 164 (s 1990) as amended by Administrative Order No. 103 (s 1992) on the Creation of the DOLE Focal Point and Technical Working Group.

16. Personal communication with several members of NCRFW staff, 1993.

17. The smallness of the BWYW's share of the Department's regular budget has made it imperative for the BWYW to access external funds (such as through the NCRFW) to finance activities in connection with its role as Secretariat to the Focal Point and the Technical Working Group.

18. The originator of the instruction is of great importance in terms of obtaining compliance, especially in matters relating to gender. This is why I think it will

be interesting to see the effect of the change of the DOLE Focal Point. The current Chair is the Under-secretary in charge of the Workers' Welfare and Protection cluster who, strictly speaking, has no direct clout over the other clusters in the Department.

19. As of May 1993, more than 200 members of DOLE staff belonging to various grades (to the inclusion of ministerial-level officials) have been recipients of gender-sensitivity training (GST), training on gender-responsive planning and other forms of in-house gender awareness programme within the Department.

20. These are my personal observations during a gender-sensitivity session conducted for top DOLE officials. By comparison with sex distribution of attendance in departmental meetings/workshops on other issues (e.g., industrial relations, employment), it is notable that few male top officials were in attendance in such sessions, reflecting lack of interest, and possibly lack of commitment, in women's issues.

21. It is because of this narrow conceptualization of women's work and the failure to recognize the links between the various types of work done by women that issues such as prostitution and the mail-order bride phenomenon have not been seen as legitimate concerns of the Department (see del Rosario, 1994).

22. Contradictions in policies emanating from different branches of the government are also a problem. For examples and discussion of this problem, see del Rosario (1987).

23. 'State masculinism' is a term borrowed from Brown (1992). Emphasizing the non-unitary nature of state power and male dominance, Brown encourages us to understand state masculinism as one operating through an intricate grid of often conflicting strategies, technologies and discourses of power.

24. Since the early 1980s, the need for collecting gender-specific statistics as a crucial aid towards more responsible policy-making in the labour and employment sector has been articulated by the BWYW both within and outside the Department. However, there was great reluctance, especially on the part of regional office personnel, on the grounds that regional offices are under-staffed and under-resourced, making it impossible to respond to such a 'demand' from the BWYW.

25. This has become increasingly clear to me as a former bureaucrat performing the roles of Chair of the Technical Working Group and Division Chief in the BWYW, as well as an activist. The demands of such roles have frequently required the use of specialized knowledge both in terms of commanding credibility and designing effective strategies. For example, as Chair of the Technical Working Group, I was the first person to be called upon to design a module on gender and deliver the actual lecture during two occasions in 1993. In this context, specialized knowledge has assisted in penetrating a traditionally male-dominated sphere such as industrial relations, whereas failure to act and respond on the basis of lacking specialized knowledge would have meant a lost opportunity in advancing gender issues. For an illustration of the importance of expertise and specialized knowledge in feminist strategizing, see also Barroso (1991).

6

Women's Movements, the State and Democratization in Chile: The Establishment of SERNAM

Georgina Waylen

With the return to competitive electoral politics in a number of Latin American countries, the viability of 'state feminism' has come under scrutiny as one mechanism with which to achieve change. So far most of the analyses of 'state feminism' have taken place in the context of the developed world, but a number of the articles in this volume demonstrate the importance of undertaking such analyses in the developing world (Stetson and Mazur, 1995). This chapter examines SERNAM (*Servicio Nacional de la Mujer*), the Chilean women's bureau, established during the consolidation of competitive electoral politics by the incoming civilian government. As such it provides an interesting case study of state feminism in the context of democratization. Because it is impossible to analyse the nature and efficacy of an institution like SERNAM in isolation from the wider context, this case study also highlights the nature of the relationship between different women's movements, the state and political parties in one political movement, and therefore has a wider focus than some of the other chapters. This type of example highlights a number of themes. What possibilities exist for women's movements in their relationships with political parties and the state? How much space and manoeuvrability can exist within the state for women's movements and institutions such as SERNAM to achieve their aims? Or do movements simply get co-opted, lose autonomy and have to submit to the agendas of others (Waylen, 1993)? What happens to others which stay outside the state? The exploration of these issues can only be historically and conjuncturally specific.[1]

The assumption that the nature of the state is not fixed provides the starting point. Indeed, the state has no necessary relationship to gender relations, but this is evolving, dialectic and dynamic. 'The state' can rarely if ever be seen as a homogeneous category. It is not a unitary structure but a differentiated set of institutions, agencies and discourses, the product of a particular historical and political conjuncture. It is far better to see the state as a site of struggle, not lying outside society and social processes, but, on the one hand, having a degree of autonomy from them which varies under particular circumstances, and on the other, being permeated by them. Gender (and race and class) inequalities are therefore buried within the state, but through part of the same dynamic process, gender relations are also partly constituted through the state (Pringle and Watson, 1992). The state therefore partly reflects and partly helps to create particular forms of gender relations and gender inequality. State practices construct and legitimate gender divisions. Gendered identities are in part constructed by the law and public discourses which emanate from the state (Showstack Sassoon, 1987).

Because the relationship between the state and gender relations is not fixed and immutable, battles can be fought out in the arena of the state. Consequently, while the state has for the most part acted to reinforce female subordination, the space can exist within the state to act to change gender relations (Alvarez, 1989; Charlton, Everett and Staudt, 1989). At different times and within different regimes, there are opportunities to alter the existing pattern of gender relations. Women's relationship to the state, particularly its welfare element, can also be seen as a site of contestation which provides the context for mobilization, and the welfare state can function as a locus of resistance. The actions of the state can also become a focus for political activity by groups outside the state; an example would be poor women campaigning for an extension of services. Alvarez (1990), for example, has argued that the extension of the remit of the state into the realm of the private has the effect of politicizing the private, through issues such as abortion, rape and domestic violence. This politicization then gives women's movements a handle to campaign around and influence the political agenda. Shifting the boundary between the public and the private then becomes an important point of influence (Alvarez, 1990).

Different groups of women thus interact with the state in different ways, and can have some influence over the way in which the state acts. Feminist analyses therefore have advanced from looking at the way the state treats women unequally in relation to men, to examining the ways in which particular states act to construct gendered state subjects, and the public/private divide in different contexts (Waylen, 1996). As part of the process of engagement with the state, interests and identities can also be constructed. It is therefore important to analyse how and under what conditions women's movements can influence the state and policy agendas. Debate has centred around whether women's movements should attempt to work with the state and political parties. Australian 'femocrats' argue that the state is a potential agent of empowerment and feminist strategies should involve winning gains from it (Watson, 1990).

Some Chilean feminists have shared this view and attempted to influence the state directly in the course of the transition to democracy. An important characteristic of this transition was the role played by heterogeneous women's movements, particularly in its early stages. But it has also seen the reconstitution of a strong and traditional party system and the subsequent demobilization of popular movements including women's movements. The transition has been narrowly defined to focus on the political to the exclusion of the social and economic, as the civilian governments have maintained the liberal economic policies of the military government and had a narrow economistic perspective on social questions such as poverty alleviation. During the initial opening, concerted campaigns were undertaken by some feminists and women party activists to influence the political process. The resulting centre-left government, dominated by the Catholic-influenced Christian Democrats, was committed in its programme to the establishment of a national women's bureau, but with an unclear brief. The complex and contradictory fate of SERNAM can therefore only be understood as part of this wider process of democratization and consolidation.

In order to explore how these processes unfolded in the transition and consolidation of competitive electoral politics it is useful to divide the transition into three phases. Events which occurred in the two periods prior to the civilian government taking power – 1983 to the end of 1986, and from 1987 to the elections – had important implications for the return to competitive electoral politics in the post-1990 period.

1983–86: The Breakdown of Authoritarianism and the Period of Social Mobilization

The year 1983 saw the emergence of a mass opposition movement in Chile, moving away from the pattern of sporadic and isolated protests that had been occurring since the military coup of 1973, and marked the beginning of the widespread reconstitution of civil society. The mass mobilizations were seen by many as providing the key both to overthrowing Pinochet and his authoritarian regime, and to the creation of a new type of more open and democratic politics. Also running alongside the mass mobilizations was the re-emergence of the political parties whose activities became increasingly central in the opposition movement (Petras and Leiva, 1988; Garreton, 1989).

During this period of mass opposition to the dictatorship, diverse women's movements had a high visibility. The human rights organizations, the *agrupaciones*, comprising mainly women, highlighted disappearances and other abuses perpetrated by the military government; popular movements, active around social and economic issues, grew rapidly in response to the severe economic crisis faced by Chile; and feminist movements, including 'popular feminist' groups, campaigning around gender inequality (re)emerged onto the public scene (Arteaga, 1988; Valdes and Weinstein, 1989; Kirkwood, 1990; Valenzuela, 1991). Feminists played a visible role in the opposition, participating in the mass mobilizations and days of protest and organizing demonstrations for international women's day.

Once political parties began to reconstitute, all social movements (including feminist ones) were under pressure to decide on a strategy: whether it was to be autonomy from or integration into the unfolding political process (Valenzuela, 1990). Some feminists decided on integration as the best way of pursuing a feminist agenda and moved into the political parties. They tended to be middle-class professional women, and they were active in the more moderate parties of the centre and renovated left. The political opposition formed into two groups in 1983, the moderate Alianza Democrática (AD) which increasingly favoured a strategy of *negociación* (negotiation) and the left-wing Movimiento Democrático Popular (MDP) which advocated *ruptura* – the violent overthrow of the military dictatorship. Women's organizations tried to remain united in the face of a divided political opposition through broad umbrella movements such as Mujeres por la Vida, which was formed in 1983 and attracted over 10,000 women to its first meeting. It was active under the slogan 'Democracia en el País y en la Casa' (democracy in the country and in the home), underlining the feminist demand that democracy would have to be rethought if it really was to include women.[2] Mujeres por la Vida also played a role in the Asemblea de la Civilidad, a broad and moderate opposition front opposing the dictatorship formed in 1986. A women's petition was included in the *Demanda de Chile*, a document submitted to the military government in 1986, and the feminist and socialist Maria Antioneta Saa sat in assembly as the women's representative. However, in a trend which was to recur, it was the middle-class women's organizations which became more integrated into national politics and some popular women's organizations felt Mujeres por la Vida did not represent them in the assembly (Angelo, 1990).

1987–89: The Transition Begins and Political Parties Regain Hegemony

In this period, two events set the tone for the transition to competitive electoral politics and had important implications for the nature of the civilian government that could take power in Chile. First, as the military regime began to allow a limited political opening, the political parties gained control over the unfolding process to the detriment of the social movements. Second, the centre and centre-left decided that a change of government would not be achieved solely through the process of social mobilization and moved towards a strategy of reaching agreement with the military government, by a negotiated transition of pacts made within the political elite. The centre and centre-left parties became the dominant force, and negotiation the dominant strategy within the transition. The left and other organizations, such as human rights groups and popular organizations, adhering not to the strategy of *negociación* but to *ruptura*, became increasingly marginalized in this middle-class transition of nego-tiated pacts. In 1988 a plebiscite was held in which people voted yes or no to Pinochet continuing as president. As a result of his defeat, com-petitive elections were held in 1989.

Women's organizations were also affected by these dynamics. The questions of what role they should play in relation to wider political developments became even more pressing. These developments, in com-bination with the experience of the Pliego and the Asamblea, reinforced the belief of some feminists that more than ever it was necessary to enter the political process but in the context of an autonomous movement, while others decided to remain outside (Molina, 1990). Much of the feminist movement reoriented itself and debated the ways in which women should 'do politics' (*hacer política*), the alliances they should make, and the aims they should have. A number of feminists made increased efforts to enter politics during this period and appeared to make significant head-way within the political parties of the centre and centre-left. Old tensions which had existed between the *feministas* and the *políticas* (female activists within political parties) were reduced as many *políticas* became more sym-pathetic to the aims of feminists. Many women activists began to value an autonomous women's axis whose existence could help them in their activities in political parties (Angelo, 1900).

Women had the greatest visibility and presence within renovated socialism in the Partido por la Democracia (PPD), the new umbrella party of the renovated left, and the Socialist Party. The emergence of a feminist agenda was also noticeable in the Christian Democrats (DC) and the newly formed Humanist Party. It was these parties that formed the Concertación, the centre-left coalition which contested the 1989 elections, and was in many ways a continuation of the moderate alliance tentatively established after 1983. However, while several parties were prepared to make general statements about women's equality, they were not prepared seriously to restructure power to allow women greater access to decision-making processes within them, often segregating them in separate organizations.

The perception of women's continued lack of influence in the run up to the 1988 plebiscite and the selection of very few women candidates (around 5 per cent of the total) for subsequent elections provided the major impetus for the creation of the autonomous Concertación de Mujeres por la Democracia in 1988. It was formed by women from a wide range of parties in the coalition contesting the elections together with independent feminists (including academics and activists, many of whom were middle-class professionals). The Concertación de Mujeres can be seen as growing both out of a tradition of attempts to create a united women's movement to influence the political agenda and out of the attempts by feminists to influence the centre and centre-left political parties. However, as had been the case with some of the earlier attempts to create a united movement, some women active in the popular organizations again felt that the Concertación de Mujeres did not represent their interests (Angelo, 1990).

The Concertación de Mujeres had a three-fold aim: first, to raise women's issues on the national political scene; second, to work in the presidential and parliamentary campaigns on behalf of the Concertación; and third, to formulate a programme on women for future democratic government. The eleven commissions of the women's Concertación produced a document which included a proposal for a ministry for women (and for changes in education, law, employment, health and the family). These proposals were presented to the Concertación as demands and most of them were incorporated into its electoral programme (Montecino and Rosetti, 1990). The visibility of women's movements during all phases of the transition in combination with the activities of feminists within centre-left parties had meant that those political parties felt that they could not ignore the demands of the Concertación de Mujeres.

'Women's issues' had been firmly placed on the political agenda in the following form: the Concertación was now committed to 'fully enforce women's rights considering the new role of women in society, overcoming any form of discrimination'. However this on its own was not acceptable to all in the coalition and the statement that the 'government will enforce the measures required to adequately protect the family' was added, leaving the proposal with what were perhaps contradictory aims from the start.

The goals were to be enforced through:

- legal changes: improving women's legal position;
- social participation: the incorporation of women into the political system and labour market;
- the creation of a national machinery at state level which would propose policy and oversee its implementation by other ministries.

It was therefore anticipated that these goals would be implemented through policies specifically aimed at women, but that these would not be ghettoized away from mainstream development policy but integrated into the work of all relevant government departments.

These proposals came out of the strategy of direct engagement of parts of the Chilean feminist movement with the political process and it is highly unlikely that, without this pressure, the Concertación would have adopted these ideas. According to Valenzuela (1992) (an academic, feminist activist and later part of SERNAM), members of the Concertación de Mujeres assumed that the government (and by implication the state) was a gender-neutral tool that could be used in gender-based ways. They thought that engaging with the state would be a relatively straightforward process to bring about an expansion of rights and democratic procedures through which women would also be incorporated as full citizens. There was also an assumption that relationships with women's organizations outside the state would be relatively unproblematic. Neither of these two assumptions has been borne out in practice.

1990 Onwards: The Consolidation of Competitive Electoral Politics

The centre-left Concertación was elected convincingly in the elections of 1989 (although with very few women deputies) and took office in 1990. Clearly some space did then exist within the state to introduce gender-based policies, but the government's programme on women has only been partially implemented. In order to explore why this has occurred, it is useful to consider which parts of the programme have been initiated and to what effect, and thereby understand why there have been complex and contradictory outcomes both within and outside the state.

The major way in which the Concertación programme on women discussed above has been implemented has been through the establishment of SERNAM, the National Service of Women (or Women's Bureau) in 1990, modelled on similar bodies in Spain and Brazil. After pressure from the feminist movement, SERNAM was created through a law rather than a presidential decree, unlike similar bodies in Argentina and Peru, so it is less vulnerable to abolition.[3] However, as a result of right-wing opposition the bill was toned down. The functions of SERNAM were reduced, its capability to execute programmes was removed, its personnel reduced, and while its director was at cabinet level, SERNAM was placed under the auspices of MIDELPAN, the Ministry of Planning. A number of SERNAM's personnel, many of whom were involved in drawing up the Concertación de Mujeres' original proposals, were activists drawn mainly from NGOs or academics. But while they are not civil servants with experience of government, many are members of the Chilean political class with connections to Concertación politicians. In the first four years of its existence, SERNAM's president and vice-president were partners of the leaders of the Christian Democrats and the Socialists (Macaulay, 1995).

SERNAM's budget has been relatively small. According to some sources it was initially established with $US 2 million plus $US 1.5 million from outside. Almost three-quarters of the initial budget for 1990–91 was allocated to pay for the 59 staff and the remaining quarter for goods and services (*Mensaje Presidencial* on Bill to create SERNAM, 1990). Outside funding came primarily from foreign governments (Sweden, Norway, Denmark, Holland and Spain), and NGOs and other international organizations such as the EU, IDB, the FAO and UNICEF. Foreign funding could potentially have given it greater autonomy from government, but much of it has been short-term and some is now being replaced by state funding. SERNAM initially benefited from the shift of foreign funding from the grassroots NGOs which had received resources directly during the dictatorship, to the new civilian government.

The role and functions of SERNAM were unclear at its establishment as it was not made into a full ministry. While its institutional location in MIDEPLAN means that it should be at the heart of planning and policy-making, it has no concrete mechanisms to influence government decisions and, as we will see, is therefore dependent on other methods such as negotiation and personal contacts (Goetz, 1994). However, four priorities were determined:

1. the establishment of a programme for women heads of household;
2. the establishment of a network of information centres on women's rights;
3. the establishment of an anti-violence against women programme;
4. the introduction of legal reforms.

What SERNAM Has Done

SERNAM has carried out multiple roles, although its limited functions, particularly its weakness in overseeing other departments and in making policy, has resulted in a concentration on public awareness building, implementing pilot projects and pushing for legal changes (Goetz, 1994).

SERNAM has experienced its greatest problems in its role within the state. Its brief within the government to coordinate with other ministries, particularly those concerned with social policy, has been problematic. There is no formal machinery with which it can oversee the work of other government departments, and contact points are neither high-ranking officials nor are they often interested in gender issues (Valenzuela, 1996). SERNAM also provides training to civil servants to increase gender awareness but this too has been problematic. Because of the voluntary attendance, only those already committed to gender awareness, with few top-level officials among them, have taken part. But again because of its small budget and lack of staff it has been largely ineffective. As a result of its lack of power within the state, progress often depends more on the existence of already committed individuals with influence within ministries than on the actions of SERNAM.

Results can therefore depend on the existence of feminist 'gatekeepers' or sympathizers at all levels, for example Jorge Arrate (then leader of the socialist party and partner of the ex-vice president of SERNAM) provided a high-level commitment to working with SERNAM in the Ministry of Labour. While some of SERNAM's contacts have been good because many SERNAM officials are members of the political class, this also leaves SERNAM vulnerable because commitment to the organization is for personal or factional reasons rather than programmatic or institutionalized ones (Macaulay, 1995).

SERNAM has been more effective in some of its other briefs. As part of its role in information gathering and dissemination, it has commissioned research from outside academics, particularly from feminist Chilean NGOs. Its communications brief was financed by foreign aid and UNICEF until 1993, and much of its publicity has been relatively successful, although limited because of underfunding. A network of Information Centres for Women's Rights (CIDEMs) has also been established (Matear, 1993). The centres were also meant to maintain links with women's movements outside the state and to promote women's organizations. They were initially funded by the EU but that money is now being withdrawn. Despite the potential autonomy offered by foreign finance, CIDEMs have been constrained in their activities, concentrating more on social benefits and poverty than on gender issues.

As SERNAM cannot set up programmes on its own account, it has concentrated on establishing pilot projects for others to continue. It has worked together with other government organizations such as the anti-poverty programme FOSIS, PRODEMU, the women's organization set up to rival CEMA-Chile, which remained under the control of the wife of the armed forces chief, and some municipalities. Most of these programmes have focused on income generation in some form or other, and maany have been seen as part of a move away from the broad emphasis on empowerment of many grassroots NGOs to a much more narrowly defined 'market empowerment' which fits in with the socio-economic policies of the government, that is, an emphasis on poverty reduction through increasing individual access to the market such as training women for the labour market (Schild, 1994). Among the programmes have been employ-ment training for women in both traditional and non-traditional jobs. Its female heads of household programme has been accused of destroying the family, and SERNAM has had to couch its support for the programme in terms of the better results for social policies that can be obtained by increasing the income-generating capacity of the needy (Valenzuela et al., 1995). Other programmes have included a micro-enterprise support pro-gramme and child care for temporary agricultural workers (Matear, 1993).

The domestic violence against women programme is an exception to this pattern. Its establishment was a result of campaigning by feminists and the commitment by feminists in SERNAM. Initially no funds were allocated but the programme secured international funding in late 1992. It has initiated research to discover the extent of the problem and organized training programmes for the police and civil servants. As a result of its activities, the issue of domestic violence now has a much higher profile than it did before SERNAM's campaign. SERNAM has also campaigned for legal reforms. It has worked for more rights for women in the labour market to be incorporated into labour law, particularly for service-sector workers such as domestic servants. It has agitated for changes in the civil code, working on changes to marriage legislation and on the rights of children born outside marriage. In the field of criminal law SERNAM oversaw the domestic violence bill which finally became law in 1994, three-and-a-half years after first being presented and after much opposition. It also produced an equal opportunities plan in 1994.

Some space has therefore existed for SERNAM to achieve some of its goals, but this has been limited. Some of the obstacles have been practical such as the limited budget, inexperienced personnel and lack of power within the government. The effectiveness of many of its projects is dependent on other ministries beyond SERNAM's control, and with de-centralization will be dependent on the municipalities over which central government has little influence. However, it is also necessary to under-stand the wider political context in order to comprehend the outcomes. SERNAM has faced opposition from a variety of sources within the state and the political superstructure. First, this has come from the right-wing political parties such as RN and UDI. Before SERNAM's establishment, the right wing opposed it. Despite the claim that its goals were to protect the family and to implement the UN convention which had been ratified by the military government, it was seen as a feminist socialist threat to social order and the family. Second, the Church has opposed some of its proposals and in part this reflects the transformation of the Chilean Catholic Church from playing an oppositional role under military rule to a more conservative one after the democratic transition (Schild, 1992). From 1988 onwards the Church began retrenching its social and educational programmes to concentrate more on *evangelización*. In addition the Catholic Church as an institution is opposed to divorce and reproductive rights and has 'traditional' views on the position of women. Its relationship with the Christian Democrats, the majority partner in the Concertación, means that it has some indirect influence over SERNAM; for example SERNAM's deputy director was removed after a row with a senior Church figure. SERNAM has also faced opposition from within the Concertación, particularly from the right of the Christian Democrats, which highlights the contradictions which exist within the coalition. Opposition was particularly evident in the debates surrounding the Beijing UN women's conference in 1995, in which SERNAM came under concerted attack from the right and the Catholic Church.

This opposition has meant that the greatest space to achieve change has existed on those issues considered least controversial. These centre around social and economic measures, such as women's employment training, which are seen as part of poverty alleviation and income generation. Huge tensions have appeared around issues such as divorce and reproductive rights, particularly abortion. Those more gender-specific measures which threaten to change the nature of gender relations directly are more difficult to get accepted. Indeed gender issues are, according to Valenzuela (1992), the most significant point of disagreement within the coalition, as there is general agreement on most other aspects of social and economic policy. However, despite these difficulties, some important legal changes have been made.

There have also been divisions within SERNAM itself, which reflect divisions between the parties, especially between the Christian Democrat oriented members who tend to have more conservative views particularly about the family, and the Socialist women who tend to have a more 'feminist' agenda (Matear, 1993). This lack of agreement on both analysis and strategy has meant that SERNAM has not been able to come up with a position on abortion and has avoided the issue instead. Personnel are often appointed along party lines to make sure of a balance between the political parties in the Concertación rather than because of links to women's movements, feminist beliefs or technical training or ability. The current director, a friend of President Frei's wife, headed the commission on the family, and is seen as more conservative.

SERNAM has also had an ambivalent relationship with women's movements outside the state. The criteria for the selection of personnel have contributed to a sense of alienation from SERNAM felt by some women's groups. Many women's organizations (some of which are often seen as radical feminist) have been wary because SERNAM is regarded simply as an arm of the state (*La Boletina*, n.d., Feministas Autonomas, 1996). In particular, popular women's movements, relegated by many of SERNAM's programmes to the role of consumers, are confused as to what SERNAM does and do not feel represented by it. There has also been some disillusionment with what is considered to be SERNAM's lack of a radical approach. The nature of the projects now being funded has shifted towards projects focused around narrow market-oriented economic aims. MOMUPO (Movimiento de Mujeres Populares) has criticized social policies that treat poor women as isolated individuals without allowing for the creation of collective spaces. It is claimed that SERNAM's policies can also have a differential impact on different groups of women. For example, it is claimed that changes to laws on property between men and women affect poor women negatively because property will be split, and as a result poor women could lose the roof over their heads.

There is a general consensus that women's movements, particularly popular women's movements along with many other social movements, have lost momentum since the return to competitive electoral politics. Schild (1994), contrary to what she sees as the analysis of some feminists within SERNAM, attributes this in part to the existence of SERNAM (1994). In this view, women's movements have been beheaded by the creation of SERNAM and the subsequent migration of feminists into the state. They have also lost potential resources because funds which used to go directly to NGOs are now channelled through the state and organizations then have to bid for them. This procedure has led to accusations that SERNAM has a clientelistic relationship with NGOs, comfortably co-existing with them and providing 'jobs for the girls' (Schild, 1994). Under these conditions resources are also more likely to go to middle-class organizations that are proficient at form-filling and know their way around the system than to popular organizations. As a result some autonomous women's organizations have lost out. SERNAM is therefore caught in a potentially contradictory position as, according to Valenzuela (1992), it loses potential power through any reduction in the strength of autonomous women's movements outside the state, as its existence is due in part to their strength and the pressure they brought to bear on the political parties which now form the government. But, at the same time, SERNAM's existence could be part of the very conditions that are undermining those movements.

Conclusions

These complex and contradictory outcomes must be seen as part of the whole process of democratization and reflect many of the trends seen in the Chilean transition more generally. They are in part a result of a narrow, middle-class transition characterized by negotiated pacts and without a radical agenda for change. Those social movements remaining outside the unfolding political process have been increasingly marginalized. However, some space for change has existed in this political conjuncture. The nature of the state was potentially more fluid at this moment of transformation than at other times, but this space was limited by the nature of the transition. The actions of organized women pressuring the state and political parties prior to and during the transition led to the establishment of SERNAM, created in a more secure and institutionalized form than similar bodies in Peru and Argentina.[4]

Clearly the state has become an arena for gender struggles. However, SERNAM's role within the state has been difficult. While the lack of consensus over SERNAM's role and its lack of finance has impeded its activities, other factors have played a key role. It is not an autonomous body but part of the government and the state; it is closely tied to the political parties that form the government and is split along those lines. But at the same time it lacks the necessary institutionalized power to influence policy-making and in its dealings with other ministries. The implications for its position of the reduction of foreign funding and its replacement by state funding are unclear.

The state has thus not proved to be the neutral tool some feminists had thought it was. It has been possible to achieve certain outcomes but not others. SERNAM has faced overt opposition for measures which threaten to alter gender relations. Those changes associated with some notion of strategic gender issues/empowerment are more difficult to achieve while more narrowly focused economic measures centred on poverty alleviation are far easier. However, SERNAM has been relatively successful in politicizing issues hitherto confined to the private sphere such as domestic violence and teenage pregnancy as well as abuse in the public sphere such as sexual harassment at work, thereby helping to challenge the public/private boundary. There has been little if any success in increasing the number of women in political processes and in positions of power in government, which was one of SERNAM's original aims.[5]

The relationship with movements outside the state is complex. While SERNAM was never established as a body to represent women's movements but as part of the Concertación government, there is some feeling that it ought to be representative (Valenzuela, 1996). But SERNAM has a differential relationship with different groups of women. Most of its personnel are professional women, while the organizations feeling most marginalized by it are made up of poor women. It is also unclear how far it would be possible for SERNAM to represent the interests of different women's movements within the state. Its equal opportunities plan was drawn up without widespread consultation with groups outside SERNAM. While SERNAM has perhaps contributed to the decline in women's movements, it needs autonomous movements backing it outside the state to give it greater power within the state. Feminist movements have lost some leverage within the government because in the process of transition, women's movements have become less active. The government can afford to reduce its commitment to a feminist-inspired programme because the agenda was originally determined from outside by women's movements and brought into the political parties by feminist activists. No easy generalizations about SERNAM are therefore possible. Without engagement with the state by feminists and other women activists, SERNAM would probably not exist, but that process has proved to be a complex and difficult one giving rise to some opportunities as well as unforeseen obstacles.

Notes

1. An earlier version of this article appeared first in 'Getting Institutions Right for Women In Development', *IDS Bulletin*, vol. 26, no. 3, July 1995, under the title: 'Women's Movements: The State and Democratisation in Chile'. It appeared in 1996 as: 'Democratization, Feminism and the State in Chile: the Establishment of SERNAM', in S. Rai and G. Lievesley (eds), *Women and the State: International Perspectives*, Taylor and Francis, London, 1996.

2. Despite the efforts to prevent it, party factionalism did have an impact on women's organizations e.g. as the umbrella organization MEMCH83 became more associated with the radical strategy of mobilization advocated by the MDP, many of the feminist and more centrist women's groups left it (Molina 1989).

3. The comparison between SERNAM and the Consejo Nacional de la Mujer, created by Menem in Argentina, and the Comisión Permanente de los Derechos de la Mujer, created by Fujimori in Peru, is interesting. Both are vulnerable to presidential whim, as has been shown in Argentina, and their heads have a much lower ranking within the governmental structure. For more details see Georgina Waylen, *Gender, Democratic Consolidation and Economic Reform*, forthcoming.

4. Although this has not been tested by the transfer of government to a different party or parties following an election.

5. Only 9 of the deputies elected in 1993 were women and the Frei government has only 2 women at cabinet level.

7

Gender and Representation: Women MPs in the Indian Parliament, 1991–96[1]

Shirin M. Rai

Questions and concerns about the issue of gender and representation are raised by the outcomes of the 1996 Indian elections. In the allocation of seats for the next parliament, women of all parties fared badly. The Bharatiya Janata Party (BJP) on the right fielded only 22 women candidates in the 464 seats it contested; the centrist Congress (I) Party 47 out of 543, and the left-wing Communist Party of India (Marxist) 5 out of 77 (*Times of India*, 8 April 1996). At the time of writing, the coalition that took power has only one woman in the Council of Ministers as the Minister of State for Human Resource Development. That this discrepancy is evident in the aftermath of the process of legislating for a 33 per cent quota for women at the grassroots representative organizations (Panchayats) is significant. This legislation resulted from a widespread process of consultation with women's groups (Kaushik, 1995), both autonomous groups and women's wings of political parties. No significant opposition was mounted by major political parties to this initiative. The role of political parties in a representative democracy as agents or obstructers to greater representation of women in politics is thus mixed.

Representation is a core concept of liberal democracy. An engagement with the idea of democracy is incomplete without examining levels and forms of participation in politics, as well as the translation of participatory movements into institutions, organizations and practices of governance. In this context, accountability and consent are essential elements of good and therefore legitimate government (World Bank, 1992: 6). All these concepts are, however, part of a universal and undifferentiated discourse which does not take into account the different needs and claims of groups constituting a particular civil and political society.

In this chapter, I raise the question of gender and representation for two reasons. First, even a cursory view of recent state initiatives to address the question of under-representation in politics of various groups reveals an institutional response based on representative politics. Whether in terms of quotas, or of creation of organizational structures, representation of interests is at the heart of state initiatives. Second, at least in the Indian context, the women's movements have also pressed for specific policies to enhance women's presence in political institutions. Representation has therefore been one issue that has been accepted as an important concept and strategy by women's groups as well as state institutions, underlining its importance to the Indian political system.

In this chapter I assess the context in which women access and perform in the Indian parliament based on interviews with 15 women parliamentarians in 1994. I will examine the issue of women's representation in the Indian parliament and argue that the growing strength of the Indian women's movement has 'politicized gender' successfully within the party system. Party-based institutional politics, however, impose significant constraints upon women organizing in their own interests. Further, the interplay between women's movements and women representatives is bounded by the party system which can form a formidable choice barrier for women representatives. Finally, representative politics can therefore form only one of the many strategies that women have to press for in their struggle to see their interests represented and translated into policies that are actually implemented. In arguing thus I will argue not against institutionalization of political participation, but point out that such a process has costs attached to the benefits it brings. These costs derive from both the universalizing discourses subscribed to by governments and political parties, and the process of institutionalization itself.

The Indian Political System

India is a bicameral parliamentary democracy. The lower house is called the Lok Sabha (Peoples' Assembly) and has 545 members. The upper house is called Rajya Sabha (States' Assembly) with 250 members. Representatives are chosen on a first-past-the-post basis by single-member constituencies for the lower house, and proportional representation by state assemblies for the upper. In 1991 women formed 5.2 per cent of the membership of the Lok Sabha and 9.8 per cent of the membership of the Rajya Sabha (Swarup et al., 1994: 362). This was lower than the preceding parliament of 1989. Further, 'it can be safely presumed that membership of women in [political] parties does not exceed 10 to 12 per cent of their total membership.' (DWCD, 1988: 157).

India has had a strong multi-party political system since 1947. There was a period of dictatorship in India for a short period (1975–77) during the national Emergency declared by Mrs Gandhi. However, political parties continued to play an important role in mobilizing and articulating interests and representing these in the political sphere. While providing political stability and a degree of accountability through elections, such strong party systems tend to marginalize issue-based politics, or to expropriate movements that are based on single issues. The women's movement in India has had to confront this (CWDS, 1994; 1995).

Another feature of this multi-party system is that while the parties have dominated politics, they have themselves largely remained organizationally weak and dependent on local elites (Bjorkman, 1987). The parties have therefore suffered both in terms of their transparency in mediating internal interests, and in their capacity to implement policies as a result of this dependence. Local elites have had important inputs into policy formulation, and have also been in a position to subvert the implementation of policies adverse to their interests. All these factors have affected the way the state addresses women's issues.

Women's Movements, Women in Political Institutions

Women have always been active in Indian political life though their visibility and autonomy have varied from one historical phase to another. Women have participated at all levels of public life, from local to national levels, and engaged in struggles both non-violent and violent. They have been accepted in public life once they have entered it both because of the iconography of motherhood – *Bharat Mata* – where participation in all forms of public life from social service for the disabled or underprivileged to more conventional political activism have been described as 'women's role in public life' and somehow in tune with their maternal character. Women have been mobilized by political movements and parties in India in different periods of their histories. While they have provided legitimacy to these movements and organizations, their own gains have been less obvious. The numbers of women, for example, that have actually been able to participate in public life has been extremely limited. Gender has not been the only variable affecting women's participation in politics; their access to the public sphere has depended on many factors, class, religion and caste being the most important. However, in no social category have women been more able to participate in political life than men. Further, *participation* in public life has not necessarily correlated with *representation* of women by women in public institutions. There are only 39 women in the current Lok Sabha (1991–96) and 17 in the Rajya Sabha.

In this section I want to explore the relationship between the growth of the women's movement in India and the politics of gender and representation in the Indian political system. My concern here is not to provide a comprehensive history of the Indian women's movement. Rather it is to make two different but related points. First, that while women are massively under-represented in legislative assemblies, women's movements have succeeded in putting the 'woman question' on the political agenda of most political parties in India; 'gender has become politicized' (Alvarez, 1990). Second, that the women representatives themselves have not necessarily been part of the women's movement and are therefore less representative of women than they might otherwise be; and they are therefore more bound by the party system within which they operate.

Women's movements: issues of representation

Women's movements[2] in independent India made significant gains through the 1970s and 1980s. The 1970s saw the rise and growth of the civil liberties movement in India in the aftermath of the crisis that led to the imposition of a national Emergency in 1975 by Prime Minister Indira Gandhi. The 1980s and 1990s have witnessed the mushrooming of women's organizations and movements as well as the rise of fundamentalism in Indian politics which has contained the advance of women's causes (Agnihotri and Mazumdar, 1995: 1869). The strength of these movements has elicited responses from state institutions, usually in favour of 'add-on' strategies whereby women and women's groups have been added on to existing institutional arrangements.

Further, for the most part women's movements (and feminist discourses) in India have been linked to the project of modernism and modernization which has had a significant impact upon public policies, institutions, and political rhetoric. While 'differing streams within the anti-imperialist ... struggle posited different, even contentious images of identities for women ... the nationalist consensus symbolized in the Fundamental Rights Resolution of the Indian National Congress, 1931, postulated freedom, justice, dignity and equality for women as essential for nation-building' (ibid.). One of the central modernist projects has been individuation in society, accompanied by a political rhetoric which has used the universalist language of equality and citizenship. The Indian women's movements supported this project: 'The women's movement in India is one of the many burgeoning efforts at reassertion of citizen's claims to participate as equals in the political and development process' (ibid.). This tension between individuation and universalism has, however, been carried into the women's movement – women have fought for full citizenship rights, but this has made them invisible as women with particular interests, leading to a more ambivalent positioning of women on the political terrain than they had expected (Phillips, 1992; Rai, 1995a). I will return to this issue in the second section of this chapter.

The demand for greater representation of women in political institutions in India was not taken up in a systematic way until the setting up of the Committee on the Status of Women in India (CSWI) which published its report in 1976. Before this the focus of the growing women's movement had been on the socio-economic position of women in India, which was regarded as the primary cause of their political marginalization. While the women's movement engaged with the project of redefining politics by imbuing it with a feminist analysis based on the dictum 'the personal is political', this project focused largely on participation in this redefined politics (CWDS, 1994: 19–25). Most of the groups involved in the women's movement in the 1970s were urban-based, and their members were drawn from the educated middle class, and from the left of the political spectrum (Kumar, 1989). The women's movement spanned a whole range of issues – civil liberties, consumer action, corruption and workplace rights. The CSWI report, while noting the links between the socio-economic marginalization and the political under-representation of women, also suggested that women's representation needed to be increased, especially at the grassroots level, through a policy of reserving seats for women (GOI, 1974). The question of political under-representation did not preoccupy most women's groups during the 1970s and much of the 1980s. The women's movement focused on issues of violence and rape, dowry and sex selection and the extension of equal opportunities, and their greater inclusion in the economic sphere through the extension of property and inheritance rights for women. In 1988, the National Perspective Plan for Women again focused on political representation of women, and suggested that a 30 per cent quota for women be introduced at all levels of elective bodies. Most left-wing women's groups saw this as a strategy of co-option of the gender issue into 'male-stream' politics (CWDS, 1994: 21). Women's groups insisted that reservation be confined to the Panchayat level to encourage grassroots participation in politics. The new consensus that was built around this demand resulted in the 73rd and 74th amendments to the Indian Constitution, were made law in 1993.

The wider political context for this initiative is the rise of fundamentalism, which has seen the appropriation of slogans of the women's movement by communalist forces (Akerkar, 1995: WS-14). As we will see below, the Bharatiya Janata Party is actively pursuing political mobilization of women using symbols of women's empowerment in both the social and economic arenas (Sarkar, 1991; Sarkar and Butalia, 1995). Further, the introduction of liberalization policies has led to a rise in social and economic disparities on the one hand, but on the other the 1980s have witnessed a decline of class-based left-wing and trade-union movements in India. Has this changed context influenced agenda-setting for the women's movement? Or is the issue of gender and representation being used by the state to divert the energies of the women's movement from socio-economic struggles? I have suggested elsewhere that using special measures to accommodate women in national politics is perhaps more feasible for political parties in a liberal democracy accommodating class differences (Hoskyns and Rai, 1996). Is this why there is an emerging trend within the Indian women's movement 'towards issues being taken up outside formal political parties' (CWDS, 1994: 20) on the one hand, and the parties' receptiveness to the formalizing of gender issues within the parameters of the party system on the other? How can the women's movement address this dilemma of seeking greater representation, and at the same time being concerned about co-option? I address this issue in the final section.

Political representation as a strategy for empowering women thus poses particular problems for the women's movement in the current political climate in India. The women's movement in India needs to rethink the linkages between its wider socio-economic agenda and its demand for greater inclusion of women in representative institutions (CWDS, 1994: 21–2). In what contexts and ways can greater women's representation help the women's movement? What mechanisms can link the issue of greater numbers of women representatives and accountability of these representatives to women's interests? These issues are raised through an examination of the political profile of women in the Indian parliament of 1991–96.

Who are the Women in the Indian Parliament?

The women representatives in the 1991–96 Indian parliament were mostly middle-class professionals, with few or no links with the women's movement. A significant number of them accessed politics through their families, some through various student and civil rights movements, and some because of state initiatives to increase representation from the lower castes in India. This selective inclusion of women into mainstream politics has tended to maintain divisions within the women's movement, posing difficult questions for representation of and by women.

Gender and caste in parliament

Caste has been an important feature of Indian public political life. Liddle and Joshi have examined how middle-class women found it easier to enter the public sphere because these groups are moving from caste- to class-oriented strategies for maintaining power and status (1986: 70–73). While in general this is correct, this analysis does not take into account the commitment of the Indian post-colonial state to address caste-based discrimination through a policy of 'reservations' or a quota system for the lowest castes and tribes. The reservation system is sensitive neither to class nor to gender in its presumptions about the causes of socio-economic backwardness of the lower castes. The system is, however, comprehensive and applies to every area of the public sector – education, employment and representation, at all levels. Women from the lower castes have been brought into representative politics through this 'reservation' system.

Even so, the number of women availing of opportunities based on caste reservation remains small. While 22 per cent of the parliamentary seats were reserved for the Scheduled Castes, women occupied only 4.1 per cent of the reserved seats. Two women MPs were from what are called the Scheduled Tribes. However, out of 39 women MPs in the tenth Lok Sabha, where they were 7 per cent of the total, five were from the Scheduled Castes. Two women MPs belonged to the 'backward' castes. Of these one was a leader of the Vishwa Hindu Parishad, the Hindu fundamentalist organization associated with the BJP. The other was a member of AIADMK, the ruling party in Tamil Nadu, led by Ms Jayalalitha, who initiated several women-oriented welfare and education programmes in the state.

Most of the women MPs were members of the higher castes. For example, there were six women from the Brahmin caste. This is a size-able 17 per cent of the women MPs, while Brahmins are only 5.5 per cent of the population. However, we have to guard against making easy correlations between caste and representation. For example, of the six women who are Brahmins, two are MPs from the Communist Party of India and Communist Party of India (Marxist). In both cases the caste factor is less important than their privileged class backgrounds. Further, both are products of political movements – the nationalist struggle, and the anti-Emergency movement.

Caste remains an important factor in the distribution of seats and voting patterns, and therefore crucially affects the profile, loyalties, and work of representatives in the Indian parliament.

Class, social positioning and gender in public life

The caste/class position of the women in parliament reflects their levels of education. Out of 39 women MPs in the 1991–96 Lok Sabha, 32 had postgraduate qualifications; in the Rajya Sabha 14 out of 17 were graduates. The class position of these women is more important to their educational levels than caste. Only one out of the seven lower-caste women MPs was not a graduate, and the one Scheduled Caste woman MP in the Rajya Sabha had postgraduate education. The levels of education are also reflected in the professional profiles of these women. Thirty per cent of women MPs in the Rajya Sabha, for example, were lawyers, and 25 per cent in the Lok Sabha were either teachers or lecturers.

Most of the women MPs (about 65 per cent) were in the late 30s to 60s age bracket and did not, therefore, have the responsibilities of bringing up a young family. Forty-five per cent of women MPs in the Lok Sabha are unmarried – 22.5 per cent are single and the same proportion are widows. Given the almost universal marriage pattern that exists in India, the figure for unmarried MPs is extraordinarily high, and indicates the social pressures on women who join public life. 'I did not get the time to get married,' said Vyas, the chair of the Congress Party's women's wing, who is now 48. For younger women too, time and position pose dilemmas: 'You join politics and somewhere along the way your private life takes a back seat,' said Selja Kumari, a junior minister in the Congress government (Savvy, 1993: 31).

For those who are married, the pressures of public life are eased a bit by their class situation. Most MPs are able to afford paid help in the home. In many cases the joint family system, or at least strong family support, also helps. However, the constraints of family life continue to be real concerns in the lives of even these privileged women. They have different strategies to cope with these constraints. One is negotiation, as Sushma Swaraj, a BJP MP and spokesperson on the economy, explained: 'We think that the woman will be successful in any profession only if she has the support of the family and her husband.' This strategy works if the family has accepted the woman's career in politics. This is more likely if the family is an elite 'political' family with more than one member participating in politics. In these instances the woman's natal family can employ its political muscle to support the woman's political career. If the woman was already in political life before she married into a family she can face tremendous pressures to conform to a traditional role which allows little scope for pursuing an active political career. A woman politician's options in this case are either to conform to the expectations of the family and retreat from public life, or to leave the family in pursuit of an uncertain future in party politics where the lack of family support and the stigma of divorce would be a further disadvantage.

Class significantly mediates the influence of religion. With only one MP in the Rajya Sabha and one in Lok Sabha, Muslim women are hugely under-represented.[3] Dr Najma Heptullah, who is also the Deputy Speaker of the Rajya Sabha, is from an elite class and educational background, with support for her work from both her natal and marital family. Margaret Alva, a Christian, Minister of State and Founder Chair of the National Commission for Women of India, is from a similar background. In both cases the families were involved in the national movement, were influenced by liberal ideology, and were highly educated.

The majority of women in the Indian parliament are thus elite women. While their public role challenges some stereotypes, their class position often allows them a far greater range of options than are available to poorer women. The pressure of the social milieu within which they operate, at the family and in some cases at the party level, has an impact not only on recruitment patterns of women into politics but also on the issues that these women representatives are willing to take up in public life.

Accessing the System

While the social positions of the women in parliament set them out as elite women, their avenues of political access are fairly limited. Within the party system women are primarily mobilized in support of already existing party policies, and placed in formal positions in the context of a tokenist politics rather than allowed space to formulate their own agendas. Active participation in the women's movement has *not* been one of the access routes into formal party politics, as the women's movement would be seen to challenge the tokenist politics of political parties *vis-à-vis* women members. Also, historically members of the women's movement have steered clear of party politics.

Kinship or more?

'Male equivalence' has been a dominant explanatory category for examining women's access to public life (Currell, 1974). The assumption here is that women access political life with the support, backing and contacts of the family, in particular of the husband. Therefore, the family is not always the site of oppression that it is made out to be, and can be

instrumental in helping women gain access to political power. In my
sample of 15, a third of the women MPs, for example, have 'family
support' in the background. However, in a well-argued critique of this
theory, Wolkowitz points out that 'male equivalence' is an inadequate
conceptual framework (Wolkowitz, 1987). First, that it is the public sphere
– state institutions, the press, and political discourse – that has to be
negotiated if the family decision to put forward a woman in politics is to
succeed; it is not a private, but a public matter (ibid.: 208). Second, in
many cases the husbands do not support the candidature of the wife at
all. It is the pressure of party political bosses that forces the issue in
many cases. Rita Verma, a first time BJP MP, for example, was courted
by three different political parties despite opposition from both her natal
and marital family, because they wanted to cash in on the popularity of
her deceased husband who died fighting bandits in Bihar. A party's concern with levels of representation of certain groups within its ranks, and
the consequences for the legitimacy of the party among the under-
represented groups might be the motive for including women. Congress
(I) MP Ms Topno, who is from a tribal, Christian background, was selected
as a candidate because Rajiv Gandhi wanted women from tribal areas
represented in parliament.

Social and political movements

Together with 'kinship link' and state initiatives, an important factor
affecting women's access to political life seems to be social and political
movements. The national movement was an important mobilizer of
women – Gandhi's contribution in bringing women into politics is well
documented (Chattopadhyaya, 1983; Joshi, 1989). On the left of the
political spectrum, women were involved in the Communist Party which
mobilized students through a network of student unions. As these unions
were based in the universities, the elite character of those who joined the
communist/nationalist movement via this route is evident.

The politics of the national movement, and of the communist movement, was such that the separatist argument for women's mobilization
was not considered appropriate by these women. At the same time the
mainstream nationalist and socialist parties did provide a mechanism for
mobilizing women by constituting 'women's organizations' under the
umbrella and control of the party – the Mahila (Women's) Congress and
the All India Women's Federation (CPI). None of the women I interviewed, however, had strong links with the women's wing of their party
prior to their entry into parliamentary politics. Some, like Vyas, were
given organizational position on the women's wing by their parties.

The civil rights and anti-Emergency movement led by Jaiprakash Narayan (JP) in 1975–77 was an important political movement which again brought students to the forefront of national politics. As a new party with a radical self-image, the Janata Party, under the leadership of Narayan, appealed to the students as a cohort untainted by the institutional corruption of electoral politics. Many women, like Swaraj on the right wing, and Bhattacharya on the left wing, joined this movement and stayed on in politics.

Finally, in the context of current politics in India, fundamentalist and communal parties are mobilizing women (Sarkar, 1991; Sarkar and Butalia, 1995). The BJP, for example, is mobilizing women not only to vote for it, but to join its organization. The BJP MP Sushma Swaraj claimed,

> We want to attract women in large numbers. Through education, but also through encouraging their increased representation. For that we have recently made a provision in our constitution. Our ward unit would not be considered valid unless two women are office bearers. This is a rider that will help women to come forward.

The BJP presents the inclusion of women as an important strategy to preserve *hindutva*, the Hindu way of life, which its leaders contend is safe in the hands of Hindu women. Symbolic empowerment of women thus becomes a particular but necessary project. Swaraj pointed out: 'We have stated that if there is any *dharmgranth* [religious text], any personal law, or any ritual, if they propagate or endorse discrimination between men and women, that section will not be acceptable to the BJP.'

One of the most charismatic women MPs is Uma Bharti, a product of the rise of Hindu militancy in Indian politics. She is the member of the Vishwa Hindu Parishad, a mobilizational wing of the BJP, a 'preacher' of Hindu texts by profession, and was in the forefront of the movement that brought down the Babri Mosque in Ayodhya. 'For me, politics is not separate from religion.... Religious people have to fight social evils, and if they have to enter politics to do so, they should.' Bharti entered politics with the patronage of Vijya Raje Scidhia, one of the women leaders of the BJP at a time when the party was deliberately switching its political strategy to a militant mobilization of the Hindu vote bank. As a 'preacher' of Hindu texts, Bharti was articulate, independent, and an actor in the public sphere since the age of eight. She is not married, does not come from an upper-caste/class family, and therefore does not embody in herself the dilemmas about political participation facing women from more conventional backgrounds. And she is militant in the defence of *hindutva* which became the rallying cry of the BJP in its attempt to mobilize electoral support. She can thus combine social and political radicalism without threatening the Hindu social fabric by subverting its gender hierarchy.

Quotas for women?

Reservation of seats as a strategy for accessing the political arena has growing support among women MPs. This is despite the fact that very few have accessed the system through that route, and are firm believers in the meritocratic argument. The ambivalence towards the quota system is understandable. Sushma Swaraj pointed out, 'I do not want the quota system – there will be a lot of heartburning among male colleagues, and they will not respect you, thinking you are a "quota-candidate", and question your ability. But if you achieve your place on merit then they will accept you as one of them.' However, in the same interview she also clarified, 'I *was* of the opinion that quotas do not work. But in the last one or two years when I witnessed how women have been discriminated against in getting seats, and in the field, then I felt that I should look at this problem again. That if there is no quota women will not be able to enter politics.' On 23 May 1994 the *Mahila* Congress, presided over by Girija Vyas, passed a resolution asking for the extension of the reservation scheme to distribution of party tickets for parliamentary and assembly elections (*Times of India*, 24 May 1994).

Women have accessed public life via different routes. While family background is still important, other factors like social and political movements, and political leaders and their policy initiatives, have also provided equally important access points to political life for women. What is evident from the data presented above is that none of the women MPs accessed the political system through activism in the women's movement.

Gender and Public Power: What Do Women MPs Do?

Out of the 20 women Congress MPs in the 1991–96 Lok Sabha, none was a cabinet minister; two were ministers of state; and two were deputy ministers of state. In the Rajya Sabha, out of seven Congress women MPs, one is a minister of state. The portfolios of these ministers included, Human Resource Development, Civil Aviation and Tourism, Health and Family Welfare, and Personnel and Public Grievances. All these are generally regarded as 'soft' portfolios, though it does not take away from the responsibility these women ministers have. One Congress woman MP is the Deputy Chair of the Rajya Sabha. At the level of the party, one MP was on the disciplinary committee of the party, and one was the President of the Mahila Congress. Among BJP women, the one Rajya Sabha member was the spokesperson on the economy and general political line of the party. Of the ten members of the Lok Sabha, one was one of the vice-presidents of the party, and two were on the national executive of their party.

The system of institutional incentives and disincentives at the level of the party and parliament imposes its gendered logic on the choices that women make in espousing issues through the parliament. Most of the women MPs I interviewed did not have women's issues high on their list of interests. Rita Verma, and V. Raje of the BJP, for example, said that they did not want to be characterized as 'women's only' MPs. Rather, they wanted to be on committees relating to economy, international relations, and trade. As ambitious women these MPs want to be where power and influence converge.

However, many women MPs felt the discriminating power of a patriarchal institution like the parliament. In its composition, functioning and assumptions about gender roles which are reflected in the behaviour of male MPs, the parliament as an institution is implicated in maintaining the status quo on gender relations. The women MPs' experience of the working of parliament has made them increasingly sensitive to issues of gender.

One of the important issues for any discussion on gender and representation is regarding the constituency that they represent. As there are no 'women only' constituencies, women MPs are not accountable to women *as women*. And yet, when there are issues regarding women raised in the parliament, these women are expected to, and do participate in the debates. Issues of women's welfare, and violence against women particularly tend to unite women MPs. As Sushma Swaraj said, 'women MPs do speak out against oppression of women irrespective of whether their party is in power. In such cases we think that women have no *dharma* (purpose) and no *jaat* (caste) other than being women. But on policy matters, like the uniform civil code, it is a different story.' These issues are discussed in the 'Ladies Room' in the parliament House, and cross-party support organized. However, as all the MPs with whom I raised this question made clear, they are, as Malini Bhattacharya of the CPI(M) said, 'party women first'; the party whip is rarely flouted.

Some women MPs are also asked by the party leadership to get involved in the women's wing of the party. While the women MPs do not necessarily see this role as an enhancement of their status within their party, some have made a success of this role and as a result gained influence with the leadership of the party. As noted earlier, Girija Vyas of the Congress (I) is one such woman MP.

This survey of women MPs also suggests that these women have benefited from the growing strength of the women's movement which has put the issue of women's empowerment and participation in politics on the national agenda, to which various party political leaders have responded in different ways. However, none of these women have come into political life through the women's movement. Their access to women's organizations is generally limited to the women's wing of their own parties. As party women with political ambitions, women MPs respond to the institutional incentives and disincentives that are put to them. All these factors limit the potential of these women MPs representing the interests of Indian women across a range of issues. As a result there seems to be little regular contact between women's groups and women MPs. The exception here is of course the women's wing of political parties which do liaise with women MPs. This does allow the possibility of women MPs becoming conduits between the party's leadership and its women members. They are also consulted from time to time by the party leadership on issues regarding the family, and women's rights. But non-party women's groups do not seem to be approaching women MPs (Rai, 1995a).

Representation and Accountability

Representation has been the focus of reformist, inclusionary strategies in public policy in many political systems. It is attractive largely in contrast to other political arrangements. Lack of representation is perceived as a problem, and democratic institutions are largely accepted as important to expanding possibilities of political participation by citizens. Further, exclusion generates political resentment, adversely affecting not only the political system but also social relations within a polity; no individual or group likes being regarded as part of an excluded, and therefore disempowered, group.

Representation as a concept makes certain assumptions which are problematic, and affect the policy-making function of political institutions based upon it. The first set of assumptions is related to defining interests – that there are identifiable women's interests that women can represent. This, of course, raises issues about what are women's interests when they are constantly being disturbed by categories of race, ethnicity and class, and whether women can be homogenized in terms of their sex/gender without regard to their race, ethnic and class positions.

A second set of assumptions regarding representation is about appropriate forms of representative politics. Despite an enduring interest in direct participative politics, representative government operates largely through a party political system. Institutional frameworks of political parties thus form an important constraint for individual representatives, especially if the representative seeks to support certain group interests. Group interests have often been regarded as too particular; 'general interests' or 'national interests' take precedence in party political rhetoric. Political parties also perform 'gate-keeping' functions – interests are given recognition through the agenda-setting of political parties. My study of Indian parliamentarians suggests that institutional constraints, and systems of organizational incentives and disincentives are important explanations of the limited role that women can play in advancing the agenda of gender justice through party-based political work.

Why do we need more women representatives?

While we cannot assume that more women in public offices would mean a better deal for women in general, there are important reasons for demanding greater representation of women in political life. First is the intuitive one – the greater the number of women in public office, articulating interests and seen to be wielding power, the more disrupted the gender hierarchy in public life could become. Without sufficiently visible, if not proportionate presence in the political system – 'threshold representation' (Kymlicka, 1995) – a group's ability to influence either policy-making, or indeed the political culture framing the representative system, is limited. Further, the fact that these women are largely elite women might mean that the impact that they have on public consciousness might be disproportionately bigger than their numbers would suggest.

Second, and more important, we could explore the strategies that women employ to access the public sphere in the context of a patriarchal socio-political system. These women have been successful in subverting the boundaries of gender, and in operating in a very aggressive male-dominated sphere. Could other women learn from this cohort? The problem here is, of course, precisely that these women are an elite. The class from which most of these women come is perhaps the most important factor in their successful inclusion into the political system. We can, however, examine whether socio-political movements provide opportunities for women to use certain strategies that might be able to subvert the gender hierarchy in politics. Finally, we can explore the dynamic between institutional and grassroots politics. As this study demonstrates, the 'politicization of gender' in the Indian political system is due largely to the success of the women's movement, and women representatives have benefited from this. There has, however, been limited interaction between women representatives and the women's movement. This, perhaps, is the issue that the women's movement needs to address as part of its expanding agenda for the 1990s.

Conclusions

The problem I have tried to highlight in this chapter is important in understanding women's role in institutional politics. Social and political institutions can (and do) form formidable choice-barriers for women representatives. Should we therefore skirt around formal institutions that are embedded in the dominant political discourses, and concentrate on mobilizing outside organizational boundaries?

There has been an ongoing debate within the feminist movement about the expropriatory power of institutions (see Brown, 1992; Rai, 1995; Ehrenreich and Piven, 1982). The various positions have covered the entire spectrum from rejecting 'dealing' with state institutions entirely, to suggesting an 'in and against' the state approach, to examining the benefits of working with/through state institutions. I have argued elsewhere that for women the state and civil society are both complex terrains – fractured, oppressive, threatening and also providing spaces for struggles and negotiations. These struggles and negotiations are grounded in the positions of various groups of women articulating their short- and long-term interests in the context of the multiplicity of power relations that form the state in any country. In turn, the state and its institutions are also 'shaped' by the forms and outcomes of these struggles. While denying any intentionality to the state, or a necessary coherence to the alliances formed in struggles against states, there are, however, particular characteristics of Third World states like India that need to be examined to form a judgement about the various possible spaces for mobilization by women. In India state institutions and dominant political parties have taken up the cause of women's representation as part of the generalized discourse of modernity to which they subscribe. This discourse, while not unified in itself, allows sections of the state to take initiatives to respond to the struggles of women for equality as well as empowerment. This results in intra-state conflict which allows further possibilities of negotiations and struggles by and in the interests of women. Further, the capacity of the state to implement its policies and enforce its laws is undermined by the weakness of the economy and of the political infra-structure, and widespread corruption which leads to the de-legitimization of government and the political system. This lack of capacity further enhances intra-state conflict (Rai, 1995a).

However, state institutions cannot be the sole focus of these struggles. Civil society, while providing a space for mobilization also constrains the construction and organization of interests that challenge the dominant discourses of gendered power. In this context, the relationship between the state and civil society becomes an important arena for negotiations and struggles. Indian state institutions are deeply 'embedded' in civil society and its 'peak interest groups'. State institutions are constrained not to propose policies that would be opposed by these peak interest groups. However, the modernist project that they subscribe to, especially when operating representative democratic political systems, means they cannot entirely neglect issues arising from women's struggles. This forces them to take issue with some of the dominant interest groups. The result is a policy framework that is at best patchy, allowing for another set of struggles to expand the domain of reform as well as improve policy implementation capacity. Thus both spaces – the informal and formalized networks of power – need to be negotiated by the women's movements in order to better serve women's interests (Rai, 1995b). Women's participation in representative institutions can be effective only in the context of such continuing negotiations and struggles.

Notes

1. A grant from the Nuffield Foundation allowed me to carry out the empirical research presented in this chapter. A version of this chapter first appeared in 'Getting Institutions Right for Women in Development', *IDS Bulletin*, vol. 26, no. 3, July 1995.

2. I use the term women's movements here as a shorthand for all the various groups of women and feminists that are engaged in political and social life and have as their central concerns justice and equality for women. I do not include in this group any right-wing women's group whose concerns are with cultural authenticity.

3. Muslims constitute about 12 per cent of the Indian population.

Part III

Institutionalizing Gender Equity in NGOs

8

Engendering Organizational Change: The BRAC Case[1]

Aruna Rao and David Kelleher

This chapter analyses the start-up phase of an ongoing structural intervention which works at the nexus of gender relations, organizational change and quality improvement. Articulating this nexus and its specific relevance to the Bangladesh Rural Advancement Committee (BRAC) and acquiring and deploying knowledge around it within the organization has involved definition and continuous reiteration of basic premises concerning gender, individual learning and systems development; an organization-wide knowledge-building exercise facilitated by a series of structured diagnostic processes; negotiating premises and visions, transferring ownership, and building on related organizational exercises in strategic visioning and planning. This chapter reflects on these processes and discusses some critical dilemmas: expanding parameters versus boundary maintenance; the prerequisites for innovation versus institutional bargaining; and change options versus change realities.

BRAC and its Gender Programme

An overview of BRAC

With approximately 15,000 staff servicing 1.6 million village-based members, BRAC is now the world's largest indigenous private-sector development organization. It has two major goals: poverty alleviation and empowerment of the poor. BRAC's history reflects less smooth transitions than strategic learning points and concomitant policy and programming shifts. From an initial focus in 1972 on relief and rehabilitation, the organization took on a community development approach to poverty alleviation but quickly graduated to a target-oriented approach to sustainable development and empowerment while also experimenting elsewhere with credit delivery. In the last decade, BRAC's credit programme has predominated though it has also taken on a host of supplementary social services ranging from income-generation skills training, human rights and legal education, a family planning and women's health programme, to non-formal education of BRAC members' children, and higher-order economic enterprises. Since the mid-1980s, BRAC has undergone a tremendous expansion in area coverage and staff strength. In the late 1980s, fuelled by its Executive Director's growing commitment to gender equity – a direction which has been encouraged over time by donors and numerous evaluation and appraisal missions – BRAC began actively recruiting women staff. At its highest, the ratio of female to male staff in the organization was 1:4; currently females comprise approximately 20 per cent of all regular BRAC staff (this excludes its primary school teachers who are part-time, 'contract' staff). Currently, the bulk of BRAC's programmes are directed to women – 85 per cent of credit is targeted to women and girls comprise 70 per cent of all students in BRAC primary schools – and women constitute 85 per cent of members in BRAC village organizations.

Why now and why gender?

BRAC's expansion together with its interest in recruiting more women staff and its commitment to women's empowerment currently pose considerable challenges organizationally and programmatically. Over the past three years, BRAC has developed policy incrementally in response to specific women staff-related issues and problems as they came up. In 1991, it appointed a Women's Advisory Committee to advise on women staff issues and in July 1993, it piloted its first staff gender-training programme. However, at the time the Gender Team began its work in January 1994, a broad consensus had yet to emerge in BRAC on what the real problems were: what were problematic attitudes and behaviours on the part of male staff? Was the organization's response adequate? What aspects of BRAC's target-driven organizational culture hinder advances toward empowerment of women members? What special provisions if any do women staff require? What gender-sensitive planning and programming skills are relevant to BRAC staff? Which of these problems are amenable to a training solution?

Before the Gender Team began its work, a broadened brief for it was negotiated with senior management – from the development of training courses in gender analysis for staff to building staff capacity to plan, deliver and monitor gender-equitable programming; and working with managers and staff to strengthen organizational systems, policies and procedures in support of BRAC's gender goals. Implicated in this approach is the need for BRAC to evolve an organizational culture and arrangements that attract and retain high quality women and men staff and allow them to be their most productive. This goes beyond the issue of gender parity to gender relations within the organizations, which is itself a determinant of female staff retention. It is important to note that changes were already under way: four of BRAC's twenty senior managers are women, the Executive Director is committed to equality of men and women staff, the number of women area managers is growing and there is a fast track to make women managers.

The Nexus between Gender, Organizational Change and Quality Improvement

Transformation of gender relations

We start with BRAC's stated goals of gender equity and women's empowerment. But just what is meant by 'gender' and 'women's empowerment' has not been clear. To guide our work, the team engaged in a process explicating these concepts in terms and language relevant to BRAC programmes and BRAC as an organization. In the process we attempted to identify areas of overlap and synergy between these two concepts and their programmatic and organizational change manifestations.

We define women's empowerment as the capacity of women to be economically self-sufficient and self-reliant with control over decisions affecting their life options, and to be free from violence. Thus, we conceptualize programming for women's empowerment goals as being constituted of three broad strands: (1) increasing women's ability to be economically self-sufficient (earn an income, own assets and manage own finances); (2) increasing women's confidence and ability to know and negotiate for their rights in the household and community; and (3) increasing women's control over their bodies, their time and their movement, including freedom from violence. We conceptualize working toward gender transformations in terms of (1) increasing women's and men's ability to analyse and reshape socially constructed gender relations in order to transform power relationships; (2) equitable access to and control over both public and private resources; (3) equitable participation in household, community and national decision-making; and reshaping social institutions and organizations to include women's and men's varied perceptions and to benefit both. We understand that these strategies can help to move beyond the male–female power nexus toward gender transformations, and that implicit in them is engagement with issues of class which both unite and divide men and women.

A key idea in our dialogue with BRAC is that gender does not mean 'women'. Moreover, we are not simply concerned with empowering women; we are also trying to alter the relationship between men and women so that it is characterized by more equity and an ability to negotiate and agree on the needs of both. Compared with other thinking, this may seem unambitious. Acker, for example, challenges one to deal with larger and more systemic issues:

> Long term strategies will have to challenge the privileging of 'economy' over life and raise questions about the rationality of such things as organizational and work commitment as well as the legitimacy of the organization's claim for the priority of their goals over more broad goals. The gendered structure of organizations will only be completely changed with a fundamental re-organization of both production and reproduction. (Acker, 1992)

Nevertheless, we choose to define gender in terms that make sense to BRAC. The essence of the normative change strategy that we are using demands that the issue be defined in the client's terms. (In fact, we are still involved in a dialogue with BRAC to build a joint agreement as to what is a gender issue.) This definition is, however, quite wide-ranging and allows a broad spectrum of intervention targets. Once you admit that a gender issue is anything that hinders, prevents or restricts women's (either staff or programme beneficiaries) involvement in the delivery, analysis and improvement of a programme, there is considerable scope for thinking. Some of the things that prevent women's full participation in quality programme delivery and improvement are cultural, some are attitudinal and some are organizational. For example, we know that women's effective participation means that they need the opportunity to earn the respect of their male colleagues, that men in BRAC need to be able to understand the situation faced by both village women and women in BRAC, and that arrangements like leave and having overnight guests at the area office need to be improved so that women can better integrate their work and their family lives and so on.

In order to translate these ideas into organizational practice, we need to consider the questions of organizational change and quality improvement.

Organizational change

Our change strategy is grounded in the practices and assumptions of collaborative change described in Bennis, Benne and Chin (1968) as normative and re-educative. This means that it is neither a coercive strategy that attempts to pressure or shame managers into change nor a rational strategy that attempts to convince them to change using what has been called brute rationality. A normative, re-educative approach works with the heart and the head by supporting a learning process that accepts the psychological resistance to the change of fundamental attitudes. This strategy for organizational change can be described as having the following aspects:

- The client must 'own' the change goals. The goals cannot be imposed by the change agents. The role of the change agent is to help the client achieve goals she/he has chosen.
- The process is long-term (2–5 years).
- It is both systemic and personal. It concerns itself with systemic changes of culture and norms and it concerns itself with the individual learning of organizational members.
- It is data-based. In other words, it is not informed by universal prescriptions but the specific requirements of that organization as demonstrated by a collaborative data collection and analysis process.
- The change agent is not expected to enter as an expert and prescribe the nature of the change. The primary role is one of a facilitator or catalyst, although from time to time she/he must be prepared to give advice, particularly in the process, timing and staging of the change.

This approach to change has resulted in a number of assumptions that guide our work. For example:

- Within the scope of the intervention, managers and programme personnel will define the priority problems and targets for intervention.
- We hold a belief in the value of action learning for bringing about individual and system change and a concomitant belief in the ineffectiveness of training that takes place out of the setting in which the changed behaviour is expected to be applied.
- Although we are committed to this approach, we are not committed to any particular configuration of intervention elements.

Quality improvement

Quality improvement or Total Quality Management (TQM) grew out of the need in the private sector to respond to intense competition by constantly improving production systems to provide customers with what they want when they want it. Companies found that they needed to focus not on profits but on the customer. It eventually meant a restructuring of the relationship between workers and management.

For an organization such as BRAC quality first and foremost means quality of programme outcomes and impact. Its very existence is premised on its ability to support poor women and men in their individual and collective efforts to better their situation. In the final analysis, its worth is measured in these terms. In BRAC, TQM could provide a balance to the focus on quantitative targets and measurements. It would focus on constant improvement of the quality of service to members, continue to push the boundaries of empowerment beyond delivery of services to strengthening women's self-reliance. It would involve members in programme design and monitoring, exploring avenues of strengthening the collective organizations of members and their participation in community decision-making bodies, and the role of men in this process. It would involve staff who deliver service in an ongoing structured analysis of how the service could be more effective and delivered at less cost.

We have discussed the 'pieces': gender, organizational change and quality improvement. How do these pieces fit together? Our current thinking can best be summed up in three assumptions about gender, quality improvement and organizational change.

Assumption 1

In order to deliver a quality programme that empowers women, you need the perspectives of various kinds of both men and women staff and primary stakeholders (village organization members in BRAC's case). Men and women staff share common skills but because of their socialization and the culture surrounding them, they also have particular strengths related to their gender. Male staff may have some strengths (mobility, collection of loans, more available time) and women have other strengths (a capacity to understand the perspectives of women in the villages, the possibility of talking to them directly). BRAC realizes this and has been working to hire, retain and promote large numbers of women to build a gender-balanced workforce.

But BRAC like all organizations is 'gendered'. The processes of interaction and systems for doing the organization's work were decided upon by men and, although they considered the needs of women, these considerations were dominated by men's perceptions. Because of this, working in the organization is easier for men than for women. For example, Men's ability to spend long hours at work is subsidized by their female partners who attend to children and home responsibilities. Also, by being part of BRAC and functioning like the men, women's security may be threatened as they work in the field; for example, being pushed off their bicycles by villagers who feel they should not be working in this way. Another problem is that being away from their families makes marriage more difficult for women.

However, there is a deeper, more pervasive issue. Globally, women are devalued *vis-à-vis* men. This sense of women's devaluation is an important part of men's socialization and may mean that certain men do not respect women staff and even may tease or psychologically harass them. The socialization of both men and women results in tension between them as they learn to work together as colleagues. Even when special arrangements are made for women's biological differences, women are reluctant to take advantage of them because, as they say, they will be viewed as not good enough or somehow disabled and therefore requiring special attention. All of these and other factors make the task of working effectively in BRAC more difficult for women than for men. These factors make hiring, retaining and promoting female staff difficult and ultimately problematic.

Assumption 2

A hierarchical target-driven organization will focus on the accomplishment of numerical targets related to programme inputs. An organization with a directive supervision ethic will focus on those targets to the exclusion of other, more subtle measurements. Problem-solving will not extend beyond the accomplishment of the quantitative targets to actual programme impacts. Therefore, if you want to deepen the quality of the programme and build a greater responsiveness to members (particularly female) you need to balance the target culture with a concern for quality of programme and its impact on the empowerment of women.

This does not mean ignoring targets like the number of loans made or the amount of money loaned. It means adding other measurements like the percentage of women who retain control over the income or the numbers of women who become more influential as a result of income generation. It also means facing the issue of perhaps decreasing the target for loan disbursement in order to allow staff to focus on increasing the impact of the programme on women's empowerment.

Assumption 3

If you are going to improve quality then you need to engage men and women front-line staff and members in the task of analysing the process and outcomes of programme delivery so as to continually improve the depth and quality of a programme and its ability to actually empower women. This analysis requires skill in programme analysis, time to do it, a climate of acceptance of new ideas and the respectful collaboration of men and women staff and members. As can be seen, these assumptions mean that gender work must go beyond training programmes. If BRAC is to become capable of retaining women, focusing on outcomes beyond loan disbursement and deepening the ability of the programme to empower women, then we must understand which organizational dynamics are facilitating and which are blocking this development.

Working at the nexus of the three domains (gender, organizational change and quality improvement) means that the project must deal with some contradictions. For example, if BRAC is a gendered organization how will a strategy that leaves the choice of goals up to the organization have any impact? Is everything a gender issue? How do you know where to start? At the same time this nexus provides us with some strong advantages. If the gender work is tied to an organizational change strategy it stands a better chance of being more than an isolated training programme without a clear plan for the implementation of actual change. By linking gender with quality we demonstrate (or not) that attention to gender dynamics results in a qualitatively better programme in BRAC's terms. Gender work will not be at the margins but an integral part of programme development.

Key Features of the Start-up Phase

At the outset, three features of the BRAC case should be noted. First, organizational entry was initiated by the Executive Director of BRAC, not imposed by outside interests. Second, the issue of gender was not new to the organization though generally it was more narrowly conceptualized (gender equity means bringing more women into BRAC) and in more women-specific terms. Third, the Gender Team consists of both outsiders and insiders: four BRAC staff all drawn from the Training Division (this is consistent with the initial outputs expected of the programme), and three external consultants who together came with credentials respected by BRAC and close knowledge of the organization.

In this section, we discuss two issues concerning the start-up phase of the structural intervention in BRAC focused on gender, organizational change and quality improvement: (1) the process of diagnosis and knowledge-building on gender in BRAC; and (2) the process of building a shared vision for change and transferring ownership. These are preliminary to designing elements of an action-learning process to explore quality issues through gender and testing the relevance and replicability of learnings across BRAC. This type of intervention was planned and implemented in 1995.

Knowledge building: the needs assessment process and findings

Diagnosis for organizational change is a collaborative attempt to aid a system to understand itself in its own terms that uses social science techniques and pays deep attention to the client's perception of what needs to change and how. Working with gender complicates the process because we are not simply responding but we are teaching and learning as well. In this work we draw on a specialized field of knowledge and experience and also create new knowledge through the process of collective engagement in conceptualization and implementation.[2]

In the spring of 1994, the team conducted a series of consultations and 23 needs assessment workshops with 400 BRAC staff at all levels, from part-time teachers to senior managers, across the three programmes: Rural Development, Non-formal Primary Education, and Health and Family Planning. The purpose of this exercise was to provide valid and compelling data for gender-related strategic planning by managers, to provide an orientation to gender thinking to a cross section of BRAC staff, and to deepen the team's own understanding of gender issues relevant to BRAC. Informing this exercise was our own work deconstructing theoretical formulations on women's empowerment and gender.

In July, the team held a strategic planning meeting over two-and-a-half days with all senior BRAC managers to analyse systematically the needs assessment data, develop a vision of what BRAC wants to accomplish in terms of women's empowerment and a strategy for accomplishing that mission. The visioning and strategizing work continued as BRAC underwent its own internal strategic planning exercise for the fourth phase of its Rural Development Programme in August.

Diagnostic tools

Each two-day needs assessment workshop addressed empowerment issues related to programmes on the first day and gender issues related to organizational life on the second. In addition, we administered a staff attitude survey consisting of 22 questions aimed at gauging staff attitudes and values regarding gender dimensions of BRAC's programme and organizational processes.

Empowerment: conceptual clarity for field-level application

The first two exercises aimed at assessing: the quality of BRAC staff's conceptual understanding of women's empowerment issues; how and to what extent staff apply these concepts to field-level situations; staff's ideas on how BRAC should change or improve its programme in order to further the empowerment of women; and what kinds of support staff need to implement these changes. The first exercise, Gender Analysis, required participants to articulate key differences between poor women and men in rural Bangladesh along the three major dimensions of empowerment: access to and control over income and resources; knowledge of and the ability to negotiate for one's rights; and control over one's own body and security of movement. Then, participants were asked to probe the reasons for these differences and to suggest what should be done to make the situation more gender equitable.

The second exercise required participants to analyse the key empowerment dimensions through case studies. A total of six cases were developed by the Gender Team for use in this exercise. The first three cases focus on the three empowerment dimensions mentioned above; the last three focus on health, education and income-generating skills.

Inside BRAC: conditions and relationships

To assess internal organizational issues, three exercises were developed. The first encouraged participants to write, individually and anonymously, about positive as well as problematic aspects of working in BRAC. The 'problems' were later redistributed to the group which categorized them by type of problem: living conditions, working conditions, relationships with supervisors, colleagues and village organization members, and career development. Groups chose the most important and discussed what could be done to deal with these. In the second exercise, participants were given two cases for discussion, both of which focused on intra-organizational gender dynamics. One case illustrates women's lack of voice and the other, norms of purity and appropriate behaviour for women.[3] The third exercise involved participants in describing, pictorially and verbally, their preferred organizational shape for the future, based on their conceptions of appropriate gender roles and appropriate organizational responses in support of these.

Findings

The findings of the needs assessment exercise fall into three broad areas: staff attitudes about women's empowerment and female staff; gender analysis and programming; and gender and organizational issues.

Staff attitudes

Staff, both male and female, at all levels and programmes, believe BRAC should pursue women's empowerment and change men's attitudes and values as a prerequisite to accomplishing this goal. Beyond this, however, there are uncertainties and disagreements on programming strategies, particularly in the areas of women's mobility, intra-household decision-making and conflict, and ensuring freedom from violence. The majority of staff also believe that women should be promoted up the management ladder because they can do the job and do it well. But there is a good deal of disagreement over questions of reconciling women's family and work responsibilities, special provisions and an accelerated career path for women. Gender relations in the workplace are often not smooth and women face varying levels of teasing and/or harassment. Thus, while conditions have improved for women in the last few years, a great deal is left to be done.

Empowerment

Three issues stand out regarding BRAC staff's conceptual understanding of gender issues and an application of this understanding to programmatic situations. First, staff's intuitive understanding of gender differences does not translate often into creative strategic solutions for dealing with the core issues of empowerment. Instead, proposed strategies and solutions either tend to reflect system imperatives of achieving targets, a process through which empowerment goals can be sacrificed in the name of efficiency, or standard supply-side responses to problem symptoms. Second, while conflict inheres in common conceptualizations of empowerment, staff lean toward searching for harmonious solutions to problems of women's subordination in the family and community rather than confrontation. In the Bangladesh cultural and political context this is instructive and strategic and at the same time worrisome because it leaves the power imbalance and gender ideology intact. And third, BRAC staff place inordinate emphasis on and have enormous faith in the ability to change behaviours and values through training. To this extent, they discount (and therefore inadequately address) the tremendous impact of forces external to the individual (family, kinship, factions, cultural norms, gender ideology, etc.) in shaping individual behaviours.

Inside BRAC

Put together, staff responses paint a complex picture. BRAC is an organization in transition from a collective to a corporation pursuing empowerment goals in a volatile socio-economic and political environment. Externally, it is grappling with an enormous expansion in area coverage and an increasing complexity and technical sophistication in programme content. Internally, organizational complexity is enhanced by a series of features: a race for target achievement that leaves experienced supervisors with little time to nurture and guide newer entrants; newcomers fresh out of the universities who are moving up the corporate ladder and are being handed programme responsibility quickly; a management style geared toward target achievement which militates against the search for lasting solutions to difficult problems of women's subordination and gender equitable change on the ground; an organizational environment in which opportunities for open discussion on personal and professional issues are becoming scarce; a brewing conflict between traditional patriarchal norms and behaviours and a nascent culture of gender equity supported at the very highest levels of policy-making within the organization; a need to forge ways of working between men and women in an organization that espouses counter-cultural values but among people who do not necessarily believe in them; a fatigue among longstanding cadres to the front-line fight; and a desire for work–family balance among men and women alike.

Strategic issues

How do BRAC's dual goals of poverty alleviation and empowerment of women play out on the ground? The evidence suggests that participation in BRAC's programmes has strengthened women's economic roles and, to some extent, increased women's empowerment measured in terms of mobility, economic security, legal awareness, decision-making, and freedom from violence within the family (see for example Schuler and Hashemi, 1994). However, widely acknowledged among BRAC staff is the fact that the imperatives of credit delivery are eclipsing the objectives of social change.

Moreover, the complexity intensifies the closer you look. A recent study examining women's high demand for credit and access to loans in Bangladesh found that in close to one-third of cases, BRAC women members have little or no control over their loans (Goetz and Sen Gupta, 1994). By excluding, for the most part, men from credit access, is BRAC merely setting women up as conduits for credit to men and if so at what cost? What does BRAC do with the knowledge that many of the loans given to women are hijacked by men? Can it enter the conflictual household arena through programme interventions and re-emerge relatively unscathed having achieved useful outcomes? What other responses are possible? BRAC now believes that working with men to bring about changes in the perceptions and valuations of women is essential and that men should be included in small numbers in the female village organizations. This may help to counter opposition to BRAC from husbands and village elites as men will be able to present BRAC in village fora from which women are excluded, but it opens up a host of complications for building women's self-reliance and solidarity as well. How can BRAC work to build women's capacity to pursue their strategic interests including security and freedom from violence; issues which a majority of staff believe BRAC should focus on? How can BRAC re-focus its institutional development work to build the organizational effectiveness and public bargaining strength of women?

Has BRAC as an organization come to terms with its corporate nature? For the most part, its systems and standard operating procedures, including the level of autonomy for decision-making among staff, are ones that worked well when the organization was a fraction of its current size and during a different era of the organization's history. These very systems and procedures are straining now with negative consequences for work quality and staff morale. BRAC's human resource function, for example, is atomized among different line functions and is perceived by staff to be an arcane process in which they have no voice. Moreover, the current breed of recruits come to the organization with a different set of motivations from those that shaped it in its early years. Livelihood issues predominate over ideology, creating new demands over working conditions and career development issues. The changing gender mix within the organization is also throwing up new challenges to standard practices and cultural norms.

Must women become men to succeed? Over the course of the last two years, BRAC has made a series of special arrangements to accommodate women staff's need (such as giving them the option to work at their desks rather than do fieldwork during menstruation). Interestingly, women are reluctant to take advantage of some of these special arrangements either because in this culture of extreme modesty it would make public the very private, or because they will be viewed as not good enough or somehow disabled and therefore requiring special attention. While the organization is attempting to accommodate women's needs, it is doing so in an incremental fashion essentially leaving intact the dominant organizational culture, space and ways of working which are themselves gendered. Thus, women in effect have to fit into a system that was made to fit men. In the Bangladesh cultural context it is easy and acceptable for men to carry out fieldwork at night, ride bicycles and motorbikes, and live singly in villages; for women it is not. Women face harassment from villagers and from their own male colleagues. If they protest, they are blamed for their own vulnerability to physical violence, and are held to be weak and inefficient, with the strong implication that they are themselves responsible for behaviours forced on them by patriarchal norms that sort out what is appropriate and what is not. Thus, most women are faced with the difficult choice of conforming to counter-cultural values without the support of their male colleagues within a system that espouses them but in effect practices the opposite. Those who have fought their way up the system have proved they are as good as any man but are their struggles organizational requirements? Must women become men to succeed? Most male BRAC staff say that's not the case but many women contest that.

Ownership, Visioning and Negotiating Next Steps

Coming up with a series of issues is one thing; what an organization chooses to do with them is quite another. Although the findings of the needs assessment were not unknown to BRAC senior managers, coming together the way they did caught them off guard. (This, however, was not the case with the Executive Director who though not present at the meeting was briefed on the findings prior to it, and approved presentation of the findings to the second tier management group.) Reactions ranged from shock and denial to quiet contemplation and thoughtful attempts at distilling implications for BRAC and its work. The meeting did not result in any common visioning or conclusion about next steps.

But BRAC has moved quickly from its initial response to grapple seriously with the issues. In a second round of internal meetings chaired by the Executive Director to plan the organization's strategy for the next five years, the gender needs assessment findings were once again discussed. The strategy document summarizing those discussions states the organization's commitment *inter alia* to 'deepening existing programmes, with greater responsiveness to target group needs and expectations', and improving 'the internal organizational culture' – issues also raised by the gender needs assessment.

When, after a hiatus of two months, the team leader went around to each senior manager to ask what they thought and how they felt about the work of the Gender Team, they gave three messages: first, that the team had done a useful task in putting important issues on the table; second, that BRAC as a whole and specific programmes in particular are committed to addressing specific aspects of these issues; and third, that most of the second tier of management had internalized these issues and articulated them as their own. During a second round of one-on-one's, it became clear that while senior managers remained interested in the issues, they were uncertain about what exactly gender meant to organizational development in concrete terms including areas of overlap and distinctions. They were also uncertain about what an intervention aimed at creating organizational spaces for learning through doing on issues of gender, programme quality, and organizational change would look like.

These are legitimate questions to which there are no easy answers. In the next phase of our work, the team organized a series of work sessions with senior managers to address collectively these questions and come to agreement on an intervention design.

Dilemmas and Cautions

Expanding parameters versus boundary maintenance

Expanding parameters in this case means three things. First, it means expanding understanding of gender as a synonym for women to gender as referring to the social construction of what is male and what is female, as a way of signifying power relations. It means moving from referring to women's specific needs within the organization (such as separate living facilities and arrangements for desk rather than field work during pregnancy), to understanding organizations as gendered spaces. Second, it is related to broadening understanding of how individuals learn – by exposure to relevant concepts and tools, applying them in one's work setting, and reflecting on problems and outcomes in an iterative fashion – rather than classroom learning alone. Third, it means understanding that the application of concepts and tools leading to new ways of working will become institutionalized only when they are supported by a range of other policy, institutional and advocacy interventions aimed at bringing about organizational change. Pursued alone their effect will remain limited. BRAC needs both committed individuals and a strategy for change; when the two come together change takes place. At the same time, however, three other related processes also have to occur: making these concepts real to BRAC and its programme processes, drawing boundaries around gender work in BRAC so that it retains meaning and is not subsumed for example under 'management', and delimiting the scope of the intervention to what is manageable within a specific period of time and to one that will show results. These two sets of processes pull in opposite directions and managing them centres on conceptualizing and concretizing the boundary areas.

Innovation versus institutional bargaining

Organizational theory suggests that innovation requires influence but that institutional bargaining requires contractual rather than confrontational terms. In the BRAC case this plays out in two ways. First, the team's credibility built as it is on its own merit and through support from the Executive Director strengthens its potential to innovate. But bringing senior managers on board involves more than discussions and clarifications. In a hierarchal organization like BRAC in which the Executive Director has an extensive hand in setting policy directions, it also requires clear signals from the very top that this programme deserves attention. This poses a dilemma because it reinforces a model of organizational behaviour which is at odds with our conception of individual and systemic learning for organizational change. This irony is not lost on a number of senior managers who nevertheless believe that it is one we have to live with especially in the start-up phase of the programme. The second way in which this plays out is that because gender relations as constructed within society and mirrored to a greater or lesser extent within the organization are to men's advantage, the institutional learning process which we are promoting requires men to collaborate in a process aimed at dismantling their privilege. We believe, however, that this does not explain the whole picture because men's gender roles stereotype them too in some ways which are disadvantageous to them. Getting both men and women beyond this may point to directions for different ways of conceiving and structuring power in ways that take in differences. But developing processes and attitudes that deal with men's jealousy without alienating either women or men and bringing both into a learning process is a constant challenge.

Change Options or Change Realities

The third fundamental dilemma in the work on quality improvement in the BRAC context which we face is distinguishing what is theoretically desirable (for example, pushing the boundaries of women's empowerment) and what is programmatically possible, at what costs, and with what effect, in a socio-political environment where demand for changing gender relations is weak, fundamentalist forces are increasingly dominant, and where existing structural realities ensure that the process of women's empowerment is both non-additive and non-linear. What to do about the dilemma of women's lack of control over BRAC loans is a case in point. Given that entering into the household, an arena of power relations drawn on lines of gender and age, is a path fraught with pitfalls, does BRAC leave well enough alone? If it can work for change in a small handful of households, can it replicate small-scale change experiments across all areas without losing the quality? And how does BRAC support people's struggles over resources and ways of thinking *vis-à-vis* larger and more powerful groupings in the community? How does an organization like BRAC sort out what it wants to keep in itself from what it wants to change? Some things are clear: BRAC can deliver credit and a range of social services. But whether or not deeper qualitative approaches are feasible is still to be discovered. Answers to these issues are possible only by creating organizational learning spaces for creating and testing innovations.

Notes

1. A version of this chapter first appeared in 'Getting Institutions Right for Women in Development', *IDS Bulletin*, vol. 26, no. 3, July 1995.

2. For details on the BRAC Gender Programme design, instruments and tools, see 'An Action-Learning Approach to Gender and Organizational Change', BRAC, August 1996

3. The cases were based on taped interviews of staff from BRAC and the Bangladesh government poverty alleviation programme conducted by Anne Marie Goetz and Rina Sen Gupta in the course of their study on Women's Leadership in Bangladesh carried out in 1993.

9

What's in a Design? The Effects of NGO Programme Delivery Choices on Women's Empowerment in Bangladesh[1]

Brooke Ackerly

Bangladeshi credit programmes work in an environment of social, political and economic values, practices, norms and laws that are biased such that they are harmful to women. Credit organizations loaning money to women have in some respect sought to change the circumstances of women through their programmes. Where 'empowerment of women' is the primary goal, credit programmes have devised creative programme design features that work within, while at the same time working to change, those aspects of the Bangladeshi institutional context that are harmful to women.[2] However, as I will demonstrate, other goals can compete with empowerment of women for priority consideration in formal programme design and informal programme operations. Competing goals create incentives for workers, borrowers, and borrowers' families to act in ways that potentially undermine women's empowerment. Based on a study of four credit organizations, I demonstrate ways in which credit programmes affect their borrowers through their programme design.

In recent years, issuing credit to women has developed wide acceptance as a means of economic development targeting the poor. Empowerment of women is a frequently articulated goal of these development strategies. Although there is no agreed definition, empowerment is an active concept in both development and academic work because it approximately articulates a change development professionals hope to encourage and researchers look to document. 'Empowered', the borrower wisely invests money in a successful enterprise, her husband stops beating her, she sends her children to school, she improves the health and nutrition of her family, and she participates in major family decisions. Although measurement is difficult (perhaps because it is difficult) empowerment, and the frequently articulated example of the empowered borrower, have become the presumed results of credit programmes.

I use a two-part definition of women's empowerment. The first depends on changes in a woman's institutional environment: circumventing, changing, or eliminating the society's values, practices, norms and laws in order to lessen the extent to which they constrain her activities and choices. The second depends on an individual woman's own ability to take action or make choices. Accordingly, empowerment is a function of institutional change and individual initiative. Importantly, the two parts are not easily distinguishable from each other because a coercive environment can limit women's ability to take action and make choices. The two-part definition identifies credit programmes' role as one of changing the institutional environment to enable borrowers to broaden their range of activity and choice.

To appreciate the ways in which organizations have worked within their institutional environment to change it, I studied credit organizations in Bangladesh. The four discussed in this chapter are the Bangladesh Rural Advancement Committee (BRAC), a Bangladeshi non-government organization (NGO) operating nationally; Grameen Bank, a Bangladeshi development bank operating nationally; Save the Children, USA/Bangladesh Field Office (SCB), an international NGO operating in a few regions in Bangladesh;[3] and Shakti Foundation, a young local NGO operating in the urban slums of Dhaka, the capital city. Each NGO utilizes a widely respected and tested methodology in its credit practices: group guaranteed savings and lending. The programmes extend loans to women to support economic activities. The women meet regularly in their villages or neighbourhoods to make savings deposits and to pay instalments. Lending costs are lower than typical bank costs because group members approve new loans and guarantee each other's loans. Peer pressure encourages high repayment rates because each individual's eligibility for future loans depends on all individuals' repayment. The borrowers absorb the otherwise high institutional costs of new issuance and collections.[4] Each programme's structure reflects formal decisions about programme design and, where left to their discretion, workers' informal interpretations of programme goals based on the incentives they face.

I argue that organizations have choices – even within an institutional context. There are two parts to this argument. First, organizations make choices about how and whether to work within and to challenge their institutional context. Credit programmes have been inventive in generating ways to work within, while at the same time challenging existing institutional constraints.[5] Given the pervasiveness of institutions of gender hierarchy, if credit organizations wish to challenge them, programme designers must consciously design their programmes to do so. Second, where organizations have conflicting goals, pursuing one can undermine pursuit of the other. I argue that without incentives for borrowers, their husbands, and workers designed to promote women's empowerment in society and in the family, where the empowerment goal competes with others, women may be the losers.

Institutional Context and Organizational Choice

Most development practitioners and researchers have a funny or sad anecdote about a programme which failed to assess accurately the institutional context of its work, but most assume that effective programmes take the local environment into consideration in their programme design. While philosophers and welfare economists debate to what extent that local environment should be respected or challenged, most programmes are designed partially in deference to existing values and partially to change them.[6] Both deference and opposition require understanding local circumstances. In this section, I present certain characteristics of Bangladeshi society which are important for understanding the institutional environment of credit programmes. I offer examples of programmatic efforts designed to work within, while challenging, those institutions. I argue that the familiar theoretical distinction between formal and informal institutions is not as useful for discussing women's empowerment as a distinction between intra-familial and other forms of hierarchy.

In *Institutions, Institutional Change, and Economic Performance*, Douglas C. North distinguishes between formal institutions, as in rules and contracts, and informal ones, as in social norms and cultural practices. Both formal and informal institutions exist in the polity, market, and social community. In the study of the ways in which social institutions perpetuate values and practices that are harmful to women, North's distinction between formal and informal institutions is helpful, but inadequate. Given the power of husbands over wives, changes in the social environment may not affect women's ability to take the initiative. When considering the institutional environment of women's action and choices, it is more important to distinguish between intra-familial hierarchy and other forms of gender hierarchy.

Much research has documented the general – and regional variations of – social and familial institutions constraining the lives of poor women in Bangladesh (for example, Chen, 1983; Shehabuddin, 1992; and White, 1992). Generally, women access markets and public fora through men. Consequently, women unattached to husbands, fathers, or sons lack an important familial resource. Because women depend on men for social access, gender hierarchy in society significantly impacts on gender hierarchy in the family, meaning patriarchy. Gender hierarchy operates within most families in some form, and in many poor families in an exacerbated form, to constrain women's activities and choices. Husbands and fathers have decision-making authority over their wives and daughters, and boy children are given preferential allocations of food, education and health care. Perhaps because social and familial hierarchy overlap, gender hierarchy within the family is often overlooked in programming decisions. In deciding which institutions to work within and which to challenge, organizations make choices.[7] Those credit programmes which choose formal and informal features designed to address both aspects of hierarchy are best able to empower women.

By virtue of its presence, a credit programme alters the context of women's lives. Rural and poor women in Bangladesh normally do not have access to institutional credit.[8] In order to operate, in order to hold meetings, and in order for husbands to allow their wives to attend meetings, credit programme designers and implementers must respect the existing constraints and work within them to some extent. At the same time, those organizations which seek to empower women try to change the institutional constraints on women's lives: those of societal gender hierarchy and patriarchy that devalue women and constrain women's activity and choice.[9]

Gender hierarchy in society and organizational choice

In group interviews, workers from all four programmes articulated (and generally challenged) socially prevalent perceptions of women as inferior – by nature physically weak, foolish and lazy. The stereotypes they attribute to biology are in fact socially induced. Women's physical weakness is generally an effect of social practices such as wives serving the largest and best portions to their husbands and sons and themselves eating after their husbands, and poor families placing a low priority on health care for pregnant women, nursing mothers, and girls.[10]

Similarly, women's 'foolishness' is a biological stereotype perpetuated by social practices such as giving girls less education than their brothers or no education at all. Education is seen as an investment in future income generation. Girls' education is not perceived as a good investment because when a girl marries the income goes to her husband's family not to the natal family. Differentials in education persist despite the fact that elementary school fees are waived for girls.

Finally, women are perceived as lazy, though social constraints on their mobility and their market access restrict their ability to contribute money to the family. Rural women are not accepted in the marketplace. Though they work to contribute to family well-being within the family compound (*bari*), they rely on men to conduct most market transactions, and thus income generation is normally attributed to men regardless of the degree of women's labour contribution.

Workers recognize that the perceptions of women as weak, foolish, and lazy and the social conditions that perpetuate them – women's limited access to health care and nutrition, education and the market – are harmful to women.[11] Although credit programmes are economic organizations, they can also affect the health and education of their borrowers through their programming if they choose to integrate education and nutrition information. Successful integration increases the quality of life for women and girls, and enhances their productive capability. In separate monthly issue meetings, BRAC workers promote the education of all children and good health and nutrition practices. In addition, through separate programmes, BRAC promotes adult literacy, non-formal primary education for boys and girls, and maternal and child health. Grameen requires memorization of its 'Sixteen Decisions', which are commitments to certain health and economic related practices including not giving or receiving dowry. Grameen also encourages its centres to save for a centre school for their children. The SCB credit programme is integrated with its programmes for early childhood development and maternal–child health such that weekly meetings provide integrated messages. Whatever a programme's messages, intra-familial hierarchy affects whether messages get translated into practice.

In addition to undermining stereotypes of women as weak, credit programmes challenge stereotypes of women as foolish by promoting women's access to, and knowledge of, the market. For example, in its subsector programmes such as poultry raising, fish culture and silk culture, BRAC brings the market to the women. These programmes enable many economic transactions to take place within the *bari*. Similarly, SCB encourages women's fish-pond management. Sales are made at the fish pond and not at the market so women do the selling and the related financial management themselves, increasing the likelihood of empowerment (Ackerly, 1995).

Further, by circumventing the market restrictions on women by moving economic transactions to the *bari*, credit programmes can also challenge stereotypes of women as lazy. For example, in its restaurant programme, BRAC encourages women to operate traditionally male-run businesses. However, contrary to the programme's intended purpose, a BRAC study indicates that, in fact, the husbands tend to run the business and the women play a supporting and less visible role (Khan, 1993). This research suggests that in order to achieve BRAC's objectives for the restaurant programme, programme design could be altered to take better account of social norms regarding women in public and familial norms of gender roles.

With programme initiatives to talk about health and education issues, to develop women's market knowledge, to have market transactions take place in the *bari*, and to introduce women to non-traditional economic activities, credit programmes have challenged gender hierarchy. However, their effectiveness is constrained by patriarchy.

Patriarchy and organizational choice

According to credit programme workers, within families, status and corresponding authority are correlated with male sex, age, income earning, education, status of natal family, ability to make wise decisions, and ability and willingness to work. In addition to the social constraints described above, women have less power in the family relative to their husbands and on many matters relative to their sons. Although the interests of women and husbands are not always or even frequently opposed, family decision-making rests with husbands. Some credit programmes work within the constraints of patriarchy by allowing women borrowers to be a means of credit and income earning for their husbands. Those programmes contribute to increasing the limits on women in the family by increasing women's liabilities without correspondingly increasing their authority to manage resources or to take action or decisions on their own initiative.

Though there is great variety in the lives of Bangladeshi women, similarities cross regional, class and religious boundaries. Generally, rural women in Bangladesh depend on the men in their families for their access to markets and for their very existence. While men depend on women for their existence as well, men's and women's mutual dependence should not be interpreted as reciprocal. Men can, and do, leave their wives and children, move to other places, and start new lives. Women can leave their husbands only by returning to their father's house. Without husbands, sons or fathers, women are economically isolated because they cannot get access to markets, and are socially ostracized.

As mentioned above, most family earnings, though perhaps earned by the labour of many, enter the family as income through the husband (or male head of household). For example, a traditional rural activity commonly funded by credit is paddy processing.[12] For this activity a woman takes credit and gives the money to her husband to purchase unprocessed paddy at the market. The woman, sometimes with her husband or other family members, processes the paddy into rice or *muri* (puffed rice). The husband then takes the processed rice to market for sale. Although the activity is funded by the woman's credit and she contributes labour to the product sold, the economic control of the activity rests with the man by virtue of his access to the market.

Thus, though lending to a family through the wife increases the family income, it leaves the woman exposed to her husband's willingness to make the instalments. The husband controls the finances and at his discretion gives responsibility and resources to his wife. When a woman gives her credit money to her husband for investment, any of a number of scenarios is possible.[13] I have grouped these into four.[14] In all four scenarios, women are means to credit for the family and they are means to reduce collection costs for the lending organization. In scenario one, the husband gives the wife most of the earnings. The wife manages the household expenses, repayment and savings. In scenario two, the husband manages the finances and gives the wife the household expense and instalment money. In scenario three, the husband gives the wife the household funds, and she must manage the instalment payment from that. Depending on how much he gives her, scenario three can result in reduced family nutrition particularly for women and children as there is less money available for food. In scenario four, the husband denies the obligation, and the wife must endure beatings and risk abandonment in order to get the repayment money. In the case of abandonment, she must borrow informally to meet repayment obligations.

Under the first scenario, the woman has increased financial responsibility and gains knowledge, respect within the family, and respect from outsiders. Under the second scenario, some of the same knowledge and respect may accrue, particularly if the wife is involved in the selling of the product or in the accounting for the activity. She can even gain respect if she is appreciated as the means to the credit although the husband conducts most or all financial transactions. In the last two scenarios, the woman's responsibility for her credit is not matched by her resources and authority within the family. For some observers, the image of a woman depriving herself in order to make a better life for her family (like the woman who saves a handful of rice from her already insufficient diet) is one of an empowered woman making important decisions. However, her decision to forgo her own needs in order to repay credit is made in a patriarchal context that constrains her activities and choices. Her 'choice' lacks the institutional context for empowerment.[15]

Some credit programmes seek to work within the familial hierarchy that oppresses women by encouraging traditional women's activities that generally use women's labor such as paddy processing, poultry raising, and animal husbandry. These activities increase the workload of women and the amount of money husbands bring home from the market. If scenario three or four results, credit actually burdens the woman and further limits her. Other organizations counter women's subordinate position in the family by promoting women's knowledge and skill development, particularly of traditionally men's activities. Mentioned above, BRAC's subsector programmes and SCB's fish-culture programmes are two examples.

SCB, Shakti and BRAC challenge intra-familial hierarchy. As described in the case of fish-pond management, SCB encourages women to take on the financial management of their loan-funded activities. Likewise, Shakti makes loans subject to husbands' sharing market information with their wives. These programmes are designed to undermine inequality within the family by encouraging women to develop market and financial knowledge. Using a different approach, BRAC discourages husbands from using their wives' loans. In some areas, BRAC loans to both the husband and the wife in a family separately. This decreases the husband's need to appropriate his wife's money for his own activity but does not limit his control of the market-related aspects of her activity. BRAC acknowledges the problem, but has not come up with a programmatic solution. By contrast, though men's use of women's loans is not intended in Grameen's programme design, since the family benefits economically, Grameen management and workers do not discourage the practice. To the contrary, Grameen has formalized this practice by offering larger 'family loans' to women who have good repayment records and who have family members able to help utilize the loan. Without programme features designed to prevent husbands' appropriation of women's loans, the institutions of rural Bangladesh make women's credit functionally her family's credit.

Though SCB and Shakti are more concerned about women's loan use than BRAC and Grameen, all three rural lenders are concerned about women's abandonment. To be eligible to receive a housing loan from BRAC and Grameen, the land and constructed house must be the legal property of the woman borrower. By educating women on their legal rights regarding divorce and abandonment, BRAC and SCB programmes try to improve women's circumstances in the case of abandonment.

The programmatic features discussed above reflect organizational choices about whether, and how, to challenge social and intra-familial gender hierarchy in Bangladesh. The variety of credit programme designs demonstrates that within the bounds of institutional constraints there remains room for choice. Credit programmes can choose to promote women's empowerment. In order to be successful, credit programmes need to address the ways in which the institutionalization of gender

Table 9.1　Percentage of women borrowers in target group[16]

	Total borrowers surveyed	no. of borrowers 'certainly' in the target group	% of borrowers 'certainly' in the target group
Total BRAC	236	195	83
Total GB	317	250	79
Total SCB	72	65	90
Total Shakti	70	69	99
Total	695	579	83

hierarchy in society and the family have been harmful to women. The management of credit programmes must choose to promote women's empowerment and structure incentives that encourage workers to choose empowerment of women as their goal too.

Conflicting Goals and Organizational Choice

In the preceding section I gave examples from each of the organizations studied of programmatic features that are empowering to women. However, a few such features do not mean that the net effect of programme design is the empowerment of most women borrowers. The ways programmes pursue other goals of the organization often undermine empowerment. In this section, I discuss ways in which the goals of Grameen and BRAC, which are not primarily the empowerment of women, conflict with women's empowerment. In contrast, I describe ways in which SCB and Shakti have been innovative in designing their programmes to empower women. While I focus on empowerment of women borrowers, I also draw attention to SCB's and Shakti's practices of empowering women employees.

Grameen's choice: lending for profitability

Grameen Bank has had one goal since its inception: profitable lending to the rural poor. How does this primary goal influence its formal design, the incentives on bank workers to operationalize that goal, and the effects of design and implementation on women's empowerment?

In seeking to form new centres, the Grameen worker looks for borrowers who are likely to be able to repay. These are not necessarily members

Table 9.2 Average loan size of borrowers by organization*

	BRAC	Grameen	SCB	Shakti
Women's average borrowings	2,805 tk ($70) (n = 317)	5,368 tk ($134) (n = 236)	3,181 tk ($80) (n = 72)	3,114 tk ($78) (n = 70)

* Housing and tubewell loans excluded.

of Grameen's formally defined target group (Table 9.1). The Grameen worker observes the borrowers' ability to memorize the Sixteen Decisions as evidence of their discipline, and ability to make regular savings deposits as evidence of their willingness to repay. She or he talks with potential borrowers' neighbours to discern their reputation and with their husbands to confirm the husbands' understanding that the loan is an obligation. She or he determines the families' resources and other sources of income. The worker is willing to lend to those with greater economic means than those of the target group because they are likely to have the means to repay if the funded activity does not yield enough income.

Grameen lends almost exclusively to married women. Workers explain that unmarried women will move when they marry and thus are at risk of leaving without repaying. Married women do not move (unless their husbands divorce them or send them away) and their husbands can help with the activity or seek employment if the activity fails. Because women have limited income earning opportunities, husbands are seen by bank workers as critical resources. Although the members' group solidarity is the 'collateral' of each individual loan, when this fails, the worker pressures the borrower and her husband. The worker's responsibility to bring back the payment shapes his or her behaviour towards borrowers.

After extending a new loan, the worker goes to the borrower's home in order to be assured that the money has been invested. The borrower is allowed to invest her credit as she wishes or to give it to her husband or son to invest. The inspection confirms for the worker that the loan-funded activity will generate an income stream. These inspections are officially required, but are performed on only a percentage of the loans, and inspection varies by branch.

Finally, in order to increase branch profitability, the worker encourages those borrowers who have the capacity to utilize increasing amounts of credit to do so. This is done by allowing the borrower to partner with other family members – generally husbands and sons – in her activity and to take out multiple loans. General, seasonal, family, housing and tubewell loans are available in most branches. In their study, average Grameen debt per borrower was 5,268 taka compared with 2,805 taka, 3,181 taka, and 3,114 taka for BRAC, SCB, and Shakti respectively (Table 9.2). Increased loan size increases the profit per borrower.

In sum, although all new Grameen borrowers are women and 94 per cent of existing borrowers are women,[17] Grameen's borrower selection process has a negative effect on women's empowerment. Borrowers with earning husbands and husbands able to work are more likely, according to Grameen workers, to be able to repay and are thus preferred borrowers. Borrowers' husbands may utilize the loan money in partnership with the wife or not, as long as the income results in regular repayments. Moreover, due to the fact that women have limited access to markets, when accepting increasing loan amounts, in most cases women borrowers must plan to partner with their husbands and sons or to transfer the loan to them entirely in order to be able to fully utilize the loan and to repay it. As a village elder explained to me, by attending the weekly meetings, women borrowers give their husbands access to credit and spare them the time commitment of the meetings.

In this light, Grameen's policy of lending to women uses women as means to achieving profitable lending to the poor and allows men to use their wives as means to credit. Workers recognize that male access to markets is necessary for women's productive activities and that when husbands are not otherwise employed, families may earn more if the husbands utilize the credit. The irony, however, is that while this increases family income, it is a liability for women and leaves them exposed to their husbands' willingness to pay the instalment money or to share the economic rewards associated with that liability.

BRAC's choice: lending for repayment rate

BRAC's formal goal is empowerment of the poor. However, competition with many other development organizations for funding has created a competing goal for the credit programme: high repayment rates. Pressure for BRAC to have high repayment rates comes from two related sources. Funding organizations treat Grameen's reported achievements in high repayment rates as a high standard for other credit programmes. Further, because it is difficult to define and measure empowerment of women, and because there is a common belief that credit is empowering, BRAC has focused on the seemingly more measurable goal of high repayment rates.[18] Regardless of its formal goal, the pressure to attract donor funds leads BRAC informally to emphasize repayment over empowerment in its programme design – including the criteria by which workers are evaluated and the criteria by which borrowers are selected. At all levels of BRAC, workers are proud that their borrowers repay at the same high rates as Grameen borrowers and are frustrated that BRAC's socially responsible programme mandate – empowerment of the poor – makes achieving those rates more challenging for BRAC workers. Management has not reconciled the goals of high repayment and empowerment of the poor such that in programme implementation pursuits of these goals are integrated and mutually reinforcing, and not harmful to poor women.

Instead the goals of high repayment and empowerment conflict, and workers resolve the tension based on the incentives they face. Workers perceive that a high repayment rate is the most important measure of worker performance evaluation criteria. As one worker said, 'Without the instalment I can't come back to the office.'[19] Consequently, workers have devised informal implementation strategies that promote high repayment.

BRAC's formal borrower selection and group development methods are intended to promote empowerment of the poor. BRAC begins working in an area with a baseline study. Through the initial survey, target group members are identified. Of the target group only two groups (*samities*) of 50 borrowers per village are formed. Because the number of *samities* per village is limited, the *samity* members are from the subset of the target group population which is most likely to be able to repay.

Workers observe the *samity*. Given demonstrated regular attendance (13 weeks of perfect attendance for a general loan) and savings of 46 taka weekly, members are eligible for credit after three months (six months for a housing loan). BRAC workers describe two approaches to borrower selection. In the first, the worker relies on the *samity* to decide on a member's creditworthiness. In the second approach, the worker conducts a thorough review of the borrower – her character, her family resources, her husband's income, and both husband's and wife's ability to work. The worker with the second approach prefers to identify a person in the family who could do day labour to repay the loan if the activity funded by the loan failed. BRAC's formal programme design gives workers the authority to determine which approach to take. However, based on their perception that they are evaluated (and potentially fired) according to loan repayment, workers generally take the second approach.

The conflicting implications of the two goals are harmful to women. Workers make membership conditional on resources rather than need, choosing from the target group those with better resources and a husband capable of working (and of appropriating his wife's loan). By loaning to poor women, BRAC and Grameen challenge some aspects of gender hierarchy, but they leave unchallenged patriarchal rule of the family. BRAC workers, like Grameen workers, allow husbands to utilize their wives' credit money and ignore the effect on women of men's expropriation of their funds.

Shakti Foundation: lending for empowerment

Unlike Grameen and BRAC, Shakti Foundation challenges familial hierarchy through its programming. Guided by the goal of the social and economic empowerment of urban poor women, Shakti modified the Grameen methodology to make credit a means to empowerment rather than women a means to credit. In order to empower women 'economically and socially', Shakti structures the incentives created by its programme design to encourage women to be familiar with the market and to discourage the use of women as means for their husbands to obtain credit. Due to the programme, even when husbands utilize their wives' credit, women gain market knowledge.

In order to receive her loan, the woman must satisfy the bank manager that she has knowledge about the activity funded by the loan. The bank manager asks the borrower about the activity – the costs of inputs, the labour required, the product's selling price, the expected profit, and who will buy inputs, make the product, and sell it. The manager quizzes the borrower on Shakti's Fourteen Rules (like Grameen's Sixteen Decisions) and the rules of repayment. Once the manager judges that the woman has significant knowledge of the loan activity and Shakti rules, the woman receives the loan. Under this disbursement system, even if the borrower's husband intends to use the credit himself, he must inform his wife of the relevant market information. Consequently, the programme design undermines familial hierarchy by creating incentives for men to share their knowledge with their wives. Rather than ignoring the effects of familial hierarchy, Shakti's design mitigates them.

Shakti further discourages husbands' use of women's credit by offering a smaller second loan amount to a woman who uses her first credit to purchase a rickshaw (a common activity for urban men). Rather than forbidding loan transfers, Shakti structures incentives so that husbands and wives decide not to use the credit money for a rickshaw. Again, the programme design undermines familial hierarchy by encouraging activities in which the wives participate or which women manage exclusively.

Concerned that these incentive structures alone are not sufficient to encourage women to participate in the market economy, Shakti also mandates that women themselves use their second loans. This may be difficult to assess given that certain loan-funded activities, like sandal-making, are traditionally family projects which involve all members.[20] Shakti uses issuing credit as a means of circumventing or eliminating social and familial hierarchies that harm women.

Save the Children's choice: lending for empowerment of the poorest of poor women

Grameen and BRAC allow workers to select borrowers to achieve higher repayment rates. By contrast, SCB has a formal mechanism for preventing informal diversions from its goal of empowering the poorest of poor women. Based on SCB's survey of household information, the Dhaka office determines four categories of village residents: A, B, C, D – D being the poorest families. All women with children of C and D households may join savings groups. The groups receive training as to the benefits and responsibilities of women's group membership. After six months of demonstrated group cohesion and regular attendance, women are eligible for credit. SCB's use of household surveys and target group determination in Dhaka is designed to make SCB staff work with the poorest of the poor households. SCB avoids exacerbating village inequalities by lending to all of the poorest women, not to a subset or to better-off women.

SCB's formal design does not allow workers to favour lending to women with husbands able to utilize their credit as Grameen and BRAC do. But it also does not have formal mechanisms in its lending practice for mitigating the harms associated with men's appropriating women's loan money as Shakti does. However, SCB complements its lending programme with programmes mentioned above – fish culture and civic education – aimed at mitigating familial gender hierarchy.

SCB and Shakti's choices: managing for empowerment

Those organizations with empowerment of women as their guiding goal have developed specific mechanisms for promoting empowerment of women borrowers. Their commitment to empowerment of women is reiterated in their management and staffing decisions. Both SCB and Shakti have made staffing decisions based on the goal of empowering women. They hire women, provide good working conditions for women, and promote the professional development of their staff – male and female.

In order to succeed with such non-traditional staffing choices in a rural setting, SCB is operationally more different from the other rural lenders, Grameen and BRAC, than they are from each other. At SCB,

Table 9.3   Percentage of staff who are women

	BRAC*	GB**	SCB†	Shakti
Total no. of staff	5,514	10,296	101	12
Total women	570	973	43	8
% women	10	9	43	67

* As of June 1993. Includes all RCP and RDP credit and programme staff.
** As of 6 September 1993.
† As of September 1993. Total staff does not include group promoters (GPs), who are all village women.

community development organizers, slightly more senior than bank fieldworkers at Grameen or BRAC, live in compounds close to the villages for which they are responsible. Each organizer works with two group promoters who are local women. Each promoter is responsible for 15 women's savings groups (WSGs) of 15 to 20 members. Group promoters earn a salary and travel outside the *bari* throughout the village for weekly WSG meetings. Organizers attend meetings monthly. With the help of the promoters, each organizer works with 450 to 600 women. By comparison, typical Grameen and BRAC workers work with 400 and 500 borrowers respectively.

SCB creates working conditions that respect the needs of female staff working in rural areas and therefore complement SCB's practice of hiring women (Table 9.3). In the Kunda working area, villages are far apart and are inaccessible by rickshaw or bicycle. The compound locations enable organizers to reduce travel time to meetings and to return to the compound between meetings. This avoids health and personal problems including dehydration-related illnesses and urinary tract infections which plague other female development workers.[21]

In addition, SCB staffing policy contributes to the empowerment of poor women. Women organizers are role models for village women and demonstrate the value of educating girls. Similarly, SCB's promoters are role models in the community. They are women working outside the *bari*, and given important responsibility by SCB. By example, these women demonstrate that women's work outside the *bari* may be in a position of responsibility, not just as a domestic labourer for someone else as is common. By hiring local women, SCB encourages women by example, increases local employment, and gains knowledge of the community from the perspective of local women. By design, all of these results are consistent with the goal of empowering women – both workers and borrowers.

Similarly, Shakti's goal of empowering borrowers is manifested in its staffing and management decisions. Although Shakti's management structure inherits corporate discipline from the Grameen model it follows, it has innovative hiring and staff development practices. In explaining her motives for starting Shakti, Executive Director Humaira Islam says, 'It is not just for me, I want to make other women feel that they can also be [at the place] in [the] hierarchy where the decision-making happens.'[22] As a result, both managers of Shakti are women and an impressive number of women fill the ranks.

Further, Shakti has an ethic of helping its workers improve themselves. Workers, including the office assistant, arrange to stay after work to receive tutoring in English provided by Shakti. At the risk of losing staff to higher-paying jobs when they gain valuable English skills, Shakti recognizes that the workers find self-improvement motivating and that the English-speaking workers will be an asset to the organization. Shakti promotes the guiding goal of empowerment of women through management that develops its staff of men and women equally.

Conclusion

In this chapter I have highlighted two obstacles to credit programmes' empowerment of women. Each is a matter of organizational design and choice. First, I argued that in order to empower women, credit programmes need to mitigate gender hierarchy, particularly familial gender hierarchy. By working within, while at the same time working to change the institutional environment, credit programmes make choices about how to effect changes in the circumstances of borrowers' lives. There are many ways in which hierarchies work to constrain women in Bangladesh. As long as women are dependent on men in families, credit programmes have to challenge familial gender hierarchy. In discussing programme design, the distinction between formal and informal institutions is less important than the distinction between familial gender hierarchy and other forms of women's subordination. Without mitigating patriarchy, programmes that try to affect other forms of women's subordination risk harming women rather than empowering them.

Second, I argued that when the goal of empowerment of women competes with other organizational goals such as profitability and high repayment rates, empowerment loses. Although Grameen and BRAC have pursued profitability and repayment at the expense of women's empowerment, both SCB and Shakti have high repayment rates without sacrificing women's empowerment. Because of their differences in lending practices, it is difficult to make meaningful comparisons of their repayment rates.[23] However, in this chapter I did compare the ways in which their programme design and implementation mitigate or exacerbate familial gender hierarchy. Women's empowerment need not be sacrificed for high repayment rates. Without choosing to give specific priority to empowering women, the pursuit of goals such as profitability and high repayment rates can exacerbate the ways in which patriarchy limits women's lives.

Those organizations that have developed creative ways of promoting women's empowerment have been successful when they have been attentive to gender hierarchy within the family and when women's empowerment does not compete with other goals for priority. They have worked within the context of gender hierarchy to change the context of women's lives. Women who take advantage of such opportunities in their actions and their choices are empowered. Organizations make design choices that affect whether credit is empowering to borrowers. Though measuring empowerment is difficult, credit programmes should be evaluated on what they actually do. Empowerment cannot be the presumed result of credit.

Notes

1. Dorothy 'Bina' D'Costa deserves special thanks for her careful research assistance, thoughtful editing and lasting friendship. Additionally, I thank Jagadindra Majumder for providing invaluable research assistance, Anne Marie Goetz and Susan Okin for their comments on a related paper, Elisabeth Friedman and Amy Jo Reinhold for discussions and comments on earlier drafts of this chapter, the J. William Fulbright Foreign Scholarship Board and the Stanford Center on Conflict and Negotiation for their support, and the borrowers and staff in Bangladesh who were so generous with their time, insights and hospitality.

2. I put 'empowerment of women' in scare quotes because empowerment has been interpreted differently by many people and organizations including those involved in this study. For discussions of each programme's definition of empowerment see Ackerly, 1994.

3. Save the Children, USA has projects in 41 countries and credit programmes in 11 countries.

4. For detailed discussion of the programmes see my unpublished manuscript, 'Empowerment by Design,' in which I describe in detail the organizations' credit programme design features (management, implementation methods, and corporate culture), the incentives they create for their workers and borrowers, and the mechanisms by which the programme design may contribute to the likelihood that a woman borrower will increase her knowledge as a result of borrowing (Ackerly, 1994). In 'Testing the Tools of Development' I demonstrate the variations in the programmes' success at promoting women's empowerment and argue that those geared toward increasing women's participation in the market aspects of the activity funded by their loans will contribute to their empowerment (Ackerly, 1995).

5. For the purposes of my argument, institutional constraints and cultural constraints are functional equivalents. However, 'institutional' is the more accurate choice because it incorporates formal legal structures, formal and informal religious rules, and local practices and norms. By referring to 'institutional change', rather than to 'cultural change', I emphasize that changes in institutions can and do emanate from within a culture and are not by definition suggestions from outsiders.

6. For versions of these debates at a philosophical level see Martha Nussbaum and Amartya Sen (1993) and Jonathan Glover and Martha Nussbaum (1995).

7. See also Sheelagh Stewart and Jill Taylor in this volume. Stewart and Taylor describe the early choice of the Musasa domestic violence programme in Zimbabwe not to provide a shelter for battered women, recognizing that given the cultural institutions of familial support, if women were to seek help outside the family future familial support would be withdrawn. However, Musasa is now planning to open a shelter, in part because of the need for an alternative space for women who are victims of domestic violence and because, since the inception of the Musasa Project, 'the general shift in public opinion on domestic violence is such as to militate against the withdrawal of support from the family' (p. 222).

8. There is an informal credit market among family and close neighbours which provides small loans for emergencies, but by virtue of their poverty, larger sums must be acquired from the rich people of the village. White describes a Bangladeshi village economy wherein women borrow from women of elite households and men from elite men. Frequently, according to White, the men and women do not know of the others' transactions (1992).

9. Elsewhere I argue that class hierarchy is also an integral component of the institutional environment of credit programmes which affects men and women differently (Ackerly, 1994).

10. For more see Thérèse Blanchet, 1984 and 1991.

11. All group interviews also mention social constraints caused by superstitions and religious beliefs.

12. In this study 37.3% of rural loans were invested in paddy processing. Other studies concur that paddy processing is a common use of loan funds: Goetz and Gupta (1994), Grameen Bank (1992), Hossain (1984), BRAC (1993).

13. In this study, women's partners in their enterprises (generally their husbands) did the marketing for the loan-funded activity. Out of 954 loans for activities (to 695 women), in 930 of the activities partners did the marketing.

14. Goetz and Gupta (1994) identify roughly the same categories of intra-household management of loan funds.

15. This is a good illustration of the point made in Fierlbeck's chapter about the problem of endowing undue legitimacy to choices women make in highly constrained contexts of choice.

16. The 'target group' is the subset of a village population with which an organization says it works, tries to work, or works exclusively. Grameen says it works with poor women; BRAC tries to work with poor women, and SCB and Shakti work exclusively with poor women. SCB's target group is defined by socio-economic data analysed in the Dhaka office and comprises 72% of the new Nasirnagar impact area populations. For Grameen, BRAC and Shakti, poor is a relative standard defined with respect to local measures of affluence. In rural areas people outside the target group have houses with metal roofs, have husbands or sons with salaried jobs, or own more than a small amount of land. Asking target group

defining questions, interviewers determined whether borrowers were 'Certainly in Target Group,' 'Questionably in TG', or 'Not in TG' according to what the borrower said about her assets, sources of income, and family resources.

I chose an analysis of variance test because it enabled me to weight the percentages by the sample size of each group. The test showed that the differences in the percentages are statistically significant at a level of 99% confidence.

17. As of June 1993.

18. For a discussion of the difficulty in comparing and interpreting repayment rates see footnote 23.

19. Interview D26, 10 November 1993.

20. Organizations wishing to duplicate Shakti's attempt an encouraging women to participate in their loan activity will have similar difficulties assessing women's involvement in rural activities. Evaluation mechanisms related to women's knowledge of the labour, material inputs, selling price, and accounting for the project will be helpful.

21. In unpublished research, Anne Marie Goetz and Rina Sen Gupta have demonstrated that living and working conditions of women fieldworkers in BRAC and the government's Rural Poor Programme create health and personal problems for single and married workers (1995).

22. Interview, 16 August 1993.

23. Because many variables affect portfolios' performances and because bookkeeping practices vary, it is impossible to make meaningful comparisons of the repayment rates of the four organizations. First, location, geographic concentration, borrower characteristics and lending practices vary by organization. The organizations work in areas of different proximity to main roads and markets and in areas subject to different risks of natural disaster. Moreover, the organizations take different risks in their lending practices. For example, SCB and Shakti expose their portfolios to greater risk than Grameen and BRAC. By working with all of a target group in only a few areas, SCB has significantly greater geographic exposure than Grameen or BRAC who work with only a subset of the population. Grameen works with a subset that is economically better off. By working in urban areas, Shakti has greater risk of borrowers disappearing, for example if a slum is razed by the government as happened in 1991.

Second, bookkeeping calculations vary by organization. At the time of this study, repayment rates were calculated as the amount of money received in a given period divided by the amount expected in that same period. Bookkeeping practices matter in interpreting repayment rates. If an organization never charges off a payment, its repayment rate denominator will never decrease, and its repayment rate will be consequently smaller than an organization that does charge off certain expected payments as lost and non-recoverable. Over time an organization which does not charge off losses will have an ever decreasing repayment rate. On a growing portfolio, without loss figures it is impossible to know if low repayment means ever increasing losses as a percentage of the portfolio, or if losses are decreasing as a percentage of the portfolio though they continue to exist.

None of these organizations was able to report late payments (unreceived payments that are still expected to be paid) and losses (amounts assumed to be unrecoverable). In order to compare repayment rates, one needs the late payments and losses of the corresponding period.

Part IV

The Role of Individual Agents

10

Actor Orientation and Gender Relations at a Participatory Project Interface

Cecile Jackson

This chapter explores the implications of an actor-oriented approach for the analysis of how institutions, and more narrowly, organizations, are gendered, and what the significance of this might be for the outcomes of development projects. It is probably fair to say that organizational analyses have remained dominated by a structural approach to social relations in which the emphasis is upon the constraints of rules, procedures and practices, for example faced by individual women as members of organizations, rather than upon the processes of structuration by which individual agency patterns and, over time, changes structures. Such approaches reflect dichotomous and absolute concepts of power and powerlessness, in which dominated groups appear weak, victimized and helpless. A structural approach is also to be seen in the continuing belief in development policy discourses that the outcomes of development projects and policies are necessarily determined by the explicit and implicit intentions in the planning and execution of projects, and that 'failures' relate to poor objectives, planning, design or implementation. To the extent that gender analysis of development projects has emphasized actor agency in the subversion of project intentions, this has focused upon varieties of male bias, in accordance with a concept of power in which action equates with power and masculinity.

An alternative perspective is to see the social relations within development institutions, and at their interfaces with local populations, not as given by institutional structures of control and subordination but as contingent and performative, reflecting choice and agency, to variable degrees for all social beings, as well as constraint. The thought that the outcomes of projects and policies are only partly and indirectly related to intentions and plans, and mediated by agency, is depressing, for ambitions for planned progressive social change can be subverted by the ability of individuals to override and redirect project intentions, as many gender analyses show. At the same time it is also a rather encouraging thought, for it suggests, conversely, that gender-biased projects do not necessarily result in equivalently gender-biased outcomes. We need to look at the ways in which 'instrumentalism' or opportunism is available not only to policy makers, where feminists rightly object to the hijacking of WID and GAD as vehicles for quite other agendas, but also to women in development organizations and indeed to women in the populations affected by development projects and policies.

Agency and Structuration

Whilst 'institutions' have multiple definitions, they are sociologically understood to be sets of rules, norms and procedures that come into being historically through the aggregate and cumulative actions of individuals, which thereby reproduce or reformulate those institutions (see Giddens, 1984). In a thesis on agricultural change in Zambia, Hans Seur quotes a Zambian farmer, Kaulenti Chisenga, who in talking about 'tradition' expresses the concept of structuration graphically:

> When you follow a path through the bush, you follow in the footsteps of those who were there before you. But as you are walking, you are not only following others, but you yourself are also making and keeping that path, because by walking you step on grasses which could make the path disappear, or you can use your axe to cut some small branches or trees. Now some day a person can think: 'Why do I always follow this path? Maybe if I cut through these bushes here I can make a shortcut'. So this person makes a new path. Now the next person, when he arrives at this junction, he can choose: 'Shall I follow the old path or the new one?' If people start following only the new path the old one will disappear. But if some follow the old path, you will have more roads in that area. The same with traditions, if you follow a tradition, you are also keeping that tradition. (Seur, 1992: 258–9)[1]

Clearly choices are not entirely unconstrained – vigilantes may patrol the pathways – but neither is choice, innovation and social change entirely beyond the influence of the acting individual.

If then the staff of projects and programmes, and the project-affected population, are subjects constituted partly by the constellation of institutions within which they exist, and at the same time act in opposition to those institutions, a number of issues take on a fresh significance. One is the instability and uncertainty of project contexts and the likelihood of unintended outcomes, since norms cannot be relied upon to deliver particular actions, rules can be broken, and institutions are continuously changing. Another is the significance of the interactive processes whereby individual actors negotiate towards joint activity in a world which cannot effectively prescribe (or easily enforce) behaviour of either development personnel or their clients. Here analyses of how development personnel exercise discretion in the performance of their professional responsibilities (see Goetz, 1992) become critically important. Within these interactions it is the symbolic as well as the material resources offered to the negotiating parties in a project context that offer opportunities and power (see Harrison, this volume). For feminists the focus shifts from prioritizing attention to changing the formal structures of institutions (removing bias from rules and procedures, more gender training, better gender planning) towards considering the circumstances within which the ability of women to appropriate project resources is increased (Olivier de Sardan, 1988: 223). It also suggests that the distinction between 'participatory' projects and 'top-down' projects is something of a fiction; for both require the cooperation of individuals with diverse, and sometimes conflicting, subject positions in a joint endeavour. The idea of the 'target group' begins to look like a vain fantasy of control.

Examples of the active subversion by women of project intentions, resources and outcomes are not difficult to find. Bierschenk (1988) writes of the successful appropriation of dam water in Benin by farming women against project intentions of provision for pastoralists' cattle; Jackson (1985) describes the capture by Muslim village women of a market in processed tomatoes on an irrigation project in Nigeria which intended to supply a canning factory; Villareal (1992) shows the use by Mexican women, in a beekeeping project, of the vocabulary of dependence (on state development agencies and on local men) as a smokescreen for their growing autonomy; and Charlotte Heath (1996) reveals the expanded and redefined gender identities won by Omani women in an 'unsuccessful' income-generating weaving project, through their manipulation of idioms of patriarchal kinship and of the cultural value accorded to creative expression. The vocabulary of agency often fails to capture the quality of such processes and remains unsatisfactory – the pretensions of the term 'empowerment' still often connotes an intentionality, and a necessity on the part of development agents; 'resistance' suggests a negative stance rather than a creative form of action; and 'struggle' implies a well-defined adversarial relationship between opponents. None of these adequately captures the process of project redefinition through the selective engagement of women. The language of interests, explicit, implicit, real and perceived, spoken or silent, is also not up to the task of portraying the simultaneity of apparently contradictory interests and positions.

The agency of women is not always consistent with the values and beliefs of GAD professionals and feminists. This of course raises the enduring feminist dilemma discussed by Fierlbeck (this volume) of how to understand women's voices and their articulated perceptions and actions. In engaging in development activity it is difficult to justify a concept of well-being which stands entirely outside the perceptions and desires and notions of well-being of the people affected by that activity, yet those notions are as likely as those of development planners to carry gendered implications which disadvantage women. Fierlbeck argues (as have Sen and others) that identity derives from cultural templates which are saturated with gender-based inequality internalized by women; therefore the context in which their 'choices' are made cannot be taken to represent 'consent' to a social order, because it is not free and conscious in the manner envisaged by liberal theorists for whom consent is the basis of social legitimacy. This is surely a serious concern, but I wonder whether such a monolithic, and unitary, concept of culture is justified? Cultures are deeply divided and fractured, they are differently interpreted by different social groups and individuals, and they are dynamic and changing. Thus, for example, 'tradition' is invented (Hobsbawm and Ranger, 1993) and identities constantly reworked. Motherhood, to take one of Fierlbeck's examples, is not historically unchanging in the identity it confers upon women, and the changes in the meaning of motherhood are not only determined by culture as a phenomenon outside women's lives but also carries the oppositional imprint of subcultures expressing subaltern alternatives and visions.

If the power to effect change is more dispersed than usually recognized in discourses of development policy and practice, then a strong argument may be made for attention to interfaces between projects and people as the critical gendered encounter for feminist scrutiny. The next section looks at the experience of a project in eastern India, the Rainfed Farming Project (RFP), with almost no women fieldstaff, a narrow view of participation, a circumscribed area of interest around agricultural technology and a vague and under-specified gender strategy, which nevertheless produced some quite radical women's groups and activities. The RFP,[2] which began in 1989, is based in rainfed areas with very little irrigation and largely tribal and low-caste populations, and aims at gender-aware poverty reduction through participation by poor farmers in accessing and adapting appropriate new upland crop varieties. It is implemented through pairs of fieldstaff, one agronomist and one village motivator (VM), whose task it is to facilitate participation.

The Rainfed Farming Project, 1989–95

Descriptions of a project 'model' are problematic, given the different actors' multiple understandings of objectives and meanings, but in this project this plurality converged around poverty objectives in a way which was less apparent and consensual in the gender objectives. The British funders, Overseas Development Administration (ODA), carried a strong commitment to gender into the project, through the gender entrepreneurs of the social development department which had been involved since inception, tempered however by what ODA staff saw as a necessary sensitivity to the less gender-aware views of the implementing institution, the Hindustani Fertilizer Corporation (HFC). The HFC was technically oriented, predisposed to a transfer-of-technology approach to agricultural development and initially unconvinced of the relevance of social science, including gender analysis, to the project. Gender objectives in the project were experienced by Indian staff as driven by ODA, in a way that the poverty agenda was not, and there was certainly 'bureaucratic resistance' (Staudt and Jaquette, 1988) from more technical and senior staff in the HFC. Gender issues were conceived in project documents as a variant of poverty problems, without specific attention to the causes of women's subordination; the role of the project was to be gender-aware and to make sure that women benefited equally from the project. The 'participatory' identity of the RFP also meant that ODA and the British consultants did not lay out detailed project plans against which performance was evaluated. In the official project approach to gender, mainstreaming women into all project activities was seen as desirable, and preferable to creating special activities for them. Attitudes to gender were not of course uniform across project staff and younger fieldworkers,[3] especially VMs, saw women as important in farming and decision-making, especially amongst tribal groups,[4] and as socially disadvantaged. VMs expressed a gentle paternalism and concern for the position of women of the villages in which they lived and worked.

The question, raised above, of women's gender interests, of who can express them and of how legitimate it is for 'outsiders' such as development agencies to impose concepts such as the separate interests of genders, and the subordination of women, in the face of the apparent 'consent' of local women to the social contracts of their cultures, is a live issue for social development professionals in development agencies such as ODA. This project experience, however, suggests that bureaucratic resistance in implementing institutions is not monolithic, and that gender discourses, from whatever source, offer points of leverage for sections of project staff. Arguments against imposing gender on unwilling development partners, on the grounds of cultural imperialism, assume incorrectly that other cultures are singular and monolithic. Gender equity was, however, less organic and less validated in popular and agricultural development discourses in India than poverty reduction, around which there are longstanding and widely supported arguments, and project fieldstaff therefore faced considerable uncertainty around implementing gender objectives. The VM fraction of project staff were both committed to gender objectives and uncertain about what exactly they might entail. This uncertainty has, however, possibly had both negative and positive effects, leaving, as it did, considerable space for village women to influence events.

Participation is a notoriously polyvalent term and it can mean many things (see, for example, White, 1995). In the RFP context it was conceived of in a relatively narrow sense as a means of technology testing, with the expectation that it would deliver institutional sustainability, in that farmers would become enabled to test, adapt and spread new technologies without project intervention. Participatory procedures which neglect the differing capabilities of men and women for attending meetings, speaking freely and expressing opinions are, of course, unlikely to elicit equal participation from both genders. The RFP fieldstaff invited men and women to crop-programme meetings, encouraged all to speak and involved women in Participatory Rural Appraisal exercises, yet they remained relatively voiceless in meetings. Neither did PRA activities identify as perceived problems the issues such as fuelwood collection and rice milling about which local women articulate concerns in conversations about their livelihood constraints. Formally, the level and quality of participation of women in the early years was low both in absolute terms and relative to men. But despite the limited form of participation offered by the project it is clear that over time the character of participation changed.

Fieldworker identity and communication

Within the project there had been intermittent discussion of the desirability of increasing the numbers of women fieldstaff in order to improve contact with women of the target groups. This, together with the prevailing levels of graduate unemployment in the region, is the backdrop against which to set the publicly articulated opinions of VMs on the necessity of employing women fieldstaff. VM views on communicating with women generally admitted to early difficulties, which they asserted had been overcome. This assertion was influenced by their concern that admitting to communication problems with women would lend support to the case for employing women VMs, and thus possibly threaten their own employment. Clearly how fieldstaff represent communications with project-affected populations is marked by the politics of their positionality. The records of the diaries (which were the suggestion of an ODA social development advisor but were in practice never inspected by the HFC), certainly show VMs struggling to open up communication with women when they first moved into the villages. In cluster B, for example, the VM writes that 'Women say that society is dominated by males so they have no right to decide anything. Most are very reluctant to talk' (January 1992), and in February 1992, 'Women are not talking, except some old ladies … women usually speak through their husbands.' It is not clear how far this reflects the 'mutedness' (Ardener, 1975) of women, or an 'exit' option (Hyden, 1980; Fatton, 1989) by women, that is, a reluctance to talk as a means of distancing oneself from encounters with officialdom. Nor indeed is it clear what it means when, as time passes, silence gives way to speech. Fieldstaff increasingly represent themselves as having 'established rapport' – a favourite phrase – with women, whilst such women, one suspects, can equally be said to have set the terms of engagement around their own chosen vocabularies, and have begun to enlist the VM in their own projects.

At one level language certainly was an undeniable obstruction for male VMs in communicating with women. VMs note frequently that women generally only speak tribal languages, unlike tribal men, many of whom also speak Hindi or Bengali, and in cluster B[5] it is noted (B, 25 March 1993) that women are not speaking at meetings because the VM cannot speak Oraon. He observes in his diary that he finds the more prosperous middle-caste women easier to talk to because they are better informed, tribal women suspicious but forceful, and low-caste women the most difficult to speak with. Interestingly this ranking of ease of communication is not consistent with the consensus view of women's 'status' in these groups, which conventionally accords more equitable gender relations to the low-caste and tribal groups which the VMs had the greater difficulty in communicating with. One might reasonably expect greater mutedness and more problematic communication from those most disadvantaged by patriarchal culture. What it does suggest is that the capability for speech and silence is not uniform amongst women, who are differentially able to construct cross-cultural interlocking projects with fieldworkers.

These comments suggest a complex mixture of linguistic, social and political issues facing a male VM attempting to communicate with women and to draw them into project activities. Visiting women project staff from the WID cell had somewhat less difficulty in communicating with women, as did the few women VMs in other project areas, although status, language and ethnicity problems remained.

The communication problem with women was a more enduring and qualitatively different one to that with local men, since it was not only a 'technical' issue of language but also reflected a troublesome gap in the perceptions and articulations around gender inequality. The mystification of gender relations in all cultures means that women seldom identify and overtly discuss their subordination, which of course should not be taken to invalidate it, but which rather makes it problematic for a fieldworker who sees himself or herself as responding to locally perceived needs. Crudely, the poor have little problem aspiring to be, and articulating a wish to be non-poor, but how much more complex, in all societies, is the vision and content of transformed gender relations.

The significance of fieldworker gender in this project lay in both the establishment of communication in the early stages, and in patterning the kinds of participation that developed. It influenced not only the quality of the relationship with the 'minimal participant' attending meetings and engaging in some project activities, but also the emergence of local leadership through the interactions of VMs with local actors. The diaries show these relationships developing mainly through friendships and affinity between men of similar ages. Given the absence of friendships across the gender divide in Indian culture, it would seem unlikely that male VMs' social interaction will be able to stimulate the same kind of local leadership, and thereby social sustainability amongst village women. This may not be entirely negative. Some women's groups may become more self-reliant in the absence of the potentially controlling presence of VM friendship, but there can be little doubt that the gender of the fieldworker *is* a significant feature of relations at the interface.

Mainstreaming versus special activities

Since the mid-1980s, and in response to the perception that special projects targeted on women resulted in marginalization, mainstreaming (that is, inserting gender sensitivity and gender accountability into all development activity) has become a dominant strategy for bringing gender concerns into development, and this was the declared RFP approach. After a year or two, however, concerns over meeting women's needs grew. The project established a Women in Development cell, in an attempt to spearhead the fuller participation of women, and employed two women of tribal origins to assist VMs, on flying visits to all three states, by holding meetings with women and gaining their confidence. The staff in the WID cell were not given adequate training and spent a great deal of time travelling between sites and supporting the VMs, but with little sustained impact and inadequate time for reflection or research. The marginalization of gender as a consequence of targeting would have been a reasonable conclusion, were it not for the contrary evidence at the interface.

The VM diaries show considerable awareness and concern about some of the major gender issues such as rape and sexual violence in the villages. In cluster B the VM mentions the anti-alcohol views of women who 'are annoyed at the drinking habits of their husbands' and who say that drink makes children 'afraid of their parents' (B, 27 May 1993). In cluster C alcohol abuse by tribal men is viewed as a problem, as is the growing dowry problem among Scheduled Castes, and the VM there also writes about the phenomena of migrant women agricultural workers.

Mainstreaming gender was understood by fieldworkers to mean ensuring that women were represented as recipients of new seeds, yet the VM awareness of local gender issues suggested that access to plant material was not a major problem for women *as women*. The limitation of seeing gender as basically a problem of poverty is revealed; when the tacit understandings of the causes of poverty (in this case poor access to appropriate agricultural technologies) are extrapolated to gender, they don't make much sense, here giving much greater prominence than warranted to crop technology whilst avoiding issues such as dowry and alcohol abuse. To some extent this tension between the project emphasis on mainstreaming and technology, and the VM realization of other gender priorities, sprang from the intense daily communication of fieldworkers with villagers. Their increasingly deeper knowledge of village society did not always fit comfortably with project priorities. (I discuss below the outcomes of this tension.) In the case of the RFP the mainstreaming approach *entailed* the collapse of gender into poverty, and inhibited the fieldworkers from approaching gender as distinct relations of disadvantage.

Mainstreaming and participation

One of the problems with a mainstreaming approach which focuses on the participation of women in the main project activities (here crop technology development and spread), rather than in separate 'women's projects' is that it is not always easy to evaluate the meaning of such participation. For example, figures which break down the sex of participants are difficult to interpret, since they refer, in the case of cropping, to recipients of new seed varieties. A woman may have her name listed when she attends a meeting on behalf of her husband and receives seed on his behalf, or vice versa a man may be listed as the recipient even when his wife received the seed since household head names were generally given by women for such purposes. Where the activity involves household production, as in the case of paddy cropping, monitoring the involvement of women cannot be done through lists of the sex of 'participants'.

Having received the seed it is then intra-household divisions of labour, responsibility and authority which affect how the seed is used and who benefits from its cultivation. Apart from consulting women on their evaluations of new varieties there was little that the project, given its approach of distributing seed for farmers to use largely as they saw fit, could do to safeguard or promote women's interests. VMs were aware of these ambiguities but uncertain about how to deal with them. Where participation involves a 'hands-off' project approach, as it usually does, it is difficult for it to co-exist meaningfully with mainstreaming. This is because mainstreaming often means mixed-gender, household-based interventions, in which fieldstaff cannot legislate for intra-household processes such as the allocation of labour and the distribution of benefits. These are the transactions which can disadvantage women; they are also the ones which are most culturally entrenched and least likely to be overtly resisted by women, or challenged by participatory fieldworkers.

Given the difficulty in demonstrating, in the main cropping programme, women's participation and benefits, and the invisibility and independence of household transactions, VMs saw virtue in women's projects which avoided, at least superficially, intra-household issues and incontrovertibly showed the project offering benefits to women. In practice women's groups came to be the focus of much of the engagement of women with the project, although these were far from easily or spontaneously formed in many areas. It is worth noting the importance of moving the often polarized debate between the virtues of mainstreaming versus targeting women into a discussion of the meaning of these terms at different levels of intervention. In the RFP the WID cell was an ineffective women-specific strategy, yet at village level women-specific activities were arguably the most effective approaches to gender objectives.

Diary entries show the extent to which VMs initiated the early 'participatory' group formation; in cluster C on 4 June 1991 the VM notes that he has selected a leader for the gardening group, and in cluster A the women's vegetable gardening group is initiated by the VM approaching a wife of a keen farmer (A, 25 September 1989). The passivity of women in these groups is indicated by a diary comment from cluster B in which the VM observes that the women in many places wish to be allocated seed rather than choose varieties for themselves, and that very few will disclose their names (B, 24 April 1992). A lack of enthusiasm is apparent; there are complaints about the small quantities of seed given, some seed is rejected and few come to take the seedlings the group raises (A, 25–28 September 1989 and 1 November 1989). Whilst women were not always enthusiastic initially, this was more related to the activity – gardening – than the separation from men, for women generally expressed a preference for separate women's activities. The reversion to women-only activities has sometimes been seen as project 'misbehaviour',[6] but here we see both male fieldworkers and female participants as agents driving the move to gender separation. Buvinic also sees women-only projects as doing little to mitigate their economic marginalization, but there is little doubt that when the women-only activities are compared with the integrated activities on this project, it is the former that are most gender progressive and give voice to women's interests.

Alongside specific activities ran the Women's Programme of meetings, the content of which show a strong emphasis on nutrition, sanitation, gardening and goat raising. Although the VM clearly controlled the early content and style of meetings a number of diary entries show the women progressively asserting themselves. In cluster C the VM reports that in one hamlet (of very poor basket-makers) the women demand female trainers, instead of male, in the Women Training Programme and also shorter meetings because of household work time. On a later occasion a woman complains that the number of women selected for field trips (to visit other NGO activities or relevant state institutions) was too low and should be increased (C, 18 January 1993). In this cluster women's rights were discussed regularly at meetings. Women in other clusters likewise demanded more local women speakers and began to shape the content and procedures of participation. The social context is undoubtedly significant in patterning the differing development of groups in different areas, but even beyond the particularities of the groups there is evidence that groups created initially by the VM have frequently evolved a character and style of their own, and that everywhere women prefer to have their own groups because they 'feel docile in a group with men' as one local woman noted.

Unintended consequences and agency

The unambitious style of participation adopted by the project was perhaps a Trojan horse through which a much more thoroughgoing participatory project emerged in some areas, via the agency of participants and fieldworkers. Project statements do not suggest that this was foreseen, and it would appear that it was something of an unintended consequence. After five years, self-sustaining local institutions for accessing and adapting agricultural technologies do not exist, but on the other hand the project has stimulated new social groupings and processes which are widening and deepening the meaning of 'participation' on the project.

In Orissa there are garden groups which now lease land and farm collectively; there are many groups in which ethnic and social differences between women have lessened as they developed group interests; successful groups have expanded their activities to include group action against alcohol abuse and domestic violence. In animated discussions women recount how they collectively lock out drunken husbands, to protect wives and to register their protest against what they see as a waste of family resources and the basis of violent behaviour, and to 'give a warning to all men!' Women in savings groups say that they prefer group savings with other women rather than family-based saving, as it prevents husbands from using the funds, and are asking for literacy classes to remove their dependence on the young literate boys who keep their records.

It would be mistaken, by focusing on agency, to imply a spurious social freedom for women, and Fierlbeck is surely right to keep the 'conditions of consent' at the forefront of her analysis. But can the conditions of consent be reduced to the concept of a socialized, and culturally validated, self-devaluation in women's identities and therefore in their perceptions and choices? How then is it that women are at times able to deny prescribed gender roles and behaviour? I incline more to the admittedly messier view that women self-consciously manage a repertoire of gendered behaviours which are context-specific and deployed towards diverse and sometimes contradictory ends; these include, but are incapable of reduction to either, the reproduction of gender norms and subversion and social change. The context within which agency is situated cannot easily be always assumed to be constraining to women; nor can it reliably predict outcomes.

A negative change can produce a positive choice; a deteriorating situation can precipitate progressive action. For example, the success of some women's groups in parts of Orissa does seem to be related to the crisis in the marriage system whereby the transition from bridewealth to dowry in tribal communities has created a hiatus in the exchange of women. As one group explained, it used to be the case that the husband's family would do the 'seeking' for a wife, and the father of a girl would wait to be approached with offers. But now men are not seeking and many girls have grown old waiting, so the fathers of girls are beginning to realize that they will have to do the seeking for a husband for their daughters. There are many single women well past the customary age of marriage who have become involved with project groups, as the vehicle for independent enterprise as well as social expression.

The relationship between VM and women participants was certainly distinct. They were both more resistant to involvement than men, then more apparently compliant but also more ultimately subversive in redirecting the project. VMs enlisted women in many of their projects, such as gardening and stockraising, but women certainly enlisted VMs in their projects too – in some ways more strikingly, since they were more distant from RFP objectives. Interestingly, many men failed to enlist the VM in their ambitions for personal accumulation, and fieldstaff were vigilant in sustaining the poverty focus and rejecting initiatives towards such ends. If the ability to enrol project staff in activities not directly related to the central concerns of the project is an indicator of participant agency then one might conclude that women proved rather stronger than men in this regard, a situation which stands in contrast to the depiction of women as especially weak and vulnerable (see Kardam, this volume). The debate about accountability perhaps needs to take account of the possibility that at the project interface women participants do have an ability to make projects responsive to their needs. The fieldworker at that interface needs to deliver cooperating beneficiaries, and in the context of a project like the RFP with the stated objective of gender sensitivity this also indicates delivering *women* beneficiaries; a situation which offers points of leverage for women over the terms and conditions of engagement.

This project began with an emphasis on mainstreaming and moved towards targeted women's activities, and it began with access to agricultural technology but found itself supporting women's groups resisting domestic violence by direct action against offenders, and campaigning against alcohol by smashing the equipment of distillers and vendors. Both these developments are rooted in the ability of fieldworkers and women at the project interface to refashion a project through their mutual interactions, compliances and resistances.

VMs did not concede to all the initiatives taken by local women, and the limits of VM flexibility with regard to women's requests are interesting to note. In cluster C the ideas and requests which VMs did not respond to included an independently expressed and sustained interest in and demand for flower cultivation (C, 7 August 1991) and knitting (C, 8 March 1991). These possibly ran aground on the VM worries about the apparent domesticity of these interests and the extent to which they departed from the food-farming orientation of the project. Another failed approach by women was that of a girls' group in Orissa who requested concrete to make paddy-field bunds permanent, to save themselves the annual task of repair, but this was refused because interventions requiring purchased external inputs (cement) were disfavoured. In some cases the VM seemed over-sensitive to gender; flower cultivation is not necessarily 'domestic'. In others cases, they were under-sensitive – a labour-saving initiative by poor women farming collectively is hardly equivalent to a bid for irrigation technology by landed men.

Conclusions

The social interface between fieldworkers and clients revealed in the RFP diaries throw a little light on questions of gender conditionality, of the significance of the gender identity of fieldworkers, of the tension between gender strategies of mainstreaming and participation, and the attractions to both fieldworkers and clients of separate women's activities within a project.

The male gender of the VM was a significant feature of VM relationships, inhibiting some participants (women) and encouraging others (men). However, the variability, regionally, of the success of women's programmes suggests that the gender of the fieldworker is not the only factor at work here. It may be that fieldworker gender is more significant in areas of Bihar (it is not coincidental that the experience of being a woman VM in Bihar is the most difficult) than Orissa and West Bengal, which have less repressive local gender ideologies, in which there are fewer communication problems, more numerous role models of active and assertive women, and greater space for autonomous participation by village women. The project may decide to deploy women VMs, if in short supply, to Bihar in the light of this. But the identity of the fieldworker cannot be expected to deliver access to all target groups, and the case for women fieldworkers is better made on the grounds of the importance of offering positive role models to women, and employment opportunities to women in development rather than on the instrumental grounds of 'doing participation better'.

VM agency has been part of a process of transformation in which the project, initially an agronomy-based project with a limited concept of participation, became much more oriented towards social change. Women participants also increasingly influenced the activities, procedures and style of the project towards unintended outcomes. An actor-oriented approach suggests that it is possibly inappropriate to label some projects 'participatory' and thereby imply that others are not, for projects cannot happen without participation, without mutually constructed cooperation between fieldstaff and local people.

The gender achievements in this project were arguably not attributable to the formal mechanisms established by the project towards meeting women's needs, that is, gender training and the WID cell. They are largely the outcome of the agency of local women who were able to create opportunities for real change from the project's broadly stated commitment to gender, together with sympathetic if uncertain fieldstaff. This might suggest that the specific character of work cultures and attitudes, as well as firmly stated project intentions for gender awareness and equity in activities, are as important as detailed gender planning. The procedures of gender mainstreaming – gender guidelines, gender training programmes and gender 'tool kits' (Razavi and Miller, 1995: vii) – cannot be relied upon to deliver WID/gender objectives; nor should the pressures for institutional change be conceptualized as deriving entirely from organized external pressure groups such as donors, women's organizations and NGOs.

Notes

1. I am grateful to Helen Derbyshire for this quote.

2. My involvement consisted of two consultancy visits to Orissa, West Bengal and Bihar, the second of which involved several weeks spent with fieldstaff in researching and writing up their histories of project involvement in three clusters of villages in Bihar and West Bengal. This chapter is based on interviews with fieldworkers, women and men project participants and especially on an analysis of three fieldworker diaries, kept on a daily basis over the period 1989–95. I would like to acknowledge the help of all project staff in the work which lies behind this paper, but especially to recognize the years of daily reflection which went into the Village Motivator diaries.

3. Fieldstaff consisted of agronomists, all male, usually high-caste, middle-aged and based in nearby towns, and village-resident Village Motivators (VMs), young social scientists, many of whom came from tribal or low-caste backgrounds and almost all of whom were male.

4. I use the term as is common in India for *adivasis* and not with a precise anthropological meaning.

5. I indicate the location, source and date of the material cited by cluster: A and B are in Hazaribag district of south Bihar; C is in Purulia district of West Bengal. A cluster is about three poor and isolated villages inhabited mostly by low-caste and tribal people, covered by a single VM who resides in one village of the cluster.

6. Buvinic (1986) suggests that women-only projects revert from 'productive' to welfare orientation during implementation because of institutional inertia and a historic tendency for women staff to be welfare-oriented.

11

Local Heroes: Patterns of Fieldworker Discretion in Implementing GAD Policy in Bangladesh

Anne Marie Goetz

Struggles over an authoritative interpretation of women's needs and interests in development are waged at every level of policy-making and implementation, from the headquarters of development organizations to the intimate confines of the household and the individual consciousness of policy beneficiaries.[1] One of the most critical, yet neglected, arenas in which these struggles are waged is in the everyday practices of the actual implementors of policy: the lower-level bureaucrats or fieldworkers in development agencies who engineer the 'fit' between national policies and local realities. Their centrality to the actual implementation of political decisions puts them in a critical position to influence the capacity of states to achieve policy objectives. When it comes to implementing policies which may be counter-cultural, or unpopular, as can be the case with gender-equity policies, their role is critical in determining whether dominant power relations will be sustained, or challenged.

This chapter examines gender differences in the practices and perceptions of field-level implementors in two rural development programmes in Bangladesh, one run by the state, the other by an NGO. Close attention to differences in the policy enactment routines of women and men fieldworkers shows that structural differences between NGO and government organizations are less significant than might be expected in fostering receptivity to the needs and interests of poor women. Other factors such as individual positions in class and gender hierarchies matter a great deal in determining receptivity and responsiveness at the grassroots.

Fieldworker discretion, however subtle and molecular, is an inherently political practice; power, stemming from positions within development organizations, institutions of personal connections, and systems of class and gender difference, is deployed in the construction and reproduction of gender or class relations. Fieldworker routines and attitudes are indicative of how they construe and construct their beneficiaries as subjects. The ways gender inequalities are experienced by beneficiaries can be affected by the ways fieldworkers symbolically mediate reality, because they can give weight to their interpretations by assigning or withholding resources and information. Such practices affect the self-interpretations of beneficiaries and their consequent capacities to utilize programme benefits or to make demands of programme staff and public resources. Of course, beneficiaries also inject their own views and develop practices to adjust programme provisions to their own needs. The domain of fieldworker discretion thus becomes a political arena in which dominant social practices can be reproduced, or what Foucault calls 'subjugated knowledges' can stage their localized insurrections (1972: 81).

BRAC and RD-12: 'Mainstreaming' Women into Credit Programmes

This chapter draws on research conducted in 1993 in Bangladesh on the experiences and perspectives of women and men staff, mostly field-level staff, in the Rural Development Programme of the Bangladesh Rural Advancement Committee (BRAC), and the government's Rural Development 12 (RD-12) programme.[2] Qualitative material analysed here draws from 121 in-depth interviews; 66 with BRAC staff, 55 with RD-12 staff – of which, in each organization, 20 were men. Material from recorded group discussions between women and men staff is also used here.[3]

BRAC is the world's largest indigenous development NGO, with 1.6 million members and over 10,000 staff across its impressive range of development programmes in the areas of health, education and credit (see Rao and Kelleher's chapter for a more detailed description of BRAC). The backbone of its work in rural areas is the Rural Development Programme (RDP), offering credit and income-generating skills and inputs to, at the time of this study, well over 700,000 members, 70 per cent of them women. RD-12 is one of several foreign-funded components of the government's Rural Poor Programme (RPP),[4] part of the Bangladesh Rural Development Board, which has managed a cooperatives-based approach to dispensing credit to rural farmers since the 1970s. The Rural Poor Programme, however, was launched in the mid-1980s as the government's largest credit-based rural development programme targeting landless people. At the time of this study, RD-12 had 350,000 members, 59 per cent women. Both organizations have pursued 'mainstreaming' women to their core credit programmes with alacrity. The proportion of women borrowers in BRAC's RDP increased to 85 per cent by late 1994, while in RD-12 it increased to 70 per cent by early 1995.

In both organizations mainstreaming women to the previously male-dominated central credit programmes began in the late 1980s. In tandem with efforts to increase numbers of women borrowers have been recruit-ment drives to expand numbers of women staff at the field level. This appears to be in response to a view that women staff have easier access to rural women in a purdah culture than do men staff. It is also in response to donor pressures for equal opportunities recruitment policies. From negligible numbers of women fieldstaff in the late 1980s, women constituted, in 1993, about 15 per cent of BRAC fieldstaff. In RD-12, women make up an impressive 45 per cent of fieldstaff.

Both organizations follow a very similar approach to credit delivery and promoting income-generating activities. Using methods pioneered by the Grameen Bank to adapt credit systems to the constraints and needs of poor borrowers, both eschew collateral in favour of peer-group guar-antees on loans, which are maintained through group discipline. Both bring banking to the village by employing large numbers of fieldworkers to conduct meetings in villages and manage savings and credit accounts. Both supplement the entrepreneurial component of their programmes with the provision of training in income-generating skills. They also contribute to human resource development through other forms of training and debate on social development issues, including institution-building and leadership, primary health care, nutrition, sanitation, and so on. BRAC differs from RD-12 in that it employs a cadre of village workers – the *Gram Sheboks* and *Shebikas* (re-named Programme Assistants in mid-1993) – whose primary function is managing the credit and savings part of the programme, while its fieldworkers, the Programme Organizers, supervise this work as well as specializing in particular features of the programme such as institution-building or skills development. RD-12's fieldworker category, the Field Organizers, combine the work of BRAC PAs and POs; they manage credit and savings and also provide some training.

There are structural differences between the two organizations. Typical of NGOs, BRAC is more decentralized than RD-12, with local Area Managers having more authority to experiment with appropriate delivery measures than their counterparts in RD-12, the Thana Rural Develop-ment Officers. BRAC has a more egalitarian working culture than the authority and status-conscious civil service culture of RD-12. BRAC is also much more explicit about challenging social inequities in its ideology, formal policies, and training programmes than is RD-12.

In their current form, both programmes promote women's economic empowerment, and eschew conventional welfarist approaches. In principle, these efforts involve an active disruption of structures of gender in-equality; they assign women management authority over cash resources, with a view to enhancing the quality of their engagement with the market, and their power in household decision-making processes. This is a radical project in a conservative context in which gender status asymmetry is established partly through denying women's right to significant asset ownership or autonomy in the market. Inevitably, some asymmetrical patterns emerge in the process of programme implementation. Recent research on women's loan use patterns has revealed that there have not yet been significant shifts in women's level of engagement with the market. Instead, it is becoming clear that some women either share loans with their husbands for joint investments, or lose varying degrees of loan control to male relatives. They may hand over the entire loan amount for husbands to invest in higher profit activities, but retain managerial control, or men may manage the loan activity while women contribute their labour, or women may have little involvement in the investment activity at all (see, for example, Rahman, 1986; White, 1991; Ackerly, 1995; Rutherford, 1995; Goetz and Sen Gupta, 1996; and Ackerly, this volume). In reaction to these findings, many argue that this process is inevitable; the house-hold is a joint venture, and in a context which so severely limits women's freedoms in the market, it is a rational household choice to cede control over new cash resources to men.

In this chapter, however, the view is taken that if the objective of credit provision to women is to increase their personal power within the household, and to shift their rate of market engagement, then it becomes a programme responsibility to try to ensure that women get the most out of their loans, at least from a managerial, income, and skills development perspective. This paper does not deny, however, that participation in credit programmes, whatever the degree of credit transfer to other house-hold members, brings women a range of personal benefits such as access to training, or greater status in the household, as has been asserted by studies which have attempted to quantify the contribution of credit to women's empowerment (Hashemi and Schuler, 1996).

Nevertheless, findings as to women's lack of managerial control over their loans suggest that a process of under-interpreting the expansive aspects of policy goals, those which might promote transformation in gender roles or relations, occurs in these programmes. Is this an inevi-table outcome of a purdah culture which imposes heavy restrictions on the room for manoeuvre of individual women borrowers and of develop-ment programmes at the field level? Or are other processes at work; aspects of programme design or incentive structures which unintentionally undermine gender-equity goals? Or is it the cumulative effect of a low commitment to more expansive policy goals on the part of fieldstaff? In investigating aspects of fieldworker discretion in the rest of this paper, the concern is to illuminate the role of the individual in mediating social structure, organizational culture and incentive systems, with a view to identifying spaces for more expansive policy interpretations.

'Kuccha' Bureaucrats: Ambiguities of Position and Practice

As J. Montgomery suggests in his review of approaches to rural development administration, fieldworkers in rural development schemes are in an ironic position. Such programmes are explicitly participatory, which makes fieldworkers, implicitly, co-participants with rural people in processes of rural development (Montgomery, 1988). In BRAC, this is symbolized by the fact that until recently, its lowest level of village worker, the Programme Assistant, was not part of BRAC's regular staff structure. In RD-12, this is signalled by the fact that its Field Organizers are not part of the civil service employment structure, but are hired on a temporary basis tied to the life of the project, not to a lifetime with the public administration. Although participants in the struggles of the poor, as bureaucrats, fieldworkers are part of a large, 'distant' development administration, and their own prospects for advance depend on whether their performance is appreciated at the central office. Even BRAC, with its decentralized administration and egalitarian culture, retains a status system calibrated according to proximity to the Head Office or higher management levels. Fieldworkers are also usually materially and psychologically distanced from the poor by virtue of education and class. As representatives and advocates of their clients' interests they are required to display a species of local heroism – to show acute receptivity to people's needs (Montgomery, 1988: 33). As bureaucrats they are expected to deliver standardized inputs and regulate client behaviour to conform with organizationally defined priorities and conceptions of deserving beneficiaries – to respond to incentives which are geared to controlling organizational processes.

Fieldworkers are distant from their clients in terms of class and social status. The majority of women and men fieldstaff studied in this research in both organizations have middle-class backgrounds, coming from solvent rural farming or urban professional families, and with high educational qualifications, ranging from two years of college to a Bachelor's degree, to Master's degrees. Almost 70 per cent of men Programme Organizers in BRAC come from the village, compared to 50 per cent of the women. And in RD-12, the background of Field Organizers is even less linked to a rural experience: 50 per cent of the men come from the village, compared to 30 per cent of the women. Only in BRAC is there a category of staff of the type associated with grassroots participatory rural development work – the village-level Programme Assistants. About 60 per cent of women PAs came from the village, as did about 80 per cent of the men, and all have secondary school education. The majority of all categories of fieldstaff are under 35 and represent a modern, professional cadre of development workers, most of them – perhaps especially the village-level Programme Assistants – with aspirations to move away from village work into higher-status managerial work. This situates them socially far from the participatory ideal which sees fieldworkers in shared struggles with the poor.

Some of the contradictions in the roles of field-level bureaucrats are captured in Montgomery's near-oxymoronic description of them as 'bureaucratic populists' (1988: xvii). In a Bangladeshi context, this contradictory notion might be rendered instead as: *kuccha* bureaucrats. '*Kuccha*' in Bengali has a number of connotations. Among its literal translations are 'raw', 'unfinished' or 'naive', in contrast to '*pucca*' or 'finished', 'professional', 'correct'. It is used to describe the rural constructions of dwellings, feeder roads, and paths of dried mud – the physical context in which fieldstaff work. The term indicates the contingent, improvised, ambiguous role of fieldworkers.

There are ambiguities in the position and work of kuccha bureaucrats peculiar to gender and development programmes, which are related to the resistance gender policy generates within and outside development bureaucracies. As noted in the introduction to this volume, resistance can be expressed in diffidence about pursuing the more radical aspects of efforts to promote gender equity in development, or in outright hostility leading to the direct undermining of policy goals. These behaviours can be shared by fieldworkers as well. Most important, however, is the fact that kuccha bureaucrats on these programmes may be in the least desirable positions in their organizations from a career point of view – careers are not made in the field (at least, not civil service careers), nor in the area of women's development.

Michael Lipsky's study of 'street-level bureaucrats' in the US (1980), provides a guide to analysing other ambiguities and constraints in the work environment of lower-level bureaucrats. Their work is structured by top-level policy directives, which they are expected to implement in environments which policy cannot predict, amongst beneficiaries who may not fit policy descriptions, using uncertain methods with inadequate resources. Their role is essentially to manage a chaotic situation, for which they invent ad hoc coping strategies. Goals are unclear, and do not always spell out implications for implementation. This is certainly true in the context of programmes addressing women's disadvantage in development. Do the goals of women's financial empowerment and poverty alleviation, for example, imply not just facilitating loan access but also monitoring the use of that income? BRAC and RD-12 'human development' goals which include functional numeracy, family health, improved sanitation and social awareness, demand considerable creativity from kuccha bureaucrats. Achievements are hard to monitor and are 'more like receding horizons than fixed targets' (Landau, 1973: 536, cited in Lipsky, 1980: 40). The lack of clear goals contributes to the ambiguity of kuccha bureaucrats' roles. Are they expected to be policers of loan use or motivators of new levels of awareness and behaviour amongst their beneficiaries? According to Lipsky, to cope with uncertainty of purpose and non-compliant work environments, kuccha bureaucrats use their discretion to develop labels to create simplified and coherent conceptions of their clients, routines to limit beneficiary demands on and expectations of their efforts, and rationalizations to modify their own understandings of the purpose of their work (Lipsky, 1980). This chapter investigates field-worker discretion by examining the representations they develop to describe beneficiaries and define their needs, their routines of policy enactment which limit beneficiary demands and expectations, and indeed their own expectations of the purpose of their work.

Simplifications: Labels and Bias

Attitudes towards women's work

Representations of gender difference, and interpretations of women's and men's needs, come out in the simplifications, routines and rationalizations of fieldworkers. These kuccha bureaucrats receive authoritative representations, in the form of labels designating the deserving 'target' of policy intervention, from their organizations. The content with which fieldworkers 'flesh out' these labels, however, is coloured by their own representations of gender and worth.

In this study, fieldworkers were asked about the kind of work poor rural women do, in order to assess gender differences in perspectives on 'work' and women's productivity and social value. Since a central tenet of the gender division of labour in many cultures is that women's work is neither productive nor socially significant, the objective was to determine whether programme staff had reflected on the injustice and inaccuracy of ideologies of the insignificance of women's labour.

Across both programmes, and almost equally for men and women, the response was that poor rural women 'do not work' – *kaj kori na.* A typical view was expressed by a male fieldworker in the NGO: 'You know, women are illiterate, they are actually not doing anything productive in society, they lack capacity, and lack the habit of working or using skills…' (group discussion, Jamalpur, 17 May 1993). This view of women as non-productive is central to an entire cultural system which justifies asymmetrical rights, access to resources and social value between women and men on the grounds that women's economic contribution is negligible. The view that only waged employment outside the home is considered 'work' is implicit in the observation of a male fieldworker in the NGO, who explained that women staff had nothing in common with women beneficiaries because 'the main difference is that our women work' (9).[5] This is a perspective which is deeply ingrained and is shared at all levels in the organizations studied, as suggested by a statement from a very high-ranking male manager in the government organization: 'Women don't have any work to do, only house work. If we can involve them in income-generating activity, whatever they earn improves household survival. It even improves family planning behaviour' (107).

Although many women respondents also shared this view that women do not work, some of them challenged the justice of ignoring or undervaluing women's reproductive labour. As one woman field manager in the government organization noted: 'In our country women are very backward. They are not getting value for their labour but men get value for their labour. Women are working in the house but there is no money for that' (20). Some women drew parallels with the way their own work was valued: 'Village women don't get proper recognition for their housework – neither do I!' (Government field manager, 63). Indeed, women staff often illustrated problems of village women by drawing parallels in their own lives. This suggests a capacity, as women, to be receptive to aspects of beneficiaries' situations to which men are less sensitive. The limits of this capacity to identify points of similarity on the basis of gender, in spite of class differences, will be discussed later.

The following extract from a taped group discussion between women and men fieldworkers on the government programme illustrates some of the above points about men and women's different perspectives on work. The debate oscillated between discussing the work of village women and the work of women fieldstaff:

Woman 1:   A woman contributes more to society.

Man 1:   You're saying that a woman works harder than a man?!

Woman 1:   What I mean is…

Man 2:   Where we spend two hours working with a *samity* (group), they work half an hour. How is that working more?

Woman 2:   Hey! That's not right! That's not the way it is!

Man 3:   Okay, let's find out what they're trying to say.

Woman 1:   A woman contributes more to the whole society. She is contributing to her household ... to her husband's household ... that is to say, in a family where both the husband and the wife work, the husband has his food prepared for him before he goes to the office. And if there is anything out of place, she'll get it. And [she] has to do all the work and look after the children given by that husband before she comes to the office. And after she goes home from the office, she has to do all the cooking and cleaning!

Man 2:   Why are you dragging domestic duties into the office?

(*All the men together*): Outside we have to do all the work!

Man 3:   We are giving the women money, as loans. The kinds of things women produce, for example, like goats, cows, ducks, planting trees – women can't go to the market for these things. They don't have the courage. They don't have that ability.

Woman 1:   Whose fault is that? It's society's fault! If we go to the markets, they won't accept it! It's society's fault!

Man 1:   Let's say a woman is given 500 takas to buy goats. The woman then gives that money to her husband. Her husband buys it for 200 takas, and tricks her. He may steal the rest of the money, or whatever. If the women could have gone to the market herself...

Woman 3:   Who is doing this? They aren't letting her go to the market! They aren't accepting it! You may not be doing it, but ten other men like you are doing it!

Man 1:   Then the problem is women's! (everyone laughs)

Woman 3:   If a woman works, her domestic duties don't disappear. She has to work even harder to manage her family as well.

Man 2:   We are accepting what you say, but it is not right to say that only women work and that men don't.

Man 3:   Do you work more than us?

Woman 1:   Why don't you compare and see?

Man 2:   They do, they do work harder. But the work that we do in one hour, they do in six!

Woman 1:   Here we aren't just talking about the field. Here we are talking about both.

Man 3:   Why are you dragging the household in here?

Evident in the above exchange is men's persistence in maintaining a separation between private and public forms of work, and a rejection of the significance of domestic labour or its relevance to the experience of 'work' – which is clear from the repeated objection to women's references to their work at home. Importantly, men also insist that their women colleagues are not working as hard or as effectively as men do. Insisting on the differential quality of women and men's labour – even if both are working in exactly the same ways, in the same arena – and insisting on devaluing women's reproductive work, is critical to justifying male dominance and privileges in the 'public' arena.

The devaluing of women's work capacity is also used by men in the above example to justify practices amongst beneficiaries of husbands investing women's loans. Women beneficiaries are described as being incapable of investing money well ('They don't have the courage. They don't have that ability'). Women fieldstaff point out that the problem is that women are actively constrained from going to the market; power relations prevent positive change.

Further indication of differential receptivity to constraints faced by rural women emerged from fieldworkers' accounts of problems in motivating and training village women. Male staff often spoke dismissively of rural women's interest in training: 'We are trying to conscientize village women through training and motivation, but without much effect – they are still dependent on men. They don't want to go for training or any learning opportunities. They're afraid of it' (NGO fieldworker, 85). In contrast, women staff suggested that problems of low turn-out for training sessions were caused by husbands preventing women's participation:

> When there is any residential training husbands don't want to let wives go. Even to get loans women have to come to BRAC offices. Husbands want to come and take the loans instead.... Women's husbands are the biggest obstacle. Husbands think that if their wives come to groups they'll learn more and won't obey them, and all the domestic work won't get done. (NGO fieldworker, woman, 36)

Where men staff used the word 'dependent' to describe rural women, women staff often used words like 'oppressed'.

Labels which stereotype women's backwardness as caused by their own ignorance, low confidence and narrow-mindedness can be useful to kuccha bureaucrats in rationalizing the gap between expansive policy objectives and meagre accomplishments. Women are presented as timorous and susceptible, and a spurious justification is provided for the fact that few women engage in high-profit non-traditional activities; or that some women cede loan control to their husbands, or that few women take up opportunities for training. Simplified perceptions of women's low productivity conveniently displace responsibility for the shortcomings of policy implementation onto beneficiaries themselves. A proclivity to blame what is in effect a policy failure – husbands using women's loans – on women's incompetence or conservatism, absolves fieldworkers of responsibility. Thus negative representations of women's capabilities become self-fulfilling prophecies.[6]

Perspectives on policy legitimacy

The content of representations also comes out in kuccha bureaucrats' views on the legitimacy of gender-equity policy. If they sense a lack of genuine commitment from policy-makers, if gender-redistributive policy is seen as a mere hollow promise designed to placate external donors, fieldworkers may feel freer to indulge their own biases and ignore or underachieve on policy objectives. After all, a demonstrated affinity with gender-equity goals is not a requirement of fieldworkers at recruitment,[7] nor is their performance ever assessed on the basis of their contribution to these goals.

Respondents were asked about the reasons for their organization's policy change with a view to discovering their perspectives on the validity or relevance of working with ever-increasing numbers of women. Hardly any respondents, men or women, in either organization, explained the policy shift by referring to the project of challenging inequities in gender relations. Instead, most offered pragmatic reasons, arguing that women were much more tractable group members and more disciplined loan repayers than men. This response from a man fieldworker on the government programme was typical: '[Earlier] experiences with male groups was bad. It is easy to work with women's groups – they work and talk nicely, … they attend meetings regularly, we can find them at home, that's why RPP is giving priority to them' (13).

Most staff consider this a perfectly legitimate reason for working with women; it contributes to what is understood as the main objective of these programmes: efficient credit management. This is implied by the candid admission of a male government fieldworker: 'We are much better at getting our loan money back now that we are using women as middlemen [sic]' (14). Most fieldworkers justify this with essentialist views on women and men's 'nature', where they associate masculinity with rebelliousness and femininity with stereotyped views of women's greater concern with maintaining family honour and propriety by keeping up loan repayments. As another man fieldworker on the government programme said: 'I believe that women have special power to manage and motivate. When we gave loans to women we found them to be very regular. Even though men are the real users of loans, women have a capacity for convincing them to repay, even when they are quarrelling' (9). A woman fieldworker in the NGO said: 'Men's groups work according to their own views and decisions and are hard to motivate. Women are easy to motivate because they are obedient' (34).

Such views stereotype men's social and economic roles as much as they do women's. They offer few prospects for considering change in gender relations towards greater autonomy for women, or indeed, responsibility for men. Instead, they justify programme delivery approaches which rely upon exploiting women's tractability in the interests of programme efficiency, not women's empowerment. These perspectives minimize the significance and legitimacy of women's independent need for policy attention.

An important issue for perceptions of policy legitimacy concerns fieldworkers' views on women's personal control over loans. All staff knew that the loss of varying degrees of managerial control over loans to male relatives was not a practice intended by policy, and it was women staff who first raised this in interviews. A substantial proportion of staff in both organizations felt that this was a problem. In both organizations, however, more women than men disapproved of the practice: 61 per cent of the women in BRAC compared to 50 per cent of the men, and 63 per cent of the women in RD-12 compared to 40 per cent of their male colleagues. Women's greater concern over the issue may reflect different feelings from men on the subject of women's rights to control financial assets within the household, as suggested by the following exchange during a group discussion between government fieldstaff:

Man: It isn't true that men have control over the women's money: husbands give their wives money, so why shouldn't wives give them money? After a woman has been married off, her husband can make her work if he wants to or not if he chooses not to. So that money is the husband's!

Woman: Just as the women take loans and hand over the money to their husbands, this happens in the case of female staff as well.

One woman fieldworker on the government programme shared a rather critical perspective on the situation:

Actually, this credit is a form of dowry. Women are giving their loans to their husbands – it replaces them having to bring money from their fathers' house – now they are getting it through the office. Because of this loan they get a release from wife battery because husbands behave better than before. (51)

She is implying a trade-off between one patriarchal arena and another, from the household to the project. With credit serving as a proxy form of dowry in the context of village groups, the basic terms of patriarchal exchanges of women are little altered, though conditions for women are somewhat improved. Dowry is a resource over which women have little direct control – it is intended for the use of the husband and his family. The analogy between credit and dowry suggests, therefore, that women's benefit is contingent, not direct; women may gain some peace in the household, but there is little contribution to her financial or entrepreneurial autonomy.

Differences in women and men's views on the legitimacy of women's husbands using women's loans do not reflect on the formal policies of their organizations, but on an informal practice which has evolved in the course of programme implementation. But as Ackerly suggests in her chapter in this volume, these informal practices do reflect on aspects of programme design and delivery; an organization concerned with the problem of male loan use could design incentive structures to discourage it. However, if fieldworkers see no problem with a range of practices which involve under-achievement on broader objectives such as women's financial empowerment – practices such as male loan use, or women investing loans in extremely low-return activities which neither shift women's rate of market engagement nor challenge the gender division of labour – they may use their discretion to ignore these practices. Indeed, if such practices do not detract from loan repayment, or actually contribute to regular repayment, fieldworkers may encourage them.

Routines of Interaction

Kuccha bureaucrats develop routines in their interactions with clients to render the complex environment of rural development problems more manageable, and to make their everyday work predictable. The subjects of routinization – programme beneficiaries – will be affected by the way kuccha bureaucrats process their work, as will, indeed, overall organizational policy, because of the recursive effect of the accretion of low-level decision-making on programme outcomes and on the knowledge environment which informs policy. Routines at the field level show whether, and how, kuccha bureaucrats choose to reinforce or challenge the institutionalization of gender hierarchy in the family and the community.

Determining eligibility: routine favouritism

Kuccha bureaucrats are expected to select out of their field environments the members of the groups they work with according to agency criteria of desert – usually this is based upon their household income status. They have to make choices over the inclusion or exclusion of certain people, in a process which involves reconciling agency targeting goals with personal preferences over the people with whom they feel best able to work.

Group creation is not just a matter of designating appropriate members. A critical component of the process is motivating people to join by persuading them of the advantages of membership. Fieldworkers must contend with the hostility and suspicion of villagers, which can be exacerbated because of the focus on women, bringing them out of their homes in ways which may be unfamiliar, or inadmissible, in the village environment. Fieldworkers are often suspected of Christian evangelizing, or involvement in the traffic in women, or of breaking up families. A familiar joke shared by village men is that their wives will be taught to reject their husbands and favour the 'bosses' in the development organization: '*Amar shami khalo, amar shahib bhalo*' ('My husband is bad, my boss is good'). Fieldworkers have to establish their credibility within the village, and find ways of forming groups without offending powerful local people. Often, the easiest way to do this is to accede to, rather than challenge, local systems of signalling prestige and social difference, working through, rather than against, local power brokers. This is not just a matter of gaining the approval of local elites. It is also a matter of working through individual men who, as husbands, are the power brokers mediating relationships between the household and the outside world. Many male fieldworkers admitted to contacting husbands and seeking their permission for their wives to join groups. Frequently, as an inducement, husbands were told that they would soon have access to a loan – though their wives. As one male fieldworker in the NGO explained: 'husbands know the wife's money is their money. And to motivate men to let women form VOs we tell husbands that they will soon get a loan' (85).

Women staff engaged much less frequently in this practice, probably because of gendered barriers to interaction between young women staff (who were often unmarried) and male strangers, barriers which have great force in a conservative village environment. The reason men staff were more prone to work through village men likewise reflects gendered behavioural norms, where it is inappropriate for male visitors to approach women directly, and would be considered an affront to the status of village men if male visitors failed to give them precedence. But this male-dominated process of mediating the relationship between the development organization and women beneficiaries reinforces conventions about women's lesser stature as village and household members. It underwrites norms giving them less authority and significance in the public arena, and means they participate in development programmes on male sufferance. As much is suggested in the following statement:

> When I talk to the VO members I have to negotiate with the men first – and it becomes a meeting for the men – instead of a women's meeting. They say:

'You have to tell us things first because the women don't understand. If you tell us first we'll explain it to them'. (NGO fieldworker, man, 73)

In terms of cumulative outcomes, this practice has the effect of subordinating a development resource designed for women's benefit to men's community and personal interests. It makes husbands the primary and legitimate interlocutors with fieldworkers, strongly signalling women's secondary and subordinate status as legitimate clients of NGO or state services.

Where fieldworker discretion comes most powerfully into play, however, is in selecting members who will actually receive loans. Ackerly's contribution to this volume describes the group selection process in four rural credit programmes in Bangladesh, where the pressure on fieldworkers to ensure that loans are repaid creates powerful incentives to discriminate amongst group members on the grounds of likely repayment capacity. She suggests this has led to a tendency to favour borrowers with other household resources with which they could repay the loan in case of default – resources such as household assets, or a husband who could do day labour to repay the loan if the loan activity failed, or who, indeed, could invest the loan more profitably than his wife. Members of borrowing subgroups in the village will probably go along with this in their own assessments of the creditworthiness of individuals, given the pressure on them to guarantee, collectively, loan repayment in case of default by individual members.

The result is that sometimes potentially deserving members – particularly women without male support – are denied loans, or are permitted to borrow only for very traditional, homestead-based gender-typed activities. In doing this, fieldworkers are involved in reinforcing some of the ground rules of the gender division of labour and the purdah system. This practice can be reinforced at an organizational level because fieldstaff often have to get approval from their local offices for their selection of eligible borrowers, and concerns to keep local aggregate repayment rates high leads to great conservatism over borrower eligibility.

Women staff tended to be most aware of these problems, and expressed frustration over their failures to defend women's rights to independent access to loans, as the following two statements from women government fieldworkers suggest:

One woman gave her loan to her husband. But he refused to repay the money. She had so many problems getting money from him – and had to repay by selling eggs, chicks, etc. He also beat her when she tried to get loan instalments from him. She managed to repay and asked for another. But she told the field workers that she didn't want money to go to the husband. She said: 'Give me

the cash, I'll buy a cow'. On the loan disbursement day, the husband came to
the office to get the money. The woman told the office to forget she had a
husband. 'Think of me as husband-less and give me the money.' When the
office tried to give it to the husband she said: 'Look, I am under double
pressure, from my husband who won't repay and you who want my money
back'. She went and bought a cow with the husband and the fieldworkers and
brought it close to her house in the village so she could control it, in case the
husband tries to take it away. (52)

One woman who had neither children nor a husband was doing domestic
labour, and became a *samity* member and applied for a loan. I supported her
loan proposal for a small trade business but the office did not approve it. The
office said she has no husband or son so how will she run the business? I think
she could have – that's why I proposed her! (58).

As will be shown shortly, women staff sometimes used their discretion
to subvert dominant loan approval practices by encouraging women
borrowers to take stronger charge of their loans, and to take advantage
of programme membership in other ways.

Limiting demand: routine dissuasion

Kuccha bureaucrats have no control over the social and economic environments of beneficiaries, and as the last on the list in their bureaucratic
hierarchies, they have the least control over the sorts of programme
inputs which their superiors deem appropriate. Where they do exercise
control is over the amount of information about the programme they
share with beneficiaries. In order to enhance the authoritativeness of
their positions *vis-à-vis* beneficiaries, they have an interest in limiting
beneficiaries' demands to what they feel is the least trouble to deliver.
The amount of information a kuccha bureaucrat will share depends on
constraints in the programme delivery system, personal workloads, their
conceptions of beneficiaries' capabilities, and their conceptions of their
own roles.

Both BRAC and RD-12 append a range of social development concerns and activities to their credit programmes. However, the dominance
of the incentive to secure high repayment, which, unlike social development outcomes, is easy to quantify and to hold up as a personal achievement, distorts fieldworker routines into an increasingly exclusive focus on
credit matters. Demand management, then, occurs over the degree to
which knowledge about women's legal rights and reproductive health is
shared. Fieldworker training, in fact, rarely equips them with the capacity
to share much more than general platitudes on these subjects. In the
Rural Poor Programme, although its 'human development' training for

fieldworkers includes an introduction to women's social and economic needs, this does not include training in legal literacy or women's rights in the family. In any case, training related to analysing inequality and the ways it is maintained is neglected in favour of technical and accounting training (Lappin, 1989). Women's personal struggles over dowry, polygamy, divorce or domestic violence are not prioritized for discussion in group meetings, nor is there space in management reports to mention these issues. In BRAC, there is more respect for the relevance of these issues, and they are addressed through separate programmes: the Women's Health Development Programme and the Human Rights and Legal Education Programme, both of which have separate cadres of fieldstaff from the credit programme. Nevertheless, fieldstaff on the credit programme often have to confront problems of abuse of women's rights – for example, where violent husbands keep their wives from attending meetings.

In both programmes women staff were much more likely than men staff to raise concerns about their programme's lack of attention to 'social awareness' training for women, and to point out that domestic violence was a serious problem in their work in the village. They also drew connections between enhancing women's legal and social status in relation to men, and improving women's chances of achieving financial independence. Men, in contrast, often saw the latter as a mere technical matter of enhancing women's skills endowment or access to wage employment, not of challenging gender relations. In other words, women staff saw their agency's neglect of issues such as violence, men's negative attitudes, and women's lack of rights in the family as direct constraints on their work. As a woman fieldworker in the NGO said: 'We are working for social awareness but all we do is teach women to sign their names – we need more than that. But in our Functional Education training that is all they learn' (92).

Men, on the other hand, claimed that issues of women's rights and male attitudes rarely came up in their meetings with women; this is evidence of the dissuasive effect of their gender on women's capacity to speak of personal problems. In meetings with village men, male staff were also reluctant to bring up these issues, partly because of the status losses they might experience if seen to be overly sympathetic with women's interests: 'Dowry, violence against women ... men aren't interested in hearing about these things and don't even react. And men who talk about these things are not respected by men. And anyway, we don't reflect these things in our own lives' (NGO fieldworker, man, 97). This comment brings out another problem male staff experience in working on gender-redistributive programmes: the disjunction between the progressive messages embedded in their work and their sometimes very different personal lives. This contrasts with the way some women staff detect and act on gender-based similarities between their own lives and those of beneficiaries. Because women staff and women beneficiaries share some gender-related problems, some women staff use their discretion to promote women's understanding of their rights, however ineffectual this may be in the absence of supportive programme structures and processes.

However, it is important not to assume any natural sisterhood between women staff and beneficiaries. In both organizations, as noted earlier, fieldworkers and beneficiaries take up vastly different positions in class and other social hierarchies. What is ironic, however, is that the women staff closest to beneficiaries in terms of class status – BRAC's village-level Programme Assistants, many of whom come from villages, and from families that may be barely solvent, are the most reluctant to identify similarities between themselves and women beneficiaries. They were anxious to stress and indeed exaggerate class differences with village women, and were uncomfortable with acknowledging any shared experiences on the basis of gender. Perhaps the very low organizational status of PAs was contributing to their efforts to insist upon status by other means, particularly by emphasizing their distance and difference from poor women. Given their position at the bottom of organizational hierarchies, it was in their interests to stress their identification with male colleagues and the organization, not village women. Another irony is that, in contrast, RD-12 women staff, who were overall more educated and more likely to have an urban background than BRAC women, showed a stronger propensity to identify gender-based similarities between themselves and village women, rather than class differences (71 per cent of RD-12 women pointed out similarities compared to 63 per cent of BRAC women).

These findings warn against assuming a simple correlation between class and attitudes. They also, very importantly, warn against assuming a commonality in women's interests. For this reason, it is best not to make the case for investing in women fieldworkers on the grounds that they are always more effective than men in reaching rural women. As Jackson suggests in this volume, 'the case for women fieldworkers is better made on the grounds of the importance of offering positive role models to women, ... rather than on the instrumental grounds of "doing participation better"' (p. 174).

Conclusions

In both the NGO and the government organization, incentive systems are increasingly geared to reward 'credit performance' above other goals. Incentive systems and organizational structures are important in determining fieldworker policy enactment behaviour. However, the differences which cut across both organizations in the perspectives and behaviour of women and men fieldworkers suggest the importance of gender in determining how staff respond to incentives and use their discretion. Evidence for this, in this study, is that there was little significant difference in women's rates of direct control over their loans between either organization, in spite of differences in organizational structures and styles: 28 per cent of the women borrowers in BRAC had complete or very high control over their loans, compared to 31 per cent in RD-12 (Goetz and Sen Gupta, 1996: 60).

The gender differences in the ways fieldworkers deploy their discretionary powers could be an important resource for programme efforts to disrupt the social organization of gender difference and inequality. However, it is important not to romanticize these subversions, to make more of them than they are. By any standards of measurement, they represent minute, molecular expressions of oppositional perspectives. Also, it cannot be assumed that these subversions are the expression of some natural solidarity or sisterhood between women kuccha bureaucrats and their beneficiaries. Whatever the class background of women fieldworkers, their primary reference group is likely to be their male colleagues and superiors, not their clients. This is especially so since they are minorities in their organizations, especially at decision-making levels. Feminist critiques of organization theory point out that even when women are not in an absolute minority – what Kanter calls a 'balanced group' (1977: 239) with staffing proportions which RD-12 is achieving – their 'minority' social status outside organizations, as well as the masculine interests embedded in organizational structures and cultures, continue to obstruct women's capacity for independence of action, reflection, or influence on practices and policies (Dahlerup, 1988). As such, Bangladeshi women fieldworkers, as socially devalued individuals doing organizationally under-prioritized work from minority positions in male-dominated agencies, are the most 'kuccha' of all bureaucrats.

This chapter has not suggested a completely clear gender difference in the policy interpretations and enactment routines of women and men fieldworkers. Some men share more expansive views on women's right to development resources; some women seem bound by dominant and limiting policy interpretations which reinforce gendered resource asymmetries. Women staff are not receptive to the needs of poor women in a predictable way, as suggested by the fact that the lowest-level women kuccha bureaucrats were at pains to deny their village backgrounds and class affinities with beneficiaries. Because of this, it cannot be assumed that women staff will necessarily promote poor women's interests in development. Nevertheless, there is a case for investing in women staff's positive use of their discretion, and for counteracting men's negative discretionary practices with regard to gender relations through new incentives and perhaps gender training. Investing in the discretion of women fieldworkers might involve not just inclusion in decision-making structures, but efforts to cultivate women's 'voice' within development organizations to validate women's perspectives on programme delivery. The latter might be achieved through promoting opportunities for women fieldworkers to develop cultures of mutual support; a critical determinant of their capacity to sustain and act upon counter-cultural perspectives.

Notes

1. 'Beneficiaries' is used here to describe the people who are designated in policy as the recipients of development inputs and services. It is an inadequate term. 'Beneficiaries' can be direct, active 'participants' or 'members' of the development programme in question, or they can be passive, receptive 'clients'. In a development context, the more formal construction of 'client' seems inappropriate for the participatory interventions intended by the kinds of rural development programmes discussed in this chapter. See Wood, 1985 for a discussion of issues involved in choosing terminology to describe the 'targets' of policy.

2. I am grateful to the UK's Economic and Social Research Council, which funded this research, and to the Canadian International Development Agency, which provided a small grant for the dissemination of the research results in Bangladesh. I thank BRAC and RD-12 for their generosity and openness in allowing me to research their operations. I am grateful to Rina Sen Gupta, my research partner, with whom the fieldwork was conducted between February and October 1993. The study also benefited from the very able research assistance of Rina Roy in Bangladesh and Cathy Green in the UK. All empirical and interpretive errors, of course, are my own.

3. All interviews, group discussions and oral histories were conducted in Bengali and were immediately translated and transcribed. This information is supplemented by a shorter survey of 455 women and men staff in both organizations at all levels. Combined with the shorter sample, this provides data on 567 employees of these programmes: 332 from BRAC (22% of BRAC RDP staff), and 235 from RD-12 (12% of RD-12 staff).

4. RD-12 is funded by the Canadian International Development Agency (CIDA).

5. Numbers in brackets refer to the individual interview from which the statement is taken.

6. Wood, 1985, provides a theorization of the role of 'labelling' in development policy which has been important to the way I have thought about the representations devised by fieldworkers.

7. In women's NGOs, however, commitment to gender equity can often be a job requirement. See Tahera Yasmin's discussion in Chapter 12 of this book of recruitment procedures for Saptagram Nari Swanivar Parishad, a respected women's development NGO in Bangladesh, 1997.

Part V

Women Organizing for Themselves

12

What is Different about Women's Organizations?

Tahera Yasmin

Do women manage differently from men? Does that make them more, or less, efficient? And how do women deal with hierarchy and decision-making? These are just some of the questions I have tried to look at in this chapter in trying to understand how and why a women-managed NGO succeeded in recruiting and retaining women where others have failed. In this chapter, the experience of Saptagram Nari Swanivar Parishad (Seven-Village Women's Self Reliance Movement), an NGO in Bangladesh, will be examined as a possible guide to these questions.

In Bangladesh, most NGOs, big or small, target women as the main beneficiaries. The assumption is that women are disempowered through pauperization and gender disparity, and by providing access to services and programmes women are initiated into a process of decision-making which ultimately leads towards empowerment. The paradox of the situation is that while NGOs stress decision-making at the grassroots level, they fail to ensure decision-making by women at the management level. Therefore, only a few organizations or programmes are managed by women. In a study conducted in 1994, only 11 per cent of ADAB's (the national coordinating agency for NGOs) 450 member organizations are shown to be managed by women (Yasmin and Huda, 1994).

Men's decisions still determine women's agenda in development activities in Bangladesh. Organizations face problems recruiting, retaining and developing women as managers because, they say, women are not as career-minded as men, they tend to take more leave, they do not like to be transferred and are not as efficient as men, since women want to go home on the dot of five. From the women's point of view, a study of women's position in the management of a private voluntary development organization in Bangladesh conducted by Yasmin and Huda (1994) shows that women face barriers right at the beginning, from the recruiting process. When interviewing candidates the organizations reveal their paternalistic attitude by asking women whether they are married, whether they have any children, or whether they plan to have children. If the job entails field assignments then the NGO inquires if the woman can leave the child behind. If she is not able to, the organization, instead of offering child-care services, will ask her to make alternative arrangements.

Women in the workplace are judged and condemned for the very qualities they are valued for by society. The institutions that talk of women's empowerment propagate the same social norms and patriarchal values that limit women's mobility, that prefer to see women as nurturers, and that believe that men are natural leaders. A woman's role in the household as wife, mother and daughter-in-law is on one hand idealized, while on the other, outside of the household, she is punished for acting according to these roles. Her roles and responsibilities within the home have precedence over other priorities and therefore, inevitably, spill over into the workplace – the mother always stays at home when a child falls sick. And yet at the workplace any absence incurred as a result of carrying out such responsibilities is viewed as inefficiency. A request for maternity leave is seen as problematic and implies a lack of professionalism. In contrast, long-term study leave taken by a man is acceptable; it is seen as a legitimate contribution both to the organization and to his personal development.

Organizations with their distorted notions of equality believe that women have to be as 'good' as men, and act like men, in order to be effective managers and decision-makers. Donor perspectives on women's organizations also play a significant role in this scenario. Most donor agencies are headed by men who can identify with and relate to men in the NGO community. The organizational structures of donor agencies, in their deference to male authority and leadership, and in their hierarchical structures, are paralleled in NGOs headed by men. Women's organizations which are managed differently are considered to be inefficient.

The key question is, therefore, can women work as women and be just as effective?

Women Working with Women: Saptagram Nari Swanirvar Parishad

There are examples which show that women do manage differently. They try to accommodate a woman's life situation and thereby create conditions conducive to recruit, retain and develop women as effective managers. Saptagram Nari Swanirvar Parishad has faced problems like any other organization but it also developed strategies and mechanisms to overcome them. I will discuss my experiences with Saptagram to show how women work with women.

Saptagram Nari Swanirvar Parishad started in 1976 to work with women: to organize, conscientize and mobilize rural landless women into cohesive groups capable of fighting on the frontiers of gender and socio-economic disparities. In 20 years it grew from a three-person project to an organization of well over a hundred staff and 30,000 members. Its growth, especially in the initial years, was slow because any change in gender relations is a slow process involving internalization of new perspectives both by the facilitator (the staff) and the village group members themselves. Though the figures show tremendous growth, Saptagram does not measure its achievements in terms of targets and numbers. Rather, it seeks to bring qualitative changes in women's lives and to encourage women's initiatives to spearhead social action on class and gender issues. It also seeks to promote women's involvement in activities reserved for men.

Saptagram currently has a total of 2,740 village groups of which 2,517 are women's groups and 217 are men's groups. Saptagram organized 58,673 women and 5,309 men through these groups. It has a managerial staff of 20, 14 of whom are women. At the field level 121 women work along with 39 men (Annual Report, 1995–96). Saptagram believes in a holistic development perspective and runs a comprehensive programme, the components of which include: conscientization, organization and mobilization of poor, landless women and men; adult functional literacy; health, water and sanitation; productive programmes in sericulture, pisciculture and agriculture; savings and credit with an emphasis on involving women in non-traditional income and employment-generating activities. Non-traditional activities are encouraged to challenge the notion of male and female spheres of activity. Saptagram believes that this separation of activities has to be broken down for effective mobilization and empowerment for women. An important part of the mobilization and training strategy is to make women visible by arranging travel to different areas of Saptagram's operation. The adult functional literacy element is its largest component with 1,639 schools where over 15,000 women and 5,000 men learn literacy and numeracy skills (Annual Report, 1995–96). The materials and curriculum have been developed by the organization, and changing gender roles in the household and in the external environment has been emphasized. Strategic issues like legal rights and how to demystify the legal system have also been highlighted to encourage women to seek solutions to their problems. The organization now has eleven field offices to implement its programmes and these are headed by women. It is an organization which considers itself to be a part of the women's movement, actively participating by taking to the streets when protesting against violence against women and the rise of fundamentalism.

Saptagram in not the only women's organization working with women in Bangladesh. Like some of the others, it has tried to place women in all levels of management decision-making and tried to deal with women's practical and strategic needs. Saptagram developed a work ethos that has remained women-centred. I will discuss some of Saptagram's management features in the belief that such features are transferable. Organizations can transform their management systems to support and nurture women rather than leaving them out in the cold.

Total commitment to women

The need to make women's needs and concerns central, rather than peripheral, to an organization's philosophy and planning is crucial. Saptagram is committed to creating a place where women are comfortable working. This means creating space for women at the practical level and at the strategic level. The managing committee is constituted by women as are the general body members, who elect the managing committee. Women are placed in managerial posts with men working under them. This is normally considered to be an impossible thing to do, as it is assumed that men will not submit to women's authority. One of the reasons they do in this case is that the working environment is non-confrontational. Women feel comfortable and confident in their work because they know they are in charge. The aggression often seen in token and isolated women working in a male-dominated environment is missing here. Hence, men too act in a non-aggressive manner. The non-confrontational environment, men's acceptance of women's authority, and women's confidence in handling management and leadership roles is a reflection of the extent to which changes in gender roles have been internalized by staff.

Hiring women

Finding women to work with Saptagram, especially at the field level, has never been a problem. This is contrary to the experience of many NGOs who have great difficulty recruiting and retaining women. Many organizations find it difficult to recruit women because women are often not as qualified as men, their attitudes are not thought to be as professional, and so on. Often organizations do not realize that the process of recruitment can itself alienate women in the workplace.

Saptagram's mandate was clear; it recruits women to work with women, especially women from similar backgrounds to those of the group members. Experience showed that women with rural backgrounds who have experienced gender discrimination are better equipped to conscientize and mobilize poor rural women around this issue. Sharing a similar background with village group members means that the workers also share common experiences of class discrimination, which is important when trying to identify common oppressors in society. The strategy of selecting staff on the above criteria was chosen after Saptagram made its first mistakes. Initially it recruited women from the richer households of the village where the organization operated. The women had college degrees and it was felt that, because of their education, they would be effective in mobilizing women. What occurred at the implementation level was the opposite. Since the staff came from elite families they were not successful in mobilizing women around class issues (such as property rights, access to government relief resources) because that meant mobilizing against their own family interests. Saptagram learned from its mistakes and later it also made efforts to recruit staff who are in some senses 'outcasts'. They may be divorced, or have been abandoned by their husbands and by society; some are physically handicapped, most have suffered from the rigours of poverty. All have suffered from living in a patriarchal society and therefore have become effective agents of change. Academic qualifications were and still are considered secondary to their commitment and interest in working with women.

Until a few years ago, staff were recruited from Saptagram's network of women and activist organizations. Interviews are held at the local field office and are relaxed affairs. Stress is placed on ascertaining the applicants' willingness to work in unknown villages, using public transport, and also on their ability to identify the causes of women's oppression. Since staff are posted in field offices which can be distant from their homes, applicants' guardians are welcome to accompany them during interviews so that they have an opportunity to discuss the nature of Saptagram's work. Otherwise the organization risks losing staff due to pressure on women from their homes; it realized that guardians have to be reassured that the staff would be working and living in a secure environment.

This process is very time-consuming and many organizations are not willing to invest that time. For Saptagram the time invested during the recruitment process yields far-reaching results – results measured not least in its high retention rate for staff, but also in the effectiveness and commitment of women staff as village mobilizers.

Investing in women

Experience shows that it is not enough to hire women. Time and money have to be invested in developing the potentials and skills of staff, especially in the case of Saptagram, since at the point of hiring staff academic qualifications are given low priority. This starts with initiating women into basic human resource development training, with emphasis on gender and class relations. A theoretical framework for understanding and analysing rural socio-economic and political structures is central to raising awareness among women on these issues. This is followed by training in accounting, group dynamics and leadership development. More crucial than the formal training, however, is the informal process of awareness-building through discussions amongst staff about problems faced at work, about conflict within village groups, or problems with local elites, the power brokers who are threatened by women's activities. These issues are also discussed with village group members, with staff from other Saptagram centres and with friends within the community.

Other than training organized by Saptagram, the staff are encouraged to complete their high school and Bachelor's degree. This allows them to climb the 'corporate ladder' and, as the programmes continue to expand, helps to develop specialized staff. Although provision for staff development is a component offered by most organizations, it tends to be more true for men rather than for women staff. Men receive more encouragement to apply for training and study-leaves since it is felt that organizations will receive their money's worth; men are less likely to leave their jobs to follow their wives, men will not apply frequently for leave and men will not need maternity leave. These assumptions do hinder a woman's chance for further training. Organizations believe that investing in unmarried women is a waste of time since the chances of them leaving the job once they are married is high. Once they are married, the spectre of motherhood (with attendant maternity leave, sick leave, my-child-is-sick leave) deters the organizations even further. The inconvenience and costs incurred due to time out from work for the above reasons outweigh the time and expenses organizations are willing to invest in women.

The Saptagram experience shows that investing in women results in confident women who are in a stronger bargaining position especially when bargaining in their own marriages. A more qualified woman means a higher position and increased pay. This in turn increases the benefits from the provident fund and gratuity, which is a percentage of their salary for each year worked and is contributed entirely by the organization. Women bargain with their husbands to retain their jobs and therefore the assumption that it is unwise to invest in women, particularly unmarried women, proves untrue.

Accommodating women

The fieldstaff live on the organization's campus, in familiar rural surroundings, yet different because the campuses are like communes. A common living arrangement, with separate dorms for women and men, is considered to be a vital learning experience for the staff. Adapting to new situations, living with strangers, helping one another, resolving personal conflicts between each other is all part of internalizing the dynamics of group formation which they are entrusted to facilitate among the village women.

Recognizing that relationships, marriage, pregnancy and motherhood are a part of women's lives, and are not, as many organizations assume, part of the problem with hiring women, Saptagram has had to find ways of accommodating these transitions in women's lives. Parents, siblings and husbands can visit the campus, marriage between women and men staff is permitted (unlike in some other NGOs where it is discouraged), and children are accommodated in the campus life. Couples usually live off-campus but in close proximity to the field office.

Women living with small children is part of the image of Saptagram and this is appealing to women. Village women often drop in during the afternoon for a chat; they bring their children, discuss problems, or gossip about what is happening in the village. Village women along with the staff are 'at home' in the field office. This aspect of Saptagram's management has brought the home into the workplace and therefore has blurred the rigid public versus private divide maintained by most organizations. Women feel comfortable with this arrangement, but others do not. Donor agencies and development organizations, which are usually headed by men, view this as unprofessional, as being dowdy and homespun in contrast to the more sleek and clean image they favour in progressive, contemporary development organizations.

These organizations, NGOs and donors, share similar hierarchical management structures and organizational cultures which place women in WID programmes and men in accounts verification. They speak the same language in terms of efficiency, targets, and a results-based approach which leaves little time to invest in women, to accommodate women and be responsive to their needs.

Travelling

The issue of travelling and the kind of vehicle used is of critical importance to women because it symbolizes women's status and social freedom. Rich women use private cars and the poor, in areas where purdah is more strictly followed, use rickshaws covered by a sari to protect them from men's eyes. The use of public transport, such as buses, symbolizes stepping into the male, public domain. All staff in Saptagram are required to use public transport such as rickshaws, rickshaw vans or buses. If the distance is not great they walk to their destinations. This brings women out into the public domain which has a demonstrative effect because rural women in a purdah culture are generally confined to using hidden pathways instead of main roads. Walking or using rickshaws has another advantage; workers get to meet villagers on the way. This contact with people helps to make workers more acceptable in the village. It also helps in establishing networks which support the women's groups in their struggles.

Other NGOs in Bangladesh have introduced motorcycles and bicycles for staff to make field work more 'efficient'. Small NGOs allow the men to ride motorcycles because they are in high supervisory positions and this is considered appropriate to their status. However, mobility policies for women, even in supervisory positions, are inconsistent, as even when women want to ride motorcycles, excuses are made such as insufficient funds for purchasing them. On the other hand, larger mixed organizations with quasi-corporate cultures have been insisting that women ride motorcycles as an expression of their empowerment, and as a broader symbol of progressive organizational cultures (Goetz and Gupta, 1995). Very few of these women actually ride these vehicles in their private lives because that makes them social outcasts. This is not to say that women riding motorcycles in male-headed NGOs have not gone through an internal transformation in the way, for example, Saptagram women have. The point is that women should decide if and when they wish to ride a motorcycle rather than the organization deciding whether they can or not.

The motorcycle culture has not entered Saptagram yet mainly due to women's lack of interest in riding these vehicles. While they agree that riding a motorcycle could be empowering, the staff would prefer to ride only when they are ready. Rather, they find using public transport, especially buses, empowering since buses are used mostly by men and it is always a struggle to get on one. Only a few seats are reserved for women and trying to find a seat becomes a battle against patriarchal values which 'protect' women, keep them in their space, and prevent any transgressions into male space. Using public transport becomes a means to establish women's right to public space. This is also found to have a strong demonstrative effect. If the staff, who live in the same village as the group members and are bound by the same social constraints, are able to ride in a bus, then surely the village women, too, can eventually ride in a bus.

Working conditions

An essential part of making space for women within an organization is creating favourable working conditions. This goes beyond making space for women in a practical way, such as providing secure accommodation. For Saptagram, this means upholding women's interests and their rights as human beings. Unlike many NGOs, Saptagram has tried to address the strategic interests of its own women staff; empowerment is not held to be a project relevant only for the women beneficiaries of the organization's work. Women staff, for example, have the right to marry when they wish and bear children according to their own plans. Besides the mandatory three-month maternity leave, extra leave with pay is allowed for post-natal recovery. Options to save through the contributory provident fund adds an impetus for staff to stay longer with the organization. Together with gratuity, each member of staff leaves Saptagram with a sum of money as recognition of their commitment to the organization.

Given the condition of health-care facilities in the country and the fact that women seldom use the poor facilities which exist, Saptagram has tried to provide medical assistance. Besides sick leave, staff can receive medical assistance to buy medicines and pay for doctors' fees. Full medical assistance is provided for accidents in the line of duty which includes paid leave to recuperate. Long-term loans for other medical expenses such as operations are also available. In this, Saptagram differs from most other NGOs, and this represents a recognition of the distinct gender-related constraints women face in taking care of their own health. Despite these measures more concrete steps need to be taken, such as group policy, to ensure substantial assistance in case of accidents or deaths.

Recognizing that one of the main problems women face is the lack of secure housing and property ownership rights, the organization created loan options for women to build their own houses. This includes loans to make the down-payment for a homestead and to construct the house. Care is taken to ensure that the rights on the land and house are retained by the women.

One of the negative factors of Saptagram's management is that, like many women's organizations, it tried to run the organization the way women run their households, stretching money to its limit and overworking. Thus the burn-out syndrome among fieldstaff is a common phenomenon. Not wishing to lose staff due to this, Saptagram reassigns them to less strenuous tasks. This may include transfer to another project office, or involve staff in a different sector or in a different capacity which requires less fieldwork. This allows staff to recover and at the same time develop interest in other activities. Thus, experienced and specialized staff are retained.

Sexual harassment is a sensitive issue to deal with in any culture, and perhaps more so in one which insists on extremes of sexual modesty. What constitutes sexual harassment, how broadly can it be defined and how can organizations deal with it sensitively? Few organizations have answers to these questions and most prefer to adopt an ostrich-like attitude towards harassment. The survey of NGOs in Bangladesh conducted by Yasmin and Huda (1994) shows that only 4 per cent of the chief executives responding to the survey admitted to the existence of sexual harassment in their organizations. On the other hand, over 20 per cent of the women and men respondents (staff of the same organizations) admitted to either having experienced or having knowledge of harassment at the workplace. Most of the incidents were dealt with surreptitiously or indirectly by the management, resulting in the victim being victimized once more by being made to feel responsible for the incident. Women took extended leave without pay to avoid the harassor, or requested transfers, or resigned from the organization rather than work with the perpetrator. Only once, in the case of rape, was the incident referred to the police. Saptagram has a policy that tries to address this: any action or words which are derogatory towards women are considered as harassment. Once proven guilty, the action against the perpetrator is swift: instant dismissal. This policy helps protect women within the organization in a way that neither their families nor society is able to.

The time factor

Saptagram's organizational culture evolved over a considerable period of time, through trial and error. Saptagram could not have predicted how long it would take to develop the management style and culture that it did. Its approach to staff recruitment and training, creating an atmosphere conducive for women, creating conditions that nurture women's empowerment took almost ten years to achieve. Of the many critical factors to consider when involving women in the various levels of an organization, especially at the managerial level, time is the most ignored. NGOs, verbose in the language of political correctness, talk about and try to implement gender parity in the number of staff. Gender parity in numbers is the evidence used to establish an organization's commitment to include women as staff members, but in many cases it ends at this point. The high turnover of women staff, especially at the managerial level, is attributed to women's problems with adjusting to the work environment. The fact that the organization's patriarchal culture and management style does not provide adequate time for women to adjust or to develop professionally is generally overlooked.

Research in management structures shows that organizations which are managed and staffed by women take up to ten years for staff to develop and specialize (Iannello, 1992). However, development organizations such as NGOs are becoming increasingly time-constrained in their programmatic approach and this trend is further strengthened by donors who also operate under time-bound priorities that are results-oriented. The current focus of management practices in both NGO and donor agencies is likely to deter women from achieving high positions because the time required for the incorporation of women into organizations is rapidly decreasing. Organizations like Saptagram, which are process-oriented and believe that empowerment can be achieved as a possible outcome of that process, will become rare. Numbers and targets for achievement are not top priority in Saptagram's agenda, and therefore the organization is regarded as less efficient than organizations which are more results-oriented.

Participation in the women's movement

Involvement with the women's movement is an indicator of an organization's concern with and commitment to women's issues. Saptagram has involved its staff, at the local level and at the national level, in issues pertinent to women's empowerment. It has participated in movements to reduce and resist violence against women, against fundamentalism and religious edicts which curtail women's rights as human beings; it has worked for the full ratification of CEDAW; it has taken these messages to the villages to mobilize the group members. Group members mobilize for women's legal rights, and participate in rallies and protest marches on issues which are of strategic importance to women. This has become a crucial mechanism in the fight for women's strategic rights in the external environment. As shown in Goetz's contribution to this volume, these are issues and methods rarely aired in more target-achievement-oriented development NGOs.

Decision-making

Decision-making within institutions reflects decision-making practices in society. Hierarchy is difficult to separate from decision-making since it regulates who decides. Besides factors like patriarchy, kinship, and wealth which stratify Bangladeshi society, the concept of deference to elders creates another level of hierarchy. The opinions and views of elders are seldom contradicted or opposed and therefore participatory decision-making, as practised by NGOs, is culturally an alien concept. Hierarchy due to age is of particular relevance to Saptagram as its founder and manager is thirty years older than the rest of the staff. Therefore, the process of developing the decision-making structure which finally evolved in Saptagram was sometimes painful.

Over a period of ten years the structure that Saptagram developed can best be described as consensual and non-conflictual (Iannello, 1992). Several committees exist at different levels which have helped to shift the decision-making responsibilities from an individual to a group. Management by committees takes time but this is a critical contribution to increasing the participation of staff and also to developing an open, transparent and accountable management structure. Each of the committees fulfils a different function. The field-level committees ensure proper implementation of the programme activities with the participation of all the staff. The central-level committee ensures coordination and cooperation among different sectoral programme components, and it reviews and modifies policy. Policies are translated into activities by another committee which directly feeds into the committee at the field level. This means that continuous feedback from the field to the policy level and back takes place, and allows for the involvement of all the staff. Saptagram believes that staff learn about decision-making, management and leadership through practice. This, however, does not necessarily mean that the organization has democratic practices because it still follows a hierarchy based on age.

The majority of NGOs in Bangladesh suffer from the 'charismatic leadership syndrome' where usually the founder of the organization continues to remain head of it. This poses problems of succession and sustainability; passing power to the second tier of leadership seldom takes place peacefully. Transferring power is seen as a sign of weak leadership and not as a sign of a strong institution with democratic features. Women's organizations also suffer from this problem. In Saptagram, the founder of the organization relinquished power for a short period, only to reclaim it without giving the second-level management a chance at leadership. It is ironic that an organization like Saptagram on one hand institutionalized decision-making by women from the grassroots levels to the management level, and yet has difficulty in allowing for participation in leadership functions at the top.

Conclusion

Women's organizations have problems handling leadership and the power that comes with it, like any other organization. However, this should not detract from the many positive features of Saptagram's management approach and organizational culture from the perspective of empowering both women staff and beneficiaries. The factors which make Saptagram one of the largest and most successful women's organizations in Bangladesh lie in its emphasis on addressing women's practical and strategic needs. But these factors need not be restricted only to Saptagram. Its management practices, the working conditions, investment in women both in terms of money and time are factors which can be incorporated into existing management practices because Saptagram has proved that it is possible to run a large and successful programme on principles which are not male-oriented. Saptagram's path has not been smooth nor straight for it had to fight battles on many fronts. But that is what it takes to work with women because one is constantly challenging the values which are repressive of and oppressive to women. While NGOs believe in change through development programmes, essentially most organizations fear to challenge the status quo where it concerns women. It is not possible to work for holistic development without involving women at every level of decision-making and leadership, without looking into women's practical and strategic needs and without believing in women. In the final analysis, it takes courage and commitment to work with women.

13

Women Organizing Women: 'Doing it Backwards and in High Heels'[1]

Sheelagh Stewart and Jill Taylor

Everyone always talks about Fred Astaire; they should remember that Ginger Rogers did it backwards and in high heels. (Unknown)

The metaphor of dance and particularly ballroom dancing is crucial to this chapter because of the clarity and fixed nature of the roles allocated to men and women when ballroom dancing. The idea of fixed roles which are part of a natural order, and the emphasis on the woman's 'following' and complementary (invisible) role, is crucial to the experience of women who enter into the 'public sphere'[2] of work, and therefore crucial to the issue of 'getting institutions right for women'. This chapter will examine how this issue affected women working in the Musasa Project, even though it was a working space occupied only by women, therefore illustrating in addition that even 'women only' jobs are gendered and that even in these environments, women can suffer from a gendered 'dis-ease' with their role.

Our interest in this topic is in the area of indigenous NGOs henceforward referred to as NGOs.[3] Broadly speaking, the question of 'getting institutions right for women in development' in NGOs falls into two areas: getting institutions right for the women who use them or are served by them (through advocacy, lobbying etc.); and getting institutions that work for women right for the women who work in them.[4] We are concerned with the second issue, but the two issues are not unconnected and this is explored.

This chapter has three main purposes: (1) to describe the organizational and structural history of the Musasa Project; (2) to consider the question of gendered 'dis-ease' with certain organizational roles; and (3) to consider how Musasa has scaled-up and what light this sheds on the question of whether and how to scale-up organizations for women.

The Musasa Project, a Zimbabwean NGO, was started to tackle the problems of rape and domestic violence in Zimbabwe. The approach developed by the project has been one of fostering change from within various institutions in Zimbabwean society (Stewart, 1992). As part of this approach we worked closely with various branches of the Zimbabwe Republic Police (ZRP) and officials from the health and legal sectors, for example the Ministry of Justice.

Musasa began as a nine-month participatory training and research project, the objective of which was to establish an appropriate model for a project of this nature in Zimbabwe. The initial membership of the project was ten trainees and the two founders. More than 70 Zimbabweans were interviewed about rape and domestic violence and appropriate ways of dealing with these problems. Interviewees included officials of the Ministry of Women's Affairs, doctors, lawyers and members of the ZRP. This was followed by the 'training exchange' component which consisted of two three-month training courses. The input from the 'training exchange' was crucial in determining the nature of the project. By the beginning of 1989, the project had opted for the name 'Musasa', 'a favourite resting place for tired and weary travellers … a temporary shelter put up by a family while they build a permanent home' (MATCH, 1993: 2). It was established in Harare, had a core membership of 22 women, a paid staff of three and relatively secure funding from international donor agencies. By 1995 the project had a paid staff of seven, including a full-time legal practitioner, a membership of 600, decentralized regional committees and was a household name throughout the country (Musasa, 1993–4).

A Structural History of the Project

The original mandate for the project was to establish, first, whether rape and domestic violence were problems which the women in the project, and the community at large, felt strongly enough about to take action on; and, second, how to take this action – with a shelter (the Women's Aid model) or in some other way.

Phase 1: Is Domestic Violence a Problem?/Hierarchical Leadership for the Time Being

This phase had two distinct components. The first was the training of a group of women who were to comprise the core membership of the project. Two groups of ten women were trained between May 1988 and January 1989. The training was conducted with two aims in mind, the first to acquaint the trainees with theories of rape and domestic violence;[5]

the second to formulate with these women strategies for dealing with the issues in the Zimbabwean context. There was a lack of knowledge on both sides which made this an exciting process in itself. By the end of the training of the first two groups, a number of decisions had been made about how to approach the problem. Decisions were based on three considerations: the Zimbabwean cultural context; strategies that had been successfully employed elsewhere; and strategies which were likely to win backing from donors and the Zimbabwean government.

An example of an issue considered in this light is the question of establishing a shelter, which was considered because it had worked elsewhere. However, the idea seemed to be inappropriate in Zimbabwe at that time. The principle reason was evidence that if a woman was provided with help from outside the family structure the family might withdraw from any future support for her (Taylor and Stewart, 1989). Given the limited resources, it seemed at the time that this type of intervention would be doing more harm than good.[6] Further reasons were that the severity of problems such as unemployment, lack of places for children in school and the lack of any social security support network, felt far too overwhelming to be taken on by Musasa at the time. There was a strong message from donors that a shelter would not receive financial backing and indications from the Zimbabwean government that they would not support the idea.

A number of other conclusions about strategies were reached during these training courses. There was very little discussion about how, organizationally, these strategies were to be implemented. A meeting of the project[7] was convened in January 1989 to discuss implementation. It was assumed by everyone that if funding was available, we would have an 'organization', but ideas about what an organization was differed. This meeting is worth considering in detail as the issues that dominated the meeting have continued to affect the project.

Hierarchy, anarchy, democracy, 'dis-ease' and organizational dissolution

The question of why we had not considered the possible organizational structure is important, partly because it is a useful exercise in this context where we are (mainly) based in the North and considering how to get organizations right for women in less developed countries, and partly because it is a core issue in the project and its future development. The core organizational assumption operating for the project's founders was that if women are to succeed in making fundamental change then they must by definition choose fundamentally different, that is, non-hierarchical, democratic modes for organization. This assumption was so deep-seated – both of us had worked in the women's movement in South Africa – as to be invisible. This meant the meeting began with us presenting how we felt the organization should be structured. The basic idea was a flat structure with various subgroups/centres of responsibility, each with a coordinator. Decisions were to be made on a consensus basis, with difficult decisions put to a vote requiring a two-thirds majority. The discussion about this way of organizing was, however, extremely negative. Flat structures were equated with having no structure at all whilst extreme unease was expressed at the idea that there was no one individual to take absolute responsibility. The result was that this option was rejected by a large majority.

A hierarchical structure was opted for with a clear delineation of authority and roles. Where we had envisaged the possibility of staff and members being able to work in a number of different roles, the membership was uneasy with this idea and generally uneasy with any suggestion of unclear roles. This was particularly marked in the area of management where members, and later staff, emphasized the need for extremely clearly defined positions and responsibilities in conjunction with clearly defined hierarchies. The view was expressed a number of times that 'those who are not professionals cannot do these things' – meaning management. (Another possible reading of this was that only men could do these sorts of things, that it was the wrong environment for women – arguably an internalization of the notion that women did not belong there, they belonged at home.) The project's ambivalent beginnings are reflected in its early terminology – for example, the Director was called the 'chief coordinator' in the early days of the project (Taylor and Stewart, 1989).

Phase 2: Hierarchies and High Finance

Phase 2 of the project began in February 1989, with the training of a third group of ten members, the commencement of the counselling service, and the beginning of a formal working relationship with the Zimbabwe Republic Police which remains a cornerstone of the work done by Musasa (Taylor and Stewart, 1989; Taylor and Stewart, 1992; Stewart, 1992; Musasa, 1993–94; Stewart, 1995). The way the project functioned in Phase 2 was a mix of hierarchical and non-hierarchical models; there were subgroups, but also subgroup 'chiefs'. The early months of the project's work were marked by subgroups who needed both very clearly defined activities and a clear indication of the structure of who was in charge within the subgroups. One concern voiced by some members during this phase of the project was whether we could run the project without men. This particular concern was voiced less often as time passed.

This phase was also marked by increasing interest and financial commitment from international donors.[8] The increasing impact of donors is reflected in the gradual movement to standard managerial labels for project positions, for example, Director, Administrator, etc. As the amount of money flowing through Musasa increased, so the pressure for us to have clearly delimited roles mounted. Pressure came from two sides: first, the trend which had been evident in the beginning for project members to feel uneasy with unclear roles became more evident; second, the donors demanded accountability from one person, the Director, who had to sign all project grants.

The increasing role played by money in the organization also resulted in a squeeze on less well educated women in the project (Stewart, 1995). This squeeze was expressed overtly by some members, as being good for the project as 'professional women were needed to do the project work'. In some instances this may have been true – some types of work, particularly work with donors (though not all donors), require professionals of various types. Nevertheless, this emphasis on educational requirements is problematic, especially as in Zimbabwe education was not generally available for any black person until 1980, let alone for black women. What is also problematic about this phase is that the pressure for financial accountability resulted in an organization headed, not facilitated, by white women in post-independence Zimbabwe. Given the context and the role of racism and colonialism in Zimbabwe's history, our politics and intentions are irrelevant. What is relevant is the recreation of the possibility of domination by race, and linked structural issues such as access to education and money.[9]

More generally this illustrates the conservative nature of aid structures and raises questions about whether and how it is possible to empower women in this context. Another issue is that the way money is donated by Northern donors often has the effect of pushing projects into standard (hierarchical) organizational patterns.

Organizational ease

More interesting, however, is to consider the one subgroup in the project where the members' dis-ease with structures and discomfort with taking a position of power did not manifest itself. This was the counselling component of the project. Members of the project were comfortable with flexible counselling roles and flexible management roles in this aspect of the project. In fact it was the only area of the project where members actually argued strongly for the need for flexibility, and roles which were not clearly defined. In terms of the way the project was described to people outside the project, counselling was often portrayed by members as the most important activity of the project. This was not 'objectively' accurate. In fact public education and the educational work with the Zimbabwe Republic Police was the primary activity, and if impact is measured quantitatively, public education and the work with the ZRP clearly had the most impact on the largest number of people.

Public education and work with the ZRP was not, however, work with which the majority of project members felt comfortable. We asked the then Deputy Director why this was and her answer is illuminating. 'Oh everyone here is used to counselling, we do it all the time at home – it is what women do. We feel we can work with other women but it is difficult to work with men and to do men's work – that's why everyone wants to know exactly what to do.'[10] The issue of flat, non-hierarchical structures was discussed again recently with the current Director of Musasa, who commented that 'the women in the project were just not ready for those structures at that time'.[11]

'It's what women do'/'Backwards and in high heels'

Biology is destiny, it would seem, in the workplace as well as everywhere else. Has the pervasive nature of continuous training only for the private sphere and a perhaps Jungian memory of increased danger in 'public', rendered us uneasy with the world 'out' there? Similar themes have long been explored in feminist writing on education and affirmative action. Kristen Golden, writing in an article called 'What Do Girls See?' comments:

> What *do* girls see? Less opportunity in the workplace for women than for men and greater responsibility in the home, the degradation of women in the media, an absence of girls and women in school curricula, conflicting messages about female sexuality, the prevalence of racism and violence and adults enforcing gender roles. (Golden, 1994: 53)

More particularly, Juliet Mitchell writing in *Woman's Estate* comments:

> Women's absence from the critical sector of production historically, of course, has been caused not just by their physical weakness in a context of coercion – but also by their role in reproduction. Maternity necessitates withdrawals from work, but this is not a decisive phenomenon. It is rather women's role in reproduction which has become, in capitalist society at least, the spiritual 'complement' of men's role in production. Bearing children, bringing them up, and maintaining the home – these form the core of women's natural vocation, in

this ideology. This belief has attained great force because of the seeming universality of the family as a human institution. (Mitchell, 1971: 106)

In Zimbabwe the clearly demarcated position of the sexes is exacerbated by the extra level of discrimination faced by black women under the colonialist regime (Mitchell, 1971: 103; Gaidzanwa, 1993). The underlying problem is the position of women in Zimbabwean society; the actual problem confronting policy-makers is women's internalization of the belief in their inferiority outside the role assigned to them. Obviously women's perception of their position in society affects the way they will operate in an organizational context.

The general conclusion one can draw from this is that 'getting organizations right for women' in cultures where there are very strictly defined roles for men and women is complex. One can propose interventions which aim to boost women's confidence, but these take time and may have little effect.

Another option is to accept that in countries where gender roles are rigid this dis-ease with management may well apply, and to work towards models of organization which can accommodate this to a certain extent while still providing space for women to learn management skills. In this connection, we turn now to consider the third 'scaling-up' phase of Musasa, and how it was accomplished, as a possible model for accommodating both the need to get larger without losing the input of those women who in many ways are closest to the core of the problem and at the same time keeping close to the needs and concerns of the constituency.

Phase 3: 'Scaling-up'

'Scaling-up' in the NGO world is rapidly becoming one of those vogue terms that is never really discussed or analysed. It is just something that Southern NGOs must do once they have reached a certain point in their development. Alan Clark, one of the most commonly quoted authors on the issue of scaling-up, illustrates this clearly in his book *Democratizing Development* (1992). Clark begins his chapter on scaling-up with the statement that 'An NGO typically starts a programme in a particular country to respond to a specific need' (1992: 73). He continues that having worked in the area of this specific need 'successfully',

> The inevitable question following success is, 'How can we do more?' Only a complacent organization would be content to continue with the same job in perpetuity when it is self-evident that its contribution is not more than a drop in the ocean, however excellent a drop it may be.

Putting aside all questions of whether an organization which chooses to carry on doing a good job on a small scale is 'complacent' and whether growth is in fact the answer, it is clear that this statement dictates looking for the route to scaling-up in certain areas. Increased professionalization is one of these areas; 'seeking to influence rather than do' (Clark, 1992: 74) is another.

There are a number of potential dangers in this for women. The first is the question of who are the professionals in a world where women have systematically been denied access to the education which qualifies them for the label 'professional'. The second danger in many ways is a core issue in the whole question of 'getting organizations right for women in development'. It is the question of how to create organizations which can at one and the same time balance a number of complex and often contradictory needs, most importantly a balance between getting bigger and more formal and keeping close to the constituency.

Brown and Covey's 1987 article on their comparative study of four Private Development Agencies (PDAs)[12] is an excellent consideration of this issue. The study had three aims: (1) to consider whether there were characteristics which distinguished PDAs from other organizations; (2) to ask if such organizations posed specific management problems; and (3) to design management strategies which take account of differences found in the study.

In answering the question about how PDAs should be organized, the authors point out that tensions inevitably arise from the shift to more bureaucratic organization (implied by Clarke's definition of scaling-up), but furthermore, this method of organizing was widely perceived by staff and volunteers in the organizations as indistinguishable from a move away from the value-base. This perception – that a way of organizing is not politically neutral but may change the value-base of the organization – is crucial when considering the question of scaling-up and still getting institutions right for women.

Perhaps even more importantly, it is a crucial issue in the question of scaling-up and still maintaining effective contact with the target constituency of the organization. The question of NGOs' accountability to their target constituencies is well-considered in the literature,[13] but practical strategies for ensuring that the target groups do not get lost when the organization expands are thin on the ground. As women represent a particularly disempowered group, the question becomes even more crucial. The way in which the Musasa Project has scaled up is one possible model for women's organizations which have a combination service provision and advocacy role. The next section will consider how this has been done without compromising accountability.

The scaling-up process

Expansion

By the end of 1991, Musasa was well established in Harare, and was doing extensive education work in Bulawayo, though it did not have a separate presence there. The relationship with the ZRP was also well established. However, a recurring problem was that women in remote rural areas had little access to the services of the project.

Faced with the need to reach women in these areas, the project had to choose between trying to expand itself or using the relationship with the police with all the advantages of the logistical capability of a state-funded organization with an extensive network of outposts. The second choice had obvious advantages, but also problems in that the ZRP's commitment to the cause was not guaranteed. Local organizations were needed to work with the police on an ongoing basis. The project therefore set itself up as a membership subscription organization and regional committees were established in all nine administrative districts of the country. Each committee consisted of a number of volunteer members familiar with the area and well known enough to have credibility both with the local population and with the police. In many instances this meant that committee members were women who were senior in their community, rather than younger professionals. These committees operate in conjunction with regional police representatives to deal with problems, counselling and other initiatives in their areas. Although the committees work with the Harare office and meet regularly with them, they are not formally employed and enjoy autonomy in their own areas. The Harare office has only taken on four extra staff since the project was established. The expansion through networking with the police and regional committees has meant that the coverage of the project has increased exponentially, whilst the budget has expanded only to accommodate the costs of three extra staff at head office.

Impact on accountability

Broadly speaking, disadvantaged groups have only two options in a power game, either to get their voices heard, or to exit if their voices remain unheard. Exit is not a realistic option where there is only one source of help, that is, only one organization dealing with violence against women. The structure of Musasa has therefore worked to reinforce the voice of the women who need the project in the following ways:

- The regional committees are aware of particular issues in their areas and can adjust the way they operate in accordance with these requirements. In terms of maintaining contact with the target group this is important, as is the presence of Musasa-trained police men and women in police stations all over the country.

- The budget has been kept low; the project has relatively modest financial requirements and therefore can choose or reject donors who make unreasonable demands.
- The regional committees and the network of members are powerful enough in the structure to demand that the project stays closely in touch with its constituency. The importance of activities apart from fundraising is continuously stressed through contact with the constituency as is the need for initiatives such as a shelter. More broadly, because needs other than donor needs are constantly being highlighted, donor needs, and therefore the type of staff who can service them (well-educated and male), do not get prioritized at the expense of other staff with other skills.
- There is a triangular power relationship within the overall power structure: the head office, the police and the regional committees all wield considerable power, and therefore create a situation where the staff and managers are continually seeking to balance this power.

Conclusion

There are particular problems in getting Southern NGOs 'right' for the women who work in them, especially for disempowered non-professional women. One of the most difficult problems is the contradiction between the organizational needs of a project handling large amounts of money, and a project which is trying to keep contact with and accountability to extremely disempowered women. One of the principal issues therefore is ensuring a balance between professionals and women who can maintain easy contact with beneficiaries. Another important issue is dealing somehow with the 'dis-ease' that women feel with certain organizational roles they are asked to play in the context of an organization dealing with the increasing complexity of managing the requirements of funders and the (often hostile) wider environment.

Notes

1. This chapter first appeared in 'Getting Institutions Right for Women in Development', *IDS Bulletin*, vol. 26, no. 3, July 1995.

2. For a general discussion of the issue of the 'private' and 'public' spheres, see Elshtain, 1981.

3. We have chosen in this paper to refer to indigenous NGOs as NGOs because of our concern with language that represents Northern NGOs as NGOs

and therefore the norm, whilst NGOs situated elsewhere are referred to as indigenous (I)NGOs, Southern NGOs or by some other delimiter, representing them not only as different but different from the 'norm'.

4. Of course the third question is that of getting mixed institutions right for the women that work in them, an issue discussed in Rao and Kelleher's chapter.

5. These theories were largely derived from similar movements in the developed world, but work conducted by Dr Christine Jones in Papua New Guinea was crucial in the early stages as it dealt with issues such as bridewealth, which are important for understanding and strategizing around the issue in Zimbabwe. (Report of the International Women's Aid Conference, 1989: 61.)

6. Musasa has taken a recent decision to open a shelter on the basis that the general shift in public opinion on domestic violence is such as to militate against the withdrawal of support from the family. Furthermore the 'nowhere to go if the source of the trouble is one's partner' problem is as intransigent in Zimbabwe as it is anywhere else.

7. Known at this stage as 'The Counselling and Research Project on Violence Against Women'.

8. Seed funding for the pilot project came from NORAD. The Oak Foundation was the first donor to Musasa, and was followed by NORAD, SIDA, CIDA and the Ford Foundation.

9. This raises a whole series of questions and issues about the politics and functioning of aid which are beyond the scope of this chapter, but crucial to the consideration of getting institutions right for women. In particular the question of whether and how the functioning of aid/money in development results in the replication of oppressive structures (race in this instance being a glaring example), needs close examination.

10. Personal conversation with Priscilla Mudzovera, New York, 1990.

11. Personal conversation with Eunice Njovana, Zimbabwe, September 1994.

12. For the purposes of this chapter, this term is used interchangeably with the term 'NGO'.

13. See for example, de Coninck, 1991; DGIS/NOVIB, 1988; DGIS/NOVIB, 1990; DGIS/NOVIB, 1993; Edwards, 1992; Fowler, 1988; Lecompte, 1986; and Muir, 1990.

Bibliography

Acker, J. (1992) 'From Sex Rules to Gendered Institutions', *Contemporary Sociology*, vol. 21, no. 5.

Ackerly, B. (1994) 'Empowerment by Design,' Report of Fulbright research.

Ackerly, B. (1995) 'Testing the Tools of Development: Credit Programs, Loan Involvement, and Women's Empowerment,' *IDS Bulletin*, vol. 26, no. 3, Sussex, July.

Afshar, H. (ed.) (1987) *Women, State, and Ideology*, SUNY Press, New York.

Agnihotri, I. and V. Mazumdar (1995) 'Changing Terms of Political Discourse: Women's Movement in India, 1970s–1990s', *Economic and Political Weekly*, vol. XXX, no. 29, 22 July, pp. 1869–78.

Akerkar, S. (1995) 'Theory and Practice of Women's Movement in India: A Discourse Analysis', *Economic and Political Weekly*, vol. XXX, no. 27, 29 April, pp. WS-2–WS-22.

ALCOM (1992) *News*, no. 5, Harare.

Allen J. (n.d.) 'Dependent Males: The Unequal Division of Labour in Mabumba Households', ARPT (Luapula) Labour Study Report, no. 1.

Alvarez, S. (1989) 'Politicising Gender and Engendering Democracy' in A. Stepan, ed., *Democratising Brazil: Problems of Transition and Consolidation*, Oxford University Press, Oxford.

Alvarez, S. (1990) *Engendering Democracy in Brazil: Women's Movements in Transition Politics*, Princeton University Press, Princeton, NJ.

Angelo, G. (1990) Nuevos Espacios y Nuevas Prácticas de Mujeres en una Situación de Crisis: Hacia el Surgiemiento y Consolidación de un Movimiento de Mujeres. El Caso de Chile, *Cuadernos de la Morada*, Santiago.

Ardener, E. (1975) 'Belief and the Problem of Women', in S. Ardener, ed., *Perceiving Women*, Malaby Press, London, pp. 1–15.

Armstrong, A. and W. Ncube (1987) *Women and Law in Southern Africa*, Zimbabwe Publishing House, Harare.

Arteaga, A. (1988) 'Politicización de lo Privado y Subversión del Cotidiano', in CEM, *Mundo de Mujer: Continuidad y Cambio*, Centro de Estudios de la Mujer, Santiago.

Baden, S. and A.M. Goetz (1997) 'Who Needs [Sex] When You Can Have [Gender]? Conflicting Discourses on Gender at Beijing', *Feminist Review*.

Bardhan, K. (1983) 'Economic Growth, Poverty, and Rural Labour Markets in India: A Survey of Research', *Working Paper 54*, Rural Employment Policy Research Programme, ILO.

Barroso, C. (1991) 'The Women's Movement, the State and Health Policies in Brazil' in G.L. Nijeholt, ed., *Towards Women's Strategies in the 1990s: Challenging Government and the State*, Macmillan, London.

Bennis, W., K. Benne, and R. Chin (1968) *The Planning of Change*, 2nd edn, Holt Rinehart and Winston, New York.

Berger, I. and C. Robertson (eds) (1986) *Women and Class in Africa*, Africana Publishing, New York.

Bierschenk, T. (1988) 'Development Projects as Arenas of Negotiation for Strategic Groups: A Case Study from Benin', *Sociologia Ruralis*, vol. XXVIII, no. 2/3, pp. 146–60.

Binks, M. (1994) 'Violence Against Women', *Taurai, Speak Out, Khulumani*, vol. 9, no. 3, September.

Blanchet, T. (1984) *Women, Pollution and Marginality: Meanings and Rituals of Birth in Rural Bangladesh*, University Press, Dhaka.

Blanchet, T. (1991) 'Maternal Health in Rural Bangladesh: An Anthropological Study of Maternal Nutrition and Birth Practices in Nasirnagar, Bangladesh', Save the Children, Dhaka.

Block, F. (ed.) (1987) *Revising State Theory: Essays in Politics and Postindustrialism*, Temple, Philadelphia.

La Boletina (n.d.) magazine of MEMCH83, no. 1, Nueva Epoca.

Boserup, E. (1970) *Women's Role in Economic Development*, George Allen & Unwin, London.

Bratton, M. and G. Hyden (eds) (1992) *Governance and Politics in Africa*, Lynne Rienner, Boulder, CO.

Brett, E.A. (1993) 'Voluntary Agencies as Development Organizations: Theorizing the Problem of Efficiency and Accountability', *Development and Change*, vol. 24, pp. 269–303.

Brown, David L. and J. Covey (1987) *Organising and Managing Private Development Agencies: A Comparative Analysis*, Institution for Social and Policy Studies, Yale University.

Brown, W. (1992) 'Finding the Man in the State', *Feminist Studies*, vol. 18, no. 1.

Butegwa, F. (1993) 'Limitations of the Human Rights Framework' in Schuler, M., ed., *Claiming Our Place: Working the Human Rights System to Women's Advantage*, Institute for Women, Law and Development, Washington DC.

Buvinic, M. (1983) 'Women's Issues in Third World Poverty: A Policy Analysis' in Buvinic, Lycette and McGreevey, eds, *Women and Poverty in the Third World*, Johns Hopkins University Press, Baltimore, MD, pp. 14–31.

Buvinic, M. (1985) 'Projects for Women in The Third World: Explaining Their Misbehaviour', *World Development*, vol. 14, no. 5, pp. 653–64.

Buvinic, M. (1989) 'Investing in Poor Women: The Psychology of Donor Support', in *World Development*, vol. 17, no. 7, pp. 1045–57.

Chabal, P. (ed.) (1986) *Political Domination in Africa: Reflections of the Limits of Power*, Cambridge University Press, Cambridge.

Charlton, S.E. (1984) *Women in Third World Development*, Westview Press, Boulder, CO.

Charlton, S.E., Jana Everett and Kathleen Staudt (eds) (1989) *Women, the State and Development*, State University of New York Press, Albany, NY.

Chattopadhyaya, K. (1983) *Indian Women's Battle for Freedom*, Abhinav Press, New Delhi.

Chen, M. (1983) *A Quiet Revolution*, Schenkman, Cambridge, MA.

Chhachhi, A. and R. Pittin (1991) 'Multiple Identities, Multiple Strategies: Confronting State, Capital and Patriarchy', paper presented at the International Workshop on Women Organizing in the Process of Industrialization, 15–26 September, Institute of Social Studies, The Hague.

Chirume, L. (1989) 'A Study of the Phenomenon of Wife Beating: Zimbabwe as a Case Study', unpublished LlB thesis, University of Zimbabwe.

Chowdhury, Najma, and Barbara J. Nelson, with K. Carver, N. Johnson, and P O'Loughlin (1994) 'Redefining Politics: Patterns of Women's Political Engagement from a Global Perspective', in B. Nelson and N. Chowdhury, eds, *Women and Politics Worldwide*, Yale University Press, New Haven, CT.

Clark, J. (1992) *Democratizing Development: The Role of Voluntary Organisations*, Kumarian Press, West Hartford, CT.

Cockburn, Cynthia (1983) *Brothers. Male Dominance and Technological Change*, Pluto Press, London.

Coleman, G. (1991) *Investigating Organisations: A Feminist Approach*, SAUS Publications, Bristol.

Connell, R.W. (1987) *Gender and Power*, Polity Press, Cambridge.

Crehan K. and A. van Oppen (1988) 'Understandings of Development: An Arena of Struggle', *Sociologia Ruralis* XXVIII.

CWDS (Centre for Women's Development Studies) (1994) *Confronting Myriad Oppressions: The Western Regional Experience*, CWDS, New Delhi.

CWDS (1995) *Towards Beijing: A Perspective from the Indian Women's Movement*, CWDS, New Delhi.

Dahlerup, Drude (1988) 'From a Small to a Large Minority: Women in Scandinavian Politics', *Scandinavian Political Studies*, vol. 11, no. 4, pp. 275–98.

de Coninck, J. (1991) *Evaluating the Impact of NGOs in Rural Poverty Alleviation, Uganda Country Study*, ODI, London.

del Rosario, V.O. (1987) 'Women and Labour Laws in the Philippines: Problems and Strategies', MA Women and Development synthesizing exercise paper, Institute of Social Studies, The Hague.

del Rosario, V.O. (1994) 'Lifting the Smoke Screen: Dynamics of Mail-Order Bride Migration from the Philippines', PhD thesis, Institute of Social Studies, The Hague.

Department of Labor and Employment (1993) 'Highlights: First Report in Compliance to R.A. 7192', Department of Labor and Employment, Manila.

DGIS/NOVIB (1988) *'Big and Still Beautiful': Enquiry into the Efficiency and Effectiveness of Three Big NGO's (BINGOs) in South Asia'*, DGIS/NOVIB, The Hague.

DGIS/NOVIB (1990) *Bigger NG(D)Os in East and Southern Africa: An Analysis of Constraints and Effects of Growth*, DGIS/NOVIB, The Hague.

DGIS/NOVIB (1993) *Big NGDOs in Latin America: Case Studies in Peru and Bolivia*, DGIS/NOVIB, The Hague.

Diamond, I. and N. Harstock (1981) 'Beyond Interests in Politics: A Comment on Virginia Sapiro's "When are interests interesting?"', *American Political Science Review*, vol. 75, no. 3.

Dietz, M. (n.d.) 'Context is All: Feminism and Theories of Citizenship', in C. Mouffe, ed., *Dimensions of Radical Democracy*, Verso, London.

DWCD (Department of Women and Child Development) (1988) *National Perspective*

Plan for Women 1988–2000, Delhi.

Edwards, M. and D. Hulme (eds) (1992) *Making a Difference, NGOs and Development in a Changing World*, Earthscan, London.

Ehlstain, J.B. (1974) 'Moral Woman and Immoral Man: A Consideration of the Public–Private Split and its Political Ramifications', *Politics and Society*, vol. 4, no. 4.

Elshtain, J. (1981) *Public Man, Private Woman*, Harvard University Press, Cambridge, MA.

Elson, Diane (1994) 'Micro, Meso, Macro: Gender and Economic Analysis in the Context of Policy Reform', in I. Bakker, ed., *The Strategic Silence: Gender and Economic Policy*, Zed Books, London.

Evans, Alison (1993) '"Contracted-Out": Some Reflections on Gender, Power, and Agrarian Institutions', *IDS Bulletin*, vol. 24, July.

Evans, P., D. Rueschemeyer and T. Skocpol (1985) *Bringing the State Back In*, Cambridge University Press, Cambridge.

FAO (1987) *Women in Aquaculture: Proceedings of the ADCP/NORAD Workshop on Women in Aquaculture*, 13–16 April 1987, FAO, Rome.

FAO (1993) *Enhancement of the Role of Women in Inland Fisheries and Aquaculture Development Project. Project Findings and Recommendations*, FAO, Rome.

Fatton, R. (1989) 'Gender, Class and State in Africa', in J. Parpart and K. Staudt, eds, *Women and the State in Africa*, Lynne Rienner Publishers, Boulder, CO and London, pp. 47–68.

Feministas Autonomas (1996) Interview with members of the group, Santiago, January.

Ferguson J. (1990) *The Anti-Politics Machine: Development, Depoliticization and Bureaucratic State Power in Lesotho*, Cambridge University Press, Cambridge.

Ferguson, Kathy (1984) *The Feminist Case Against Bureaucracy*, Temple University Press, Philadelphia.

Foucault, Michel (1972) *The Archaeology of Knowledge*, Pantheon, New York.

Fowler, Alan (1988) 'Non-Governmental Organisations in Africa: Achieving Comparative Advantage in Relief and Micro-development', *IDS Discussion Paper* 249, Sussex.

Fowler, A. (1990) 'Doing it Better? Where and How NGOs have a Comparative Advantage in Facilitating Development', *AERDD Bulletin* 28.

Fraser, Nancy (1989) *Unruly Practices: Power, Discourse, and Gender in Contemporary Social Theory*, Polity Press, Cambridge

Garréton, A.M. (1989) 'Popular Mobilization and the Military Regime in Chile: The Complexities of the Invisible Transition', in S. Eckstein, ed., *Power and Popular Protest*, University of California Press, Berkeley.

Giddens, A. (1984) *The Constitution of Society: Outline of the Theory of Structuration*, Polity Press, Cambridge.

Giddens, A. (1986) *Sociology: A Brief but Critical Introduction*, Macmillan, London.

Goetz, Anne Marie (1991) 'Feminism and the Claim to Know: Contradictions in Feminist Approaches to Women in Development', in Rebecca Grant and Kathleen Newland, eds, *Gender and International Relations*, Indiana University Press, Bloomington.

Goetz, Anne Marie (1992) 'Gender and Administration', *IDS Bulletin*, vol. 23, no. 1, pp. 6–17.

Goetz, Anne Marie (1994a) 'The Politics of Integrating Gender to State Development Processes', mimeo, UNRISD, Geneva.

Goetz, Anne Marie (1994b) 'From Feminist Knowledge to Data For Development: The Bureaucratic Management of Information on Women and Development', *IDS Bulletin*, vol. 25, no. 2, pp. 27–36.

Goetz, Anne Marie and Rina Sen Gupta (1995) 'Women's Leadership in Rural Credit Programmes in Bangladesh', unpublished research report of workshop at Savar, January.

Goetz, Anne Marie and Rina Sen Gupta (1996) 'Who Takes the Credit? Gender, Power, and Control over Loan Use in Rural Credit Programmes in Bangladesh', *World Development*, vol. 24, no. 1, January.

Goetz, Anne Marie (1996) 'Dis/Organising Gender: Women Development Agents in State and NGO Poverty-Reduction Programmes in Bangladesh', in Shirin Rai and Geraldine Lievesley, *Women and the State: International Perspectives*, Taylor and Francis, London.

Golden, K. (1994) 'What Do Girls See?' *Ms. Magazine* no. IV, p. 53.

Gordon, Linda (ed.) (1994) *Women, the State, and Welfare*, University of Wisconsin Press, Wisconsin.

Gordon, S. (1985) *Ladies in Limbo: The Fate of Women's Bureaux*, Commonwealth Secretariat, Human Resources Group – Women and Development Programme, London.

Grant, Rebecca and Kathleen Newland (eds) (1991) *Gender and International Relations*, Open University Press, Milton Keynes; Indiana University Press, Bloomington.

Grindle, Merilee (ed.) (1980) *Politics and Policy Implementation in the Third World*, Princeton University Press, Princeton, NJ.

Hart, Gillian (1991) 'Engendering Everyday Resistance: Gender, Patronage, and Production Politics in Rural Malysia', *Journal of Peasant Studies*, vol. 19, no. 1.

Hearn, Jeff, D. Sheppard, P. Tancred-Sheriff and G. Burrell (eds) (1989) *The Sexuality of Organisation*, Sage, London.

Heath, C. (1996) 'Hidden Currencies: Women, Weaving and Income Generation in Oman', PhD thesis submitted to the School of Development Studies, University of East Anglia, Norwich.

Heaver, Richard (1982) 'Bureaucratic Politics and Incentives in the Management of Rural Development', *World Bank Staff Working Paper*, no. 537, World Bank, Washington, DC.

Hirschman, Albert O. (1970) *Exit, Voice, and Loyalty*, Harvard University Press, Cambridge, MA.

Hobsbawm, E. and T. Ranger (eds) (1983) *The Invention of Tradition*, Cambridge University Press, Cambridge.

Hoskyns, C. and S. Rai (1996) 'Gender, Class and Representation: India and the European Union', paper presented at the 1996 Political Studies Association conference, Glasgow, 10 April.

Iannello, Kathleen P. (1992) *Decisions without Hierarchy: Feminist Interventions in Organization Theory and Practice*, Routledge, New York.

Jackson, C. (1985) *The Kano River Irrigation Project*, Women's Roles and Gender Differences in Development: Cases for Planners, Kumarian Press, West Hartford, CT.

Jackson, C. (1996) 'Rescuing Gender from the Poverty Trap', *World Development*, vol. 24, no. 3.

Jaquette, Jane (1990) 'Gender and Justice in Economic Development', in Irene Tinker, ed., *Persistent Inequalities: Women and World Development*, Oxford University Press, Oxford.

Jaquette, Jane, and K. Staudt (1988) 'Politics, Population, and Gender: A Feminist Analysis of US Population Policy in the Third World', in K.B. Jones and A.K. Jonasdottir, eds, *The Political Interests of Gender*, Sage, London.

Jeffries, R. (1993) 'The State, Structural Adjustment and Good Government In Africa,' *Journal of Commonwealth and Comparative Politics*, vol 31, no. 1, pp. 20–35.

Jonasdottir, A.K. (1988) 'On the Concept of Interest, Women's Interests, and the Limitations of Interest Theory', in K.B. Jones and A.K. Jonasdottir, eds, *The Political Interests of Gender*, Sage, London.

Jones, K.B. and Jonasdottir, A.K. (eds) (1988) *The Political Interests of Gender*, Sage, London.

Joshi, P. (1989) *Gandhi on Women*, Navjivan Press, New Delhi.

Kabeer, N. (1994) *Reversed Realities: Gender Hierarchies in Development Thought*, Verso, London.

Kandiyoti, Deniz (1988) *Women and Rural Development Policies: The Changing Agenda*, IDS Discussion Paper 244, Sussex.

Kanter, Rosabeth Moss (1977) *Men and Women of the Corporation*, Basic Books, New York.

Kardam, Nüket (1987) 'Social Theory and Women in Development Policy', *Women & Politics*, vol. 7, no. 4, Winter.

Kardam, Nüket (1991) *Bringing Women In: Women's Issues in International Development Programs*, Lynne Rienner, Boulder, CO.

Kardam, Nüket (1992) 'Donor Agency Priorities and Developing Country Contexts: The Case of Vocational Education Projects in Turkey', paper prepared for the Middle East Studies Association annual meeting, 28–31 October, Portland, Oregon.

Kardam, Nüket (1993) 'Development Approaches and the Role of Policy Advocacy: the Case of the World Bank', *World Development*, vol. 21, no. 11.

Kardam, Nüket (1994) 'The State, Gender Policy and Social Change: An Analysis from Turkey', in Gay Young and Bette Dickerson, eds, *Color, Class and Country: Experiences of Gender*, Zed Books, London.

Khan, M.R. (1993) 'BRAC's "Suruchi" Restaurants: An Assessment,' mimeo, Dhaka.

Kirkwood, J. (1990) *Ser Política en Chile. Los Nudos de la Sabiduría Feminista*, Editorial Cuarto Propio, Santiago.

Korten, David, (1987) 'Third Generation NGO Strategies: A Key to People Centered Development', *World Development*, vol. 15, Autumn.

Korten, David, (1990) *Getting to the 21st Century: Voluntary Action and the Global Agenda*, Kumarian Press, West Hartford, CT.

Krasner, Stephen, (1985) *Structural Conflict: The Third World Against Global Liberalism*, University of California Press, Berkeley.

Kumar, Radha (1989) 'Contemporary Indian Feminism', *Feminist Review*, no. 3, Autumn, pp. 20–29.

Kymlicka, W. (1989) *Liberalism, Community, and Culture*, Clarendon Press, Oxford.

Kymlicka, W. (1995) *Multicultural Citizenship*, Oxford University Press, Oxford.

Lecompte, B. (1986) *Project Aid: Limitations and Alternatives*, OECD, Paris.

Lappin, Jane E. (1989) 'A Qualitative Assessment of Four Rural Women's Development Programs', unpublished report for CIDA, Dhaka.

Lewis, B. (1984) 'The Impact of Development Policies on Women', in M.J. Hay and S. Stichter, eds, *African Women South of the Sahara*, Longman, London.

Liddle, J. and R. Joshi (1986) *Daughters of Independence*, Kali for Women, New Delhi.

Lipsky, Michael (1980) *Street-Level Bureaucracy: Dilemmas of the Individual in Public Services*, Russell Sage Foundation, New York.

Locke, J. (1960) *Two Treatises of Government*, ed. P. Laslett, Cambridge University Press, Cambridge.

Long N. and J.D. van der Ploeg (1989) 'Demythologizing Planned Intervention: An Actor's Perspective', *Sociologia Ruralis*, vol. XXIX, no. 3/4, pp. 226–49.

Macpherson, C.B. (1962) *The Political Theory of Possessive Individualism*, Oxford University Press, Oxford.

Macpherson, C.B. (1965) *The Real World of Democracy*, CBC Enterprises, Toronto.

Macaulay, F. (1995) 'Gender Relations and the Democratization of Local Politics in the Transition to Democracy in Brazil and Chile', paper presented to the PSA annual conference, York.

MATCH (1993) *End to Violence Against Women: African Women's Initiatives*, ZESA Training Centre, Musasa Project, Harare, Zimbabwe.

Matear, A. (1993) 'SERNAM: Women and the Process of Democratic Transition in Chile 1990–93', paper presented to Society of Latin American Studies conference, Manchester.

Matienzo, Rodolfo M. (1993) 'Loan Profitability and Impact in the RD-12 Project', Canadian Resource Team – RD-12, Dhaka, March.

Mbozi E. (1991) 'Integration of Gender Issues into Fish Farming in Chibote, Zambia', ALCOM Field Document, no. 17.

Meursing C. et. al. (1993) *Child Sexual Abuse in Matabeleland*, Matabeleland Aids Council, Bulawayo.

Meyer, C. (1992a) 'A Step Back as Donors Shift Institution Building from the Public to the "Private" Sector', *World Development*, vol. 20, no. 8, p. 1115.

Meyer, C. (1992b) 'The Irony of Donor Efforts to Build Institutions: A Case Study from the Dominican Republic', *Journal of Institutional and Theoretical Economics*, no. 148, p. 628.

Mies, Maria (1986) *Patriarchy and Accumulation on a World Scale*, Zed Books, London.

Migdal, Joel, (1988) *Strong Societies and Weak States*, Princeton University Press, Princeton, NJ.

Miller, J.B. (1976) *Towards a New Psychology of Women*, Beacon Press, Boston, MA.

Mitchell, J. (1971) *Woman's Estate*, Pelican, Harmondsworth.

Molina, N. (1989) 'Propuestas Políticas y Orientaciones de Cambio en la Situación de la Mujer', in M.A. Garréton, ed., *Propuestas Políticas y Demandas Sociales*, vol. 3, FLACSO, Santiago.

Molina, N. (1990) 'El Estado y las Mujeres: una Relación Difícil', in ISIS, *Transiciones: Mujeres en los Procesos Democráticos*, ISIS Internacional, Santiago.

Molyneux M. (1985) 'Mobilization without Emancipation? Women's Interests, State and Revolution in Nicaragua', *Feminist Studies*, vol. 11, no. 2, pp. 227–54.

Montgomery, J.D. (1988) *Bureaucrats and People: Grassroots Participation and Third World Development*, Johns Hopkins University Press, Baltimore, MD.

Montecino, S. and J. Rossetti (eds) (1990) *Tramas para un Nuevo Destino: Propuestas de la Concertación de Mujeres por la Democracia*, n.p., Santiago.

Moore, H. and M. Vaughan (1994) *Cutting Down Trees: Gender, Nutrition and Agricultural Change in the Northern Province of Zambia, 1890–1990*, James Currey, London.

Moore, Mick (1992) 'Competition and Pluralism in Public Bureaucracies', *IDS Bulletin*, vol. 23, no. 4.

Moser, C. (1989) 'Gender Planning in the Third World: Meeting Practical and Strategic Gender Needs', *World Development*, vol. 17, no. 11.

Moser, C. (1991) 'Gender Planning in the Third World: Meeting Practical and Strategic Needs', in R. Grant and K. Newland, eds, *Gender and International Relations*, Open University Press, Milton Keynes; Indiana University Press, Bloomington..

Moser, C. (1993) *Gender Planning and Development: Theory, Practice and Training*, Routledge, London.

Muir, A. (1991) *Evaluating the Impact of NGOs in Rural Poverty Alleviation, Zimbabwe Country Study*, ODI, London.

Musasa (1993–94). The Musasa Project, Sixth Annual Report. The Musasa Project, Harare.

Mustafa, Shams, Ishrat Ara, Dilruba Banu, Altaf Hossain, Ajmal Kabir, Muhammad Mohsin, Abu Yusuf (1995) *Impact Assessment Study of BRAC's Rural Development Programme*, Research and Evaluation Division, final report, BRAC, Dhaka, August.

Myrdal, G. (1968) *Asian Drama: An Inquiry into the Poverty of Nations*, Twentieth Century Fund and Pantheon Books, New York.

Newland, K. (1991) 'From Transnational Relationships to International Relations: Women in Development and the International Decade for Women', in R. Grant and K. Newland, eds, *Gender and International Relations*, Open University Press, Milton Keynes; Indiana University Press, Bloomington.

Nijeholt, G.L. (1991a) 'Introduction' in G.L. Nijeholt, ed., *Towards Women's Strategies in the 1990s: Challenging Government and the State*, Macmillan, London.

Nijeholt, G.L. (1991b) 'Policies and Strategies: a Reflection' in G.L. Nijehold, ed., *Towards Women's Strategies in the 1990s: Challenging Government and the State*, Macmillan, London..

Nijeholt, G.L. (ed.) (1991c) *Towards Women's Strategies in the 1990s: Challenging Government and the State*, Macmillan, London.

Njovana, E. (1994) 'Gender Based Violence and Sexual Assault', *African Women* 8, December 1993–May 1994.

North, D.C. (1990) *Institutions, Institutional Change, and Economic Performance*, Cambridge University Press, Cambridge.

Nussbaum, M. and A. Sen (eds) (1993) *The Quality of Life*, United Nations University, Oxford.

Nussbaum, M. and J. Gover (eds) (1995) *Women, Culture and Development: A Study of Human Capabilities*, Clarendon Press, Oxford.

O'Barr, J.F. (ed.) (1982) *Perspectives on Power: Women in Africa, Asia, and Latin America*, Duke University Centre for International Studies, Durham, NC.

OECD (1993) *Participatory Development and Good Governance*, OECD, Paris.

Okin, Susan Moller (1991) 'Gender, the Public and the Private', in D. Held, ed., *Political Theory Today*, Polity Press, Cambridge.

Olivier de Sardan, J.-P. (1988), 'Peasant Logics and Development Project Logics', *Sociologia Ruralis*, vol. XXVIII, no. 2/3, pp. 216–26.

Outshoorn, J. (1993) 'Parity Democracy: A Critical Look at a "New" Strategy', paper prepared for the workshop 'Citizenship and Plurality' ECPR, Leiden, 2–5 April.

Pankhurst, H. (1992) *Gender, Development, and Identity*, Zed Books, London.

Parker, Rani and Michelle Friedman (1993) 'Gender and Institutional Change in International Development', in Gay Young, Vidyamali Samarasinghe and Ken Kusterer, eds, *Women at the Center: Development Issues and Practices for the 1990s*, Kumarian Press, West Hartford, CT.

Pateman, C. (1988) *The Sexual Contract*, Polity Press, Cambridge; Stanford University Press, Stanford, CT.

Pearce, Diana (1990) 'Welfare is Not *for* Women: Why the War on Poverty Cannot Conquer the Feminisation of Poverty', in Linda Gordon, ed., *Women, the State, and Welfare*, University of Wisconsin Press, Wisconsin.

Petras, J. and F. Leiva (1988) 'Chile: The Authoritarian Transition to Electoral Politics', *Latin American Perspectives*, vol. 15, no. 3, pp. 97–114.

Phillips, A. (1991) *Engendering Democracy*, Polity Press, Cambridge.

Pitkin, H. (1965) 'Obligation and Consent,' *American Political Science Review*, vol. LXI, no. 4.

Pitkin, H. (1992) 'Feminism and Democracy', in J. Arthur, ed., *Democracy: Theory and Practice*, Wadsworth Publishing, Belmont, CA.

Polsby, Nelson (1984) *Policy Innovation in the United States*, Yale University Press, New Haven, CT.

Populi (n.d.) *UNFPA Magazine* (1994) vol. 21, no. 9, October.

Pringle, R. and S. Watson, (1992) '"Women's Interests" and the Post-Structuralist State', in M. Barrett and A. Phillips, eds, *Destabilising Theory: Contemporary Feminist Debates*, Polity Press, Cambridge.

Rahman, R.I. (1986) *Impact of the Grameen Bank on the Situation of Poor Rural Women*, Bangladesh Institute of Development Studies, Dhaka.

Rai, S.M. (1995a) 'Women and Public Power: Women in the Indian Parliament', *IDS Bulletin*, vol. 26, no. 3, July.

Rai, S.M. (1995b) 'Women Negotiating Boundaries: Gender, Law, and the Indian State', *Social and Legal Studies*, vol. 4, no. 3, September.

Rathgeber, E.M. (1990) 'WID, WAD, GAD: Trends in Research and Practice', *The Journal of Developing Areas*, no. 24.

Razavi, S. and C. Miller (1995a) 'From WID to GAD: Conceptual Shifts in the Women and Development Discourse', UNRISD Occasional Paper no.1, Geneva.

Razavi S. and Miller C. (1995b) 'Gender Mainstreaming: A Study of Efforts by the UNDP, the World Bank and the ILO to Institutionalise Gender Issues' UNRISD Occasional Paper no. 4, Geneva.

Rogers, Barbara (1980) *The Domestication of Women*, Tavistock Publications, London.

Rutherford, Stuart (1995) *ASA: The Biography of an NGO*, ASA, Dhaka.

Saa, M.A. (1990) Interview with Maria Antonietta Saa, *Critica Social*, May.

Safilios-Rothschild, Constantina, and Simeen Mahmud (1989) 'Women's Roles in Agriculture: Present Trends and Potential for Growth', contribution to the Bangladesh Agricultural Sector Review, UNDP/UNIFEM, Dhaka.

Sarkar, T. and U. Butalia (eds) (1995) *Women and Right-Wing Movements: Indian Experiences*, London, Zed Books.

Schaffer, Bernard (1984) 'Towards Responsibility', in E.J. Clay and B. Schaffer, eds, *Room For Manoeuvre*, Heinemann, London.

Schiavo-Campo, Salvatore (ed.) (1994) *Institutional Change and the Public Sector in Economies in Transition*, World Bank Discussion Paper, Washington DC.

Schild, V. (1992) 'Struggling For Citizenship in Chile: A "Resurrection" of Civil Society?', paper for Latin American Studies Association Congress.

Schild, V. (1994) '"Becoming Subjects of Rights": Citizenship, Political Learning and Identity Formation among Latin American Women', paper for XVIth IPSA Congress, Berlin.

Schmitz, Gerald (1995) 'Democratization and Demystification: Deconstructing

"Governance" as a Development Paradigm', in David B. Moore and Gerald J. Schmitz, eds, *Debating Development Discourse*, Macmillan, London.

Schuler, M. (ed.) (1992) *Freedom from Violence, Women's Strategies from around the World*, UNIFEM, New York.

Schuler, M. (ed.) (1993) *Claiming Our Place: Working the Human Rights System to Women's Advantage*, Institute for Women, Law and Development, Washington DC.

Schuler, Sidney Ruth and Syed M. Hashemi (1994) 'Credit Programs, Women's Empowerment, and Contraceptive Use in Rural Bangladesh', *Studies in Family Planning*, vol. 25, no. 2, pp. 65–76.

Sen, S., et al. (1991) *Gender Issues in Fisheries and Aquaculture*, ALCOM, Harare.

Serrano, C. (1990) 'Chile Entre la Autonomía y la Integración', in ISIS, *Transiciones: Mujeres en los Procesos Democráticos*, ISIS Internacional, Santiago.

Seur, H. (1992) 'Sowing the Good Seed: The Interweaving of Agricultural Change, Gender Relations and Religion in Serenje District, Zambia', PhD thesis submitted to Wageningen Agricultural University, the Netherlands.

Shapiro, I. (1990) 'Three Fallacies Concerning Majorities, Minorities, and Democratic Politics', in J.W. Chapman and A. Wertheimer, eds, *Nomos XXXII: Majorities and Minorities*, New York University Press, New York.

Shehabuddin, R. (1992) *The Impact of Grameen Bank in Bangladesh*, Grameen Bank, Dhaka.

Showstack-Sassoon, A. (ed.) (1987) *Women and the State*, Hutchinson, London.

Skjeie, H. (1991) 'The Rhetoric of Difference: On Women's Inclusion into Political Elites', *Politics and Society*, vol. 19, no. 2, pp. 233–63.

Skocpol, T. and E. Amenta (1986) 'States and Social Policies', *Annual Review of Sociology*, no. 12, pp. 131–57.

Smith, T.B. (1985) 'Evaluating Development Policies and Programmes in the Third World', *Public Administration and Development*, vol. 5, no. 2.

Staudt, K. (1985) *Women, Foreign Assistance, and Advocacy Administration*, Praeger Special Studies, New York.

Staudt, Kathleen (1987) 'Women, Politics, the State, and Capitalist Transformation in Africa', in Irving L. Markovitz, ed., *Studies in Power and Class in Africa*, Oxford University Press, New York.

Staudt, Kathleen (1990) 'Gender Politics in Bureaucracy: theoretical issues in comparative perspective', in K. Staudt, ed., *Women, International Development, and Politics: The Bureaucratic Mire*, Temple University Press, Philadelphia.

Staudt, K. (1991) *Managing Development: State, Society And International Contexts*, Sage, London.

Staudt, K. and J. Jaquette (1988) 'Bureaucratic Resistance to Women's Programmes: The Case of Women in Development', in E. Boneparth and E. Stoper, eds, *Women, Power and Policy*, Pergamon, New York, pp. 1–19.

Stetson, D.M. and A. Mazur (eds) (1995) *Comparative State Feminism*. Sage, London.

Stewart, S. (1992) 'Working the System: Sensitizing the Police to the Plight of Women in Zimbabwe', in *Freedom from Violence, Women's Strategies from Around the World*, UNIFEM 157, New York.

Stewart, S. (1994). Interview with Eunice Njovana, Director, Musasa Project. unpublished typescript.

Stewart, S. (1995a) 'Cutting Off One's Nose – The Impact of Donor Funding on the Strength of NGOs', *Development in Practice*, forthcoming, Oxfam, Oxford.

Stewart, S. (1995b) 'Women and a Radical Agenda for Change in Zimbabwe – the Musasa Project', *Gender and Development – Oxfam*, vol. 3, no. 1, Oxford.

Stewart, S. (1996) 'Bringing the Law Home: Action on Gender and Rights, Workshop Report', Oxfam, Oxford.

Swarup, H.L. et al. (1994) 'Women's Political Engagement in India', in B. Nelson and N. Chowdhury, eds, *Women and Politics Worldwide*, Yale University Press, London.

Taylor, C. (1991) *The Malaise of Modernity*, Anansi Press, Concord, Ontario.

Taylor, C. (1992) *Multiculturalism and the Politics of Recognition*, Princeton University Press, Princeton, NJ.

Taylor, J. and S. Stewart (1989) *Musasa: A Project for Zimbabwe*, MATCH International, Ottawa, Canada.

Taylor, J. and S. Stewart (1991) *Sexual and Domestic Violence. Help, Recovery and Action in Zimbabwe*, A. von Glehn and J. Taylor, in collaboration with Women in Law in Southern Africa, Harare.

Times of India (1996) 'Women Once Again Disappointed', 8 April, p. 3.

United Nations (1987) 'Report: Seminar on National Machinery for Monitoring and Improving the Status of Women', United Nations Office Centre for Social Development and Humanitarian Affairs, Vienna.

Valdes, T. and Weinstein, M. (1989) 'Organizaciones de Pobladoras y Construcción Democrática en Chile. Notas para un Debate', *Documento De Trabajo*, FLACSO, Santiago.

Valenzuela, M.E. (1990) 'Mujeres y Política: Logros y Tensiones en el Proceso de Redemocratización', *Proposiciones*, vol. 18, pp. 210–32.

Valenzuela, M.E. (1991) 'The Evolving Roles of Women under Military Rule', in P. Drake, and I. Jaksic, eds, *The Struggle for Democracy in Chile 1982–92*, University of Nebraska Press, Nebraska.

Valenzuela, M.E. (1992) 'Women and Democratization in Chile', paper presented to Conference on Women and the Transition to Democracy in Latin America and Eastern Europe, Berkeley.

Valenzuela, M.E., S. Venegas and C. Andrade (eds) (1995) *De Mujer Sola a Jefa de Hogar: Género, Pobreza y Políticas Públicas*, SERNAM, Santiago.

Valenzuela, M.E. (1996) Interview with Jefa de Departmento de Planificación y Estudios, SERNAM, Santiago, January.

van der Schoot, A. (1989) 'Some Ideas on Involvement of Women in Small-Scale Aquaculture', ALCOM, unpublished, Harare.

Villareal, M. (1992) 'The Poverty of Practice: Power, Gender, and Intervention from an Actor-oriented Perspective', in N. Long and A. Long, eds, *Battlefields of Knowledge: The Interlocking of Theory and Practice in Social Research and Development*, Routledge, London.

Vogelman, L. (1990) *The Sexual Face of Violence*, Raven Press, Johannesburg.

Watson, S. (ed.) (1990) *Playing the State*, Verso, London.

Waylen, G. (1993) 'Women's Movements in Latin America', *Third World Quarterly*, vol. 14, no. 3, pp. 573–88.

Waylen, G. (1996) *Gender in Third World Politics*, Open University Press, Milton Keynes.

Wertheimer, A. (1990) 'Introduction', in J.W. Chapman and A. Wertheimer, eds, *Nomos XXXII: Majorities and Minorities*, New York University Press, New York.

White, S. (1991) *Evaluating the Impact of NGOs in Rural Poverty Alleviation: Bangladesh Country Study*, ODI, London.

White, S. (1992) *Arguing with The Crocodile: Gender and Class in Bangladesh*, University Press, Dhaka.

White, S. (1994) 'Making Men an Issue: Gender Planning For "The Other Half"', in M. Macdonald, ed., *Gender Planning in Development Agencies: Meeting the Challenge*, Oxfam, Oxford.

White, S. (1995) 'Depoliticising Development: The Uses and Abuses of Participation', *Development in Practice*, vol. 6, no. 1, pp. 6–15.

Williams, D. and T. Young (1994) 'Governance, the World Bank and Liberal Theory', *Political Studies*, vol. 42, pp. 84–100.

Wolkowitz, Carol (1987) 'Controlling Women's Access to Political Power: A Case Study in Andhra Pradesh', in Haleh Afshar (ed.), *Women, State and Ideology*, Macmillan, London.

Wood, Geoffrey (1985) 'Targets Strike Back – Rural Works Claimants in Bangladesh', in G. Wood, ed., *Labelling in Development Policy*, Sage, London.

World Bank (1992) *Governance and Development*, World Bank, Washington DC.

World Bank (1994) *Governance: The World Bank's Experience*, World Bank, Washington DC.

Yasmin, Tahera (1995) 'The Way Women Work: Internal Dynamics of Saptagram', mimeo, IDS, Sussex.

Yasmin, Tahera, and M.N. Huda (1994) 'Understanding Women's Position in PVDO Management', PACT–PRIP, Dhaka.

Young, I.M. (1989) 'Polity and Group Difference: A Critique of the Ideal of Universal Citizenship', *Ethics*, vol. 99, pp. 250–74.

Young, I.M. (1990) *Justice and the Politics of Difference*, Princeton University Press, Princeton, NJ.

Young, Oran (1989) 'The Politics of International Regime Formation: Managing Natural Resources and the Environment', *International Organization*, vol. 43, no. 3, Summer.

About the Contributors

Brooke Ackerly is a Visiting Assistant Professor in Political Science at the University of California, Los Angeles. She is a political theorist who integrates her theoretical work with the study of feminist activism and GAD programming, specifically credit programmes and popular empowerment initiatives.

Katherine Fierlbeck is Associate Professor of Political Science at Dalhousie University in Halifax, Canada. She is a political theorist and has published a number of articles in political theory in such journals as the *Canadian Journal of Political Science*, the *Canadian Journal of Development Studies*, and *History and Theory*. She also conducts research in comparative health policy, and her articles in this area have appeared in the *International Journal of Health Studies* and *Studies in Political Economy*. She has contributed a number of book chapters in both fields, and is currently finishing a book on democratic theory in the global context for Manchester University Press.

Anne Marie Goetz is a Fellow of the Institute of Development Studies, University of Sussex. She is a political scientist and her research focuses on the politics of gender in development institutions. She has studied the politics of implementing GAD policy at the grassroots level, in rural credit programmes in Bangladesh, and at the state level, through 'national women's machineries' in a range of developing countries. She has also researched the politics of implementing poverty-reduction policies in Africa. She is currently studying processes of political liberalization in sub-Saharan Africa from a gender perspective.

Cecile Jackson is a senior lecturer in the School of Development Studies at the University of East Anglia where she directs the MA Gender Analysis in Development, and researches her interests in gender analysis of environmental change, and in policy issues including population, poverty and well-being discourses. She has lived and worked mainly in Nigeria, Zimbabwe, the Sultanate of Oman and India, and currently lives with her three children in Norwich.

Elizabeth Harrison is a Lecturer in Social Anthropology in the School of African and Asian Studies, University of Sussex, and currently co-directs the MA in Gender and Development which is run jointly with the IDS. She has worked on issues of intra-household resource allocation and decision-making, and on institutional–local linkages in the practice of rural development in southern Africa.

Nüket Kardam is Associate Professor at the Monterey Institute of International Studies and heads the MA programme on International Public Administration. She has written on the response of gender issues by several donors, on theories of gender, on women's movements, and women in Turkish Society. She is currently working on two themes: international governance on gender issues, and women's Islamic NGOs in Turkey.

David Kelleher is an independent organizational consultant operating from Ste Anne de Prescott, Ontario, Canada. He is also a Visiting Fellow at the Simmons Institute for Leadership and Change at Simmons College in Boston.

Shirin M. Rai is a Senior Lecturer in Politics and Women's Studies at the University of Warwick. She has edited a book on gender issues in transition economies (the Soviet Union, Eastern Europe, China), a book on Chinese politics, and one on issues of gender, state, and political representation. She is the Deputy Director of the Centre for Studies in Democratization at Warwick University, and co-editor of the book series 'Perspectives on Democratization' (Manchester University Press).

Aruna Rao is a gender and development consultant and writer. She is adviser to the Gender Team of the Bangladesh Rural Advancement Committee (BRAC). Currently, she is involved in building a global network of theorists working on gender and organizational change. She has just completed a two-year study on the dynamics and sustainability of local groups formed by social mobilization NGOs in Bangladesh. She has coordinated the Population Council's Gender and Development Programme in Asia, and has worked for many years to advance knowledge and practice in the field of gender training. She has written extensively on gender analysis and training, women and development projects, NGOs and organizational change.

Virginia O. del Rosario is a Lecturer in the Department of Sociology, University of Leicester. Her main research interests include institutionalization of gender in state policy, gender aspects of migration and other social mobility strategies, women and globalization, sex tourism and the international traffic in women. She has extensive experience in South-east Asia and has been acknowledged by UN-ESCAP as an expert on women in Asia and the Pacific. She has worked for 13 years as a senior civil servant in the Philippines, part of which time was spent chairing the Technical Working Group for Mainstreaming Gender Concerns in the labour and employment sector. Additionally, she has conducted a number of policy research and action programmes in collaboration with the ILO and UN-ESCAP.

Sheelagh Stewart is a lawyer. She co-founded and was the Director of the Musasa Project from 1988 to 1991. She is currently a Research Officer and PhD student at the Institute of Development Studies, University of Sussex, where she is researching the question of how donor funding impacts on NGOs in Zimbabwe and Nepal.

Jill Taylor is a psychologist. She co-founded the Musasa Project in Zimbabwe with Sheelagh Stewart and worked with the Project until 1989. She is currently studying for a PhD in organizational psychology at the Institute of Psychiatry, London, and is a consultant with Psychology at Work.

Georgina Waylen is a Lecturer in Politics at the University of Sheffield. She has researched and published on colonialism, gender, structural adjustment and democratization in Latin America and the Caribbean. She has just published a book on gender in Third World politics, and is currently working on a book on gender, democratic consolidation and economic reform.

Tahera Yasmin worked with Saptagram Nari Swanirvar Parishad from 1985 to 1993 as programme officer and later as its director. She has been involved with various forums in the women's movement and played an active role in the preparations for the Fourth World Conference on Women in September 1995, where she was a member of the National NGO Delegation to Beijing. Currently, she is working as a consultant with the Canadian International Development Agency in Bangladesh as its Funds Coordinator where she is focusing on capacity-building for organizations, especially those headed by women.

Index